MW01101406

ICE

ICE

BEAUTY. DANGER. HISTORY.

PAULINE COUTURE

McArthur & Company
Toronto

First published in 2004 by
McArthur & Company
322 King St. West, Suite 402
Toronto, Ontario
M5V 1J2
www.mcarthur-co.com

Library and Archives Canada Cataloguing in Publication

Couture, Pauline, 1954-
        Ice / Pauline Couture.

ISBN 1-55278-447-9

        1. Ice. I. Title.

GB2403.C69 2004   551.31   C2004-904219-X

The publisher would like to acknowledge the financial support of the Government of Canada through the Book Publishing Industry Development Program, The Canada Council for the Arts, and the Ontario Arts Council for our publishing activities. We also acknowledge the Government of Ontario through the Ontario Media Development Corporation Ontario Book Initiative.

Design and Composition by Tania Craan
Printed in Canada by Friesens

10 9 8 7 6 5 4 3 2 1

TO IAN, SARAH AND ANNE

ACKNOWLEDGMENTS

This book has benefited from the support and encouragement
of many people and institutions. While ice is of international
concern, and research and monitoring activities are supported
and coordinated by many countries, I found that the Canadian
Atmospheric Service's *MANICE* manual contained the most useful and succinct descriptions of the various kinds of ice to be
found in the cryosphere, and have mostly used definitions from
that source. I owe David Phillips, Senior Climatologist at
Environment Canada, a great vote of thanks for his help and
support, and for Environment Canada's generous permission to
reproduce their materials as needed. I have also counted heavily on expertise, data and images from the National Aeronautics
and Space Administration (NASA), the National Oceanic and
Atmospheric Administration (NOAA), the National Science
Foundation (NSF), the Canadian Space Agency (CSA), Natural
Resources Canada (NRCan), the Whyte Museum of the Rockies,
the National Snow and Ice Data Centre (NSIDC)—in particu-
larly Dr. Ted Scambos there, Dr. Lonnie Thompson at Ohio
State University, Jamie Rossiter of CANARIE in Ottawa, Peter
Mackinnon of Synergy Technology Management, also in
Ottawa, Dr. Norikazu Maeno of the Institute of Low
Temperature Science at Hokkaido University, Dr. Victor
Petrenko of Dartmouth College in New Hampshire, Dr. Jason
Donev, Professor of Physics at the University of Puget Sound in

Washington, Dr. Edwin Fitzgerald, Professor Emeritus of Johns Hopkins University, who acted as science editor for several chapters of this book, Philip Ball, author and contributing editor of *Nature* magazine, who allowed me to use his "little men" diagram, Dr. George Ewing, Professor Emeritus of Chemistry at Indiana State University, Professor Helmut Dosch of Max-Planck-Institut Fuer Metaccforschung in Stuttgart, Germany, Pramod Kumar Satyawali, of the Snow and Avalanche Study Establishment in Chandigrah, India, Dr. Dan McCarthy, Associate Professor in the Department of Earth Sciences at Brock University, Ken Dryden, then Vice-Chairman of Maple Leaf Sports and Entertainment, Dan Craig, Facility Operations Manager, National Hockey League (NHL), Jacques Desbois, CEO, L'Hôtel de glace Québec-Canada.

I am deeply indebted to the Banff Centre for the Arts, which supported my use of the Evamy Studio while I was mapping out this book (particularly Joanne Morrow and Sara Diamond), the Paul D. Fleck Library and the Banff Centre for Mountain Culture (particularly Woody MacPhail) for their generous and unfailing support of this work. They opened their archives to me, ensuring that my search for materials was always efficient and rich with meaning. They made available books, films and audio recordings that introduced me to a whole world of exploration, science, athleticism and art—all related to the mysteries and beauties of ice.

I am especially grateful to all those at Memorial University of Newfoundland who were so generous with their time and their resources: Dr. Ian Jordaan and Dr. Paul Barrette of the Faculty of Engineering and Applied Sciences, Dr. Stephen Jones, of the National Research Council of Canada's Institute for Marine Dynamics (NRC-IMD), Richard McKenna of the Centre for Cold Ocean Research Engineering (C-CORE), and Dr. Noreen Golfman, Memorial's Associate Dean of Graduate Studies and her husband, Dr. Stephen Bornstein, who extended their legendary hospitality to me and facilitated my contacts in St. John's. Thank you also to Victoria King in St. John's, who helped take care of me there.

In Toronto, Barbara Woolley and her team at Hambly and Woolley provided invaluable expertise and support early on. Bruce Westwood of Westwood Creative Artists blessed the idea originally, and my agent, Hilary McMahon, has carried it with me and continues to be a font of wisdom and grace. Glen Milne was a golden sounding board. Gracey Hitchcock, Julia Johnston, Elizabeth Dowdeswell, Rose O'Neill, Peter James Haworth, Julie Legal Brodeur, Eric Rothschild, Susan Lynch, Veronica Tennant, R.H. Thomson, Rosemary Dunsmore, Roland Beauregard, Donna Logan, Mary Aitken, Susan Chapman, Rona Maynard, George Chiu, Amanda Batchelor, Patrick Morrison, Mark Boudreau and many others were wonderful supporters and facilitators of this project and of me while I was undertaking it. Early on, Ivan Fecan, the best client anyone could ever have, encouraged me and supported me in my decision to change the orientation of my career.

My publisher, Kim McArthur, has been unfailingly enthusiastic and supportive, along with her staff, particularly Janet Harron. Copy-editor Pamela Erlichman and designer Tania Craan also deserve a vote of thanks for their grace under pressure. I have learned a great deal from my U.S. editor, Allison McCabe, and thank her for that.

On a personal note, I am grateful to the team that has kept

me mobile and mostly off crutches while working on this book: Xiaolan Zhao, Trista Zinn, Jennifer Hunter, Dr. Lise Paquette and Dr. Wayne Marshall. Thank you also to Mimi Weisband and everyone at Crystal Cruises and to Kate Stingley and Christa Guidi of Alice Marshall Public Relations for their support and collaboration in making beautiful places and images accessible to me.

My entire family (biological, inherited and chosen), but especially my beloved husband, Ian Morrison, my daughters, Sarah and Anne Gravel, and my sister Monique Couture were staunch supporters and critical readers. I can never thank them enough.

INTRODUCTION

"Ice has always been a great teacher, as winter continues to be today.
It determined our economical, technical and moral style.
It tempered our will and taught us to think. It is likely that
the existence of ice and the history of thinking coincide on
our planet, belonging to the same universal style."
—Ernst Jünger

My journey to the ice has been a long and winding one, and I
nearly missed the signpost that set me on this path. It was a
sunny day in June. We were headed up the Icefields Parkway
north of Lake Louise, Alberta, in a red convertible with the top
down. I was preoccupied, barely taking in the spectacular
Rocky Mountain scenery, when I looked up for a moment and
saw the steely aqua talons of the Crowfoot Glacier gripping the
sedimentary rock. There were just two claws, where there used
to be three. "Ice!" I said aloud to my husband.

"Ice?" he asked. He is very patient. "What do you mean?"

I meant that I had found the subject I wanted to write
about: ice. Ever since, I have been explaining the fascination
that entered my life that day: to puzzled friends and family, to
new acquaintances and old. After years in the frenetic pursuit of
daily journalism, followed by more years of writing complex
policy documents for corporate clients, I was at the point in my
life where I wanted to delve into a project of my own, that

would captivate me—and the readers I hoped would accompany me on my journey. I was to find it useful that my background was so eclectic, and that I had spent so much time over the years with a broad range of specialists—scientists, engineers, bankers, doctors, regulators, artists—helping them connect with broader audiences. Ice is a very broad subject, and there seemed to be a dearth of people who had contemplated its many facets all at once.

Most people don't think much about the solid form of water, unless, like many Canadians, they are addicted to an ice sport like hockey, figure skating or curling. But today more and more people all over the world are thinking about it—sometimes in ways that seem more like science fiction than practical reality. I was interested in everything about ice: the science that was exploring it and explaining it, the people who lived on it or with it, the lessons it has for each of us about the past and the future—and perhaps about the origins of life itself. I was interested in its beauty, its strength and fragility, and its associations with both agony and pleasure.

The more I learned about ice, the more new elements appeared that I had to consider. Even though water is everywhere in our bodies and in our world, its physical properties and its behaviour as a solid are still being explored and discovered, still the subject of controversy. There are all kinds of people worldwide preoccupied with gaining a better understanding of ice. I was to meet many of them in person, at conferences, by phone, over the Internet and through their work. I also began to ask people who had never given it much thought to think about ice and what it meant to them, or to their disciplines. That too, was interesting and enlightening, sometimes for them and always for me.

For some people, ice evoked miserable memories of bitter cold and hardship, pain and discomfort they couldn't wait to escape. Others had happy memories of backyard games of "shinny" hockey or ice fishing in carefree childhood. Ice made them think of rosy cheeks and hot chocolate and team spirit. Margaret Macmillan, the brilliant historian, thought of the Siege of Leningrad and the legend of the Teutonic Knights in the Battle of the Ice. An old friend remembered a cheerful deliveryman bringing a dripping block covered by insulating sawdust to his grandmother's icebox every other day, still coming with a horse and carriage in the 1950s.

A great chef thought of ice as the bed of a jewel box for his precious supplies of oysters and caviar. An aging beauty remembered a Hollywood starlet who pressed it to her breasts daily to keep them firm and high. My Chinese doctor said ice was bad for injuries, while my physiotherapist swore by its use to combat swelling and inflammation.

The scientists I spoke to looked at it differently. Some wanted to capture the secrets of the ice before it was too late: there were now seven hundred thousand years worth of ice cores stashed away in the freezers of expert ice interpreters in several countries. Those cores, layer by layer, could be read like tree rings to relay the history of planetary climate and atmospheric conditions. The experts have learned that for the entire evolution of human beings, the equilibrium of greenhouse gases in the earth's atmosphere was 30 percent less than it is now, and that large bodies of ice are collapsing and melting faster than they ever have before. These experts are still grappling to understand and communicate what these unprecedented circumstances will mean. For Canadians, the pressure to rethink the country's sovereignty over a High Arctic that is changing rapidly from an immense solid mass to navigable trade routes is enormous.

Other scientists saw the ice as a proxy for life itself, and their knowledge of earthly ice as the key to success in space exploration. A growing school of thought considered that extraterrestrial ice, or even parts of Antarctica, might be the home of "extremophile" life forms that could resemble the way life began here on earth.

Still other scientists and entrepreneurs wanted to harness the ice for one purpose or another—either to help humanity, to advance global knowledge, or just to make money. One, Dr. Kenneth Libbrecht of Caltech in Pasadena, California, spent time growing ice crystals in his lab and recording their subtleties and beauties for posterity. When he wanted ice crystals from nature, I discovered, he liked to hole up at a modest little place called the Bon Air Motel in Timmins, Ontario, where he could observe huge snowflakes and still have high-speed Internet access.

I met a poet from Wisconsin who waxed lyrical about ice, and an artist from Massachusetts who had gone to live beside a glacier in Alaska because she found the light frequencies of the ice nurturing and peaceful. She didn't mind living alone, a seven-hour drive from Anchorage, and chopping a hole in the ice every morning just to get water to drink and to wash in. Her paintings fairly sang with joy. I chatted over the Internet with a photographer who made ephemeral ice creations such as bowls and then shot them under beautiful studio lighting, in whole and in such close-ups that you could no longer tell what they were.

I holed up with my daughter at the beautiful ice hotel near Quebec City, where I had the best night's sleep of my life. The air there felt as if it was brand new and never breathed before. I listened to staff on a luxury cruise ship compete for assignments to Antarctica and Alaska over tours to the Caribbean.

I stood where Viking ships had braved the ice to conquer new worlds; I touched the wood in the living quarters below deck on the sturdy *Fram* in Oslo—the world's most famous polar exploration ship—and felt the spirits of Fridtjof Nansen, Otto Sverdrup and Roald Amundsen were there beside me. I tried to identify with the failed ice heroes Sir John Franklin and Sir Robert Falcon Scott—and just couldn't do it.

I sailed up the Gulf of Finland to St. Petersburg, and went to the shores of Lake Ladoga, whose frozen waters provided the only "road of life" during the nine hundred days of the Siege of Leningrad. Where I couldn't go in person, I went vicariously— to the ice festival in Harbin, China, for example, where I hope I will make it someday. I saw more ice sculptures on the Internet than I ever want to see in person, and discovered the Kenyan ice-carving team at Quebec's Carnaval. I subscribed to an ice news alert on Google, and watched, mesmerized, as ice catastrophes and rescues piled up in my inbox every day for months.

I still haven't driven a Zamboni, though I know how Dan Craig, the man in charge of operations for the National Hockey League, works hard to give players the best, most consistent ice in the world for hockey . . . while satisfying the marketing department that sponsors' logos show through crisply and clearly on television.

A single book cannot do justice to each and every one of these themes and experiences. But it can provide a taste of the adventures and learning to be had, and places to look for more. The experience of writing it has changed me forever: I can no longer travel anywhere in the world without watching the landscape for the telltale signs of sculpting, gouging, scraping and polishing left behind by the ice sheets. I am attracted by translucence and brilliance, and the refraction of light, the unfathomable beauty and mystery of it all. Finally, I am much more conscious of the radical changes we have launched in our environment; like turning a huge oceanliner, we cannot undo these quickly. Ice is the first place to look for clues as to what is to come.

CHAPTER ONE

"They were monolithic; their walls, towering and abrupt,
suggested Potala Palace at Lhasa in Tibet,
a mountainous architecture of ascetic contemplation."
—Barry Lopez in *Arctic Dreams*

UBIQUITOUS MYSTERY

One of nature's abiding mysteries is this: when the disordered molecules that make up liquid water are exposed to a certain temperature, some kind of signal whips them into shape. The molecules jump to attention, forming millions and billions and trillions of pristine hexagonal crystals gripping each other, as astonishing in their perfection as in their boundless numbers. It is as if an immense square dance suddenly stopped on a dime, transfixed into a crystal lattice. Despite the extent of current knowledge and the increasing sophistication of scientific instruments, we still do not know exactly why this happens. It is the mission of legions of scientists and scholars in a range of disciplines around the world to seek the truth about the most ubiquitous material on the surface of the planet: H_2O.

Because more than three-quarters of its surface is covered with open water or ice, our planet looks mostly blue from space. The layers deposited year by year on the ice sheets and glaciers are like the growth rings of trees, telling the story of the planet's past. Our human bodies are, on average, about 60 percent water,[1] and no form of life can survive without H_2O. In fact, water has been called the matrix of life itself, and current space exploration focuses on finding water or ice on faraway planets and moons, as a proxy for potential extraterrestrial life forms.

One might think that all this would ensure that we know everything there is to know about ice, the solid form of water. Not so. Beneath the familiar business of water freezing to ice lies a process so complex it took Japanese researchers six years to make the first realistic computer simulation of it.[2] The simple water molecule, in its various forms, still holds myriad secrets, and will for many years to come.

The range of exploration required is vast, encompassing many disciplines. There are people studying ice in the ground, on the ground, in the water, on the water, in the atmosphere, and in space. They study its mechanics, its surfaces, its chemical composition, and its electrical conductivity. The physics and chemistry of ice determine whether a person can skate across a frozen pond, or whether an oilrig can drill safely in the North Atlantic. Reactions among ice crystals in the upper atmosphere can determine the intensity of a tropical storm, even where people never see ice on the ground.

In winter, ice determines when and whether planes can fly, motor vehicles can drive safely, and ships can ply the seas. It can bring power lines crashing down, interrupting the flow of electricity to millions of people, or it can curtail the independence of an elderly person who slips and breaks a hip.

People write poetry about ice and play with it; they try to master it and they submit humbly to it. They use it, they rely on it, they do everything they can to avoid it. They seek it out curiously, recklessly and fanatically. In places where people live through long winters with ice all around them, they bet good money on the exact moment of its breakup, the start of melting into the blossoming warmth of spring. People use ice in therapy, to reduce swelling and to dull the pain of an injury. They preserve food with it, and use it to try to retain the elasticity of their skin. They skate on it, slide on it, fish through it, carve it, ride it and use it as a building material. Some cultures think of it as an essential natural resource, while others abhor it. No one is indifferent to ice—at least, not once they stop to think about it.

In its most dramatic form—the floating, aqua-veined marble castles called icebergs—ice inspires awe and dread among sailors and tourists, as well as writers from Coleridge and Melville to Vonnegut and Lopez. Perhaps the most lyrical of all modern writers on the Arctic, Barry Lopez speaks of "a picket line of ice the size of cathedrals," and evokes a stunning sight:

I would walk from one side of the ship to the other, wondering how something so imposing in its suggestion of life could be approached so closely, and yet still seem so remote. It was like standing in a dirigible off Annapurna and Everest in the Himalayas.

On a planetary level, ice sheets and sea ice protect vast bodies of water from evaporation and help regulate the earth's temperature. Land-based glaciers and ice sheets form the bulk of the world's freshwater reserves, so essential for drinking and growing food, and to life itself. Altogether, the cryosphere, the world's frozen water taken as a whole, plays an important role, perhaps not yet fully understood, in the regulation of ocean currents and global climate. And although most of us do not spend much time thinking about it, leading-edge scientists are concerned with how ice evolves and behaves under different pressures and temperatures. Some are concerned with current problems, such as the protection of people whose lives depend on safe passage through ice—those who work on ice-battered oilrigs in northern oceans, or who fly airplanes through winter storms, for example. Others believe we need to know more about ice because of its key role in our future. The cycle, in which ice forms and melts to nourish life on earth, as we know it, relies on a certain slow rhythm. They worry that the growing burden of human activities, combined with the earth's own mysterious evolution, could speed up this cycle, pushing us into a situation where it suddenly becomes much more difficult to maintain life on the planet. These scientists are used to longer-term thinking than most of us. They see a very serious and growing possibility of sudden climate change in as little as twenty years.

Even the Pentagon is sitting up and taking notice, commissioning a study that sounded the alarm in 2004 about the significance of climate change to American strategic interests.[3] When the catastrophe film *The Day After Tomorrow* appeared shortly thereafter, many scientists pooh-poohed the sensational story line, showing New York City petrified under an ice avalanche over just a few days—but many also said we should take seriously the idea that something similar could actually happen over a somewhat longer timeframe. (The film simply wrote off Canada—"too late for them," said the wild-eyed heroes.) A four-year scientific investigation by 600 scientists, the Arctic Climate Impact Assessment (ACIA) concluded that the 155,000 Inuit and Eskimo people who live in the eight polar nations will no longer be able to live in their traditional hunting culture because marine mammals like polar bears, walrus and some species of seal will become extinct by the middle of the twenty-first century.[4]

The most compelling reason for much of the current scientific research on ice, then, is to help track climate change here on earth. Moving beyond earth, there are scientists looking to explore other planets and celestial bodies. So far, researchers have determined twelve phases of ice—ways in which ice crystals take different forms as they are subjected to pressures and temperatures outside the range of what occurs naturally on our planet. No one except scientists in highly sophisticated laboratories has ever seen one of these high-pressure ices, and even then, sometimes only computer-generated graphics representing what expensive machines are detecting. To a non-scientist such as myself, graphic representations of the crystal structure in some of these various phases of ice—usually numbered in Roman numerals from I to XII—appear both surprisingly playful and aesthetically pleasing.

Almost all the ice that occurs naturally on earth is the six-sided crystalline kind called ice I_h, (for hexagonal), although if water vapour condenses onto a surface at −120 to −140°C, you will get a cubic structure called I_c. But if you follow the news from the space probes and from Mars, for example, you will know that there is acute interest in the existence or non-existence of ice elsewhere in the solar system and beyond, as a proxy for the potential for life. Ice ɪx, as it turns out, does not have the properties of the Ice Nine Kurt Vonnegut described in his 1963 novel *Cat's Cradle*. He imagined a form of ice that could cause all of the earth's water to freeze at once, and no doubt piqued the interest of more researchers than he knew at the time. However, Vonnegut was on to something with his idea of an agent that could provoke freezing. Every snowflake that drifts down from the atmosphere is made of ice crystals that attach themselves to some kind of dust particle, and "nucleating agents" play a major role in the nature and speed of freezing.

Those who specialize in this area are mostly the kind of scientists who just want to know—the way Sir Edmund Hilary climbed Mount Everest "because it's there." Often, they have no idea how, when or why this knowledge will ever serve a useful purpose. For now, suffice it to say extraterrestrial ices are important because they help to explain the workings of the universe, from our own planet's upper atmosphere to worlds well beyond.

■ ■ ■

If you have never stopped to think about it, ice may not be a daily presence in your life. You are not necessarily aware of its handiwork in the world around you. You see hills and valleys, rivers and mountains, and may think nothing of it. It is as if they have always been there. And yet, when you become aware of what ice has left in its wake, you begin to see the world through ice-conscious eyes, and the details take on a life of their own.

First, you begin to understand that landscape is carved, and has dipped in and out of water arbitrarily over long periods, and that what we see today has not always been there. In geological time, it has not been so very long since the earth came out of its last ice age: just 10,000 years, the moment which marked the beginning of our current era, the Holocene. At various times over the last two and a half million years (the Pleistocene era until the Holocene began), colossal ice sheets have taken over and carved up something like a third of the earth's land mass as we now see it. The Pleistocene saw the thriving, then the extinction of spectacular mammals such as sabre-toothed cats, cave lions, cave bears, giant deer, woolly rhinoceroses and woolly mammoths up to 3.6 metres tall.

During the most recent glaciation, the Wisconsin, glaciers up to two miles thick covered Canada, extending from Hudson Bay as far south as Long Island (New York), and south into the Midwestern states. The mountain glaciers we can see today, majestic as they are, look miniscule by comparison. Some experts believe that the humans who lived during the Wisconsin glaciation overcame challenges that stimulated their brainpower and survival skills in ways that remain important to us today.

A mere 20,000 years ago, the top third of the globe—parts of North America, Europe and Asia, the Arctic Ocean and parts of the North Atlantic—was covered with ice sheets. So much of the earth's water was frozen that sea levels were 107 to 122 metres lower than they are today, even though the weight of the ice pressed the land downward as well, into the molten rock beneath it. When the ice sheets melted into the oceans, sea levels immediately rose. Land, once relieved of the weight of the ice, rose more slowly. This probably happened in areas as diverse as New England, Scandinavia and Scotland. The land is still rising around Lake Superior and Hudson Bay. This kind of movement, due to the long-ago withdrawal of the ice, is still making houses shift on their foundations in the old town of Stockholm. On the island of Gamla Stan, houses built on wooden pilings centuries ago have to be constantly repaired to avoid listing, because as the land rises (at a rate of 4.6 millimetres a year), the old wooden pilings are exposed to the air and begin to rot. The effects of the ice ages are always with us.

■ ■ ■

Charles Whittlesey, a geologist from Cleveland, Ohio, was the first, in 1868, to calculate the depth and extent of continental ice sheets, but many of the mysteries of the ice ages remain unsolved in the twenty-first century. The North American continental ice sheet probably started growing from Labrador or Ungava, where the rock is very hard and stable, spreading south and west. The passage of the glaciers left beautiful polished granite in what is known as Shield country, in places such as Georgian Bay on Lake Huron. These glaciers coming from the east eventually met up with mountain glaciers moving in from the west and the Arctic; they coalesced. From both directions, these ice sheets came off harder rock, digging into the softer ground of the central plains.

This digging movement created the Great Lakes, which today contain 18 percent of the world's surface fresh water. In geological time, these are young lakes, scooped out and created by moving ice. Where the underlying bedrock is very hard, or where the glaciers moved on quickly, the lakes are shallower. The Niagara Escarpment, capped by hard dolostone, remains as a high ridge today. The deepest of the Great Lakes, Lake Superior (maximum depth 405.3 metres) was reshaped by the glaciers, but it already existed as a very ancient rift valley dating back over a billion years. Lake Erie (maximum depth 64 metres) has a larger surface area than Lake Ontario (maximum depth 244 metres), but is much shallower. Both were formed by the tongue of the ice sheet (called an ice lobe) that grew from the east, moving up the St. Lawrence River Valley.

In many areas, land once weighed down by glaciers is still rising. On the shores of Lake Superior, this is happening at the rate of about 38 centimetres per century. In Maine, where the land was depressed below sea level during the ice age, the land is still rebounding at the same time as the sea level is rising, probably because of global warming, according to the Maine Geological Survey. The rebounding seems to be most incomplete in areas like Hudson Bay, which was at the centre of the Laurentide ice sheet 18,000 years ago. Both from space and from the ground, measurements of the area show that the rebound effect is linked to an anomaly in the earth's gravity: it is weaker over Hudson Bay than almost anywhere else on earth.[5] Scientists are using this information to help them understand the viscosity of the earth's mantle of molten rock, and to increase their knowledge of how the continental plates move.

■ ■ ■

Ice sheets and glaciers are strange creatures. It is hard not to think of them as living things: they are always moving, shifting, cracking, gliding, scraping, polishing, crushing—and destroying the evidence of their own earlier passage. They turn narrow V-shaped tributaries into broad U-shaped valleys. They leave deposits that can be hundreds of metres thick; over time, these deposits break down and turn into rich growing soil. They gouge the land, picking up boulders, clay, sand, gravel and soil; they drop this material, called till, when they are melting. Since I began my study of ice, I see evidence of them everywhere.

LOOKING BACK IN TIME

The history of ice ages is controversial. For example, many scientists believe in a "snowball earth" theory under which the entire planet would have frozen over and most life would have become extinct—and possibly that this happened twice. Others reject this entirely. The consensus is that there have been at least five major ice ages in earth's past, each lasting from tens of millions to hundreds of millions of years:

■   The Huronian Ice Age (from 2500 to 2100 million years ago, mostly in North America);

■ The Stuartian-Varangian Ice Age (from 950 to 600 million years ago, in Africa, China, Australia, Europe, Arabia and North America);

■ The Andean-Saharan Ice Age (from 450 to 420 million years ago, in Arabia, central Sahara, western Africa, the lower Amazon);

■ The Karoo Ice Age (from 360 to 260 million years ago in all the land masses that once formed Gondwana—Africa, South America, Antarctica, India, Arabia and Australia); and

■ The Holarctic-Antarctic Ice Age (beginning 30 million years ago in Antarctica, the Arctic, North America, Eurasia, the Andes and elsewhere). The last glaciers from this ice age, including the Wisconsin and the Laurentide ice sheets, endured until 10,000 years ago.

In each case, there were many expansions and contractions of glaciations, sometimes lasting tens of thousands of years, and mostly on continents in the mid to high latitudes. This gets very confusing when we try to adjust our brains to geological time, because over millions of years, the continents have changed places many times. The biggest challenge is learning to think about geological time in a way that is meaningful. How does one meaningfully contemplate *anything* in such large numbers, so far beyond our human lifespan? You can download a wonderful PowerPoint presentation from the Institute of Geology at the University of Texas at Austin that shows the history of the movement of the earth's tectonic plates and continents in about a minute—or about a second per ten million years![6] In fact, if you think of the earth's life as twenty-four hours, measured off from the outstretched fingertips of one hand to the other, all of human history could be removed with a stroke of a nail file: it would measure just .003 seconds out of the twenty-four hours.

There are very few places in the world where you can easily look at 450 million years of evidence with your own eyes. Within walking distance of my house in the old village of Yorkville in midtown Toronto, there is such a place: the Don Valley Brick Works Park. The exposed north wall of the quarry shows clear signs of the last two major glaciations and their impact on climate change and the environment.

Looking at the north wall of the Don Valley Brick Works quarry you can see seven distinct layers, beginning at the bottom with the limy shales of the Georgian Bay Formation, the bedrock of Toronto. This was lifted out of a tropical sea 450 million years ago and deposited there. As has happened in many places, subsequent ice ages ebbed and flowed, tearing away the entire history between that faraway time and the next record we have—the thin layer of glacial deposit above it, called the York Till. It dates back about 135,000 years. Just above that is a sandy river layer, the Don Formation. The 120,000-year-old fossils in this layer contain some molluscs, trees and other life forms that are common today, either in the Toronto area or farther south; they also contain extinct species such as the giant beaver. The presence of species that are now found only well south of here shows that the area was probably slightly warmer 120,000 years ago than it is now.

Above the warm-weather Don Beds, there is the Scarborough, which is 106,000 to 115,000 years old. This layer

12

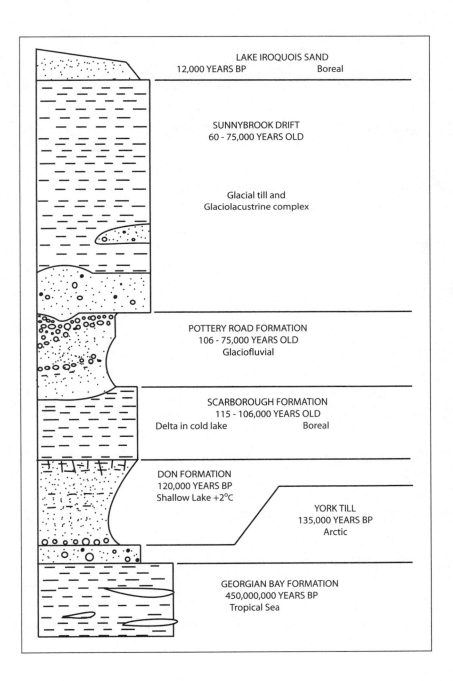

is made up of finer material that can be seen most clearly at the chalky Scarborough Bluffs east of Toronto. The Scarborough Formation was the delta of a large river, which no longer exists (the St. Lawrence was dammed up, forming a large lake behind the ice sheet at the time). This river was fed by meltwater from the growing Wisconsin Ice Sheet, descending from Labrador and Ungava. The beetle fossils in this layer lived in a cooler climate than the earlier one, with forests largely dominated by evergreens like pine, spruce and fir.

Higher, nearly at the top, the Sunnybrook Drift is a mix of glacial till and other substances showing that the Wisconsin Ice Sheet had still not receded completely. Early in Toronto's urban history, this layer, with its high red-clay content, became a desirable source of brick and pottery clay, so that the upper part of it is sometimes called the Pottery Road Formation (75,000 to 106,000 years ago). How odd to think that glaciers are responsible for Toronto's distinctive red-brick architecture!

Much of today's Greater Toronto Area remains covered by the debris of this massive ice sheet, known as the Halton Till. The Wisconsin pushed as far south as the Ohio Valley, and was at its largest about 18,000 years ago. At its maximum, which lasted until 14,000 years ago, the ice was a mile thick over Toronto and much of the northeastern seaboard of the United States. On the north wall of the quarry, there are 12,000-year-old sandy beach deposits formed by the waves of Lake Iroquois after the ice sheet finally melted.

My house sits right beside a buried glacial stream called Castle Frank Brook, probably formed in the grooves between ridges (called drumlins) left behind by the glaciers during their final retreat about 13,000 years ago. By then, the ice was still pushing, but the warming climate was melting it faster than it could flow forward. The back-and-forth movement created thousands of grooves and ridges in Southern Ontario, natural beds for freshwater access to the Great Lakes system, and interesting fanlike movements that left big deposits such as the area now known as the Oak Ridges Moraine. This glacial deposit area acts as a natural filtration system for groundwater, and plays an essential role in replenishing the freshwater supply upon which millions of residents in this area depend. The ebb and flow of the glaciers was linked to every change in geology and climate in this area, through that whole 450 million years.

■ ■ ■

My curiosity about ice led me to St. John's, Newfoundland, where there was a critical mass of expertise at Memorial University, in the spring of 2002. On that visit, I got to know several ice specialists, particularly Stephen Jones, Paul Barrette and Ian Jordaan. They invited me to attend the International Conference on the Physics and Chemistry of Ice taking place at Memorial in July of that year. I accepted eagerly: this opportunity to watch 140 of the world's top ice scientists in action only happens once every four years.

The trip itself—2,987 kilometres from Toronto to St. John's—became a kind of game, as we watched for ice effects everywhere along the way. There was no shortage of them. As we drove along the St. Lawrence River Valley towards Montreal, I remembered how much my father used to love the

Thousand Islands. If you come off the Trans-Canada Highway and spend some time exploring, it is hard to believe that this magical place is right between Canada's two largest cities, and along the country's most densely populated corridor. As a child, I used to try and count the islands as we drove across the Canada-U.S. border here, not quite believing there could be a thousand of them (there are not).

At other times, I remember boat rides through these beautiful, densely wooded little bits of paradise on a human scale. I never realized what I was looking at: the tips of a Precambrian mountain range called the Frontenac Axis, a kind of granite bridge, 40 kilometres wide, linking the southern edge of the Canadian Shield and the Adirondack Mountains in New York. During the last ice age, it was buried under 3 kilometres of ice. When the glaciers receded 12,000 years ago, the St. Lawrence River Valley was flooded, and these waters began to drain into the Atlantic Ocean.

What remains today is a rocky, rugged shoreline that harbours a rich array of flora and fauna in adjacent wetlands. It was Canada's twelfth area to be designated a Biosphere Reserve by UNESCO, and it continues to provide a stepping-stone corridor between two large wild areas in Canada (the Algonquin Forest) and the United States (the Adirondacks). There are many enclaves of charming older cottages where families have been coming for generations from all around the valley: Quebec, Ontario, upstate New York, Pennsylvania, Ohio and even farther afield. Since 1914, some twenty-one granite islands and about ninety rocky shoals and islets have formed St. Lawrence Islands National Park, the smallest of Canada's crown jewel wilderness areas, and the first National Park created east of the Rocky Mountains.

As we continued down the St. Lawrence, past Montreal, past Quebec City and towards the east coast, we marked the passage from a freshwater system to a tidal system. By the time the river meets up with the Saguenay fjord between Quebec City and the Magdalen Islands, you are looking at one of the great unsolved mysteries of North American geology. Part of the process of becoming ice-conscious is to become earth-conscious—and the earth does not end at the water. This area is still very seismically active, with underwater landslides and deep troughs resulting from tectonic movements and rebound from the passage of glaciers. It has been very difficult to research, even for specialists: the water is deep, the tides are very strong, the seabed is unstable, and there are gas hydrates, which can cause explosions or fire hazards. Joint teams from Canada, the United States and Europe are working to learn more about it.

As we turned away from the St. Lawrence, south towards Fredericton, New Brunswick, the gentle remnants of the ancient Appalachian Mountains reminded us that here, the tectonic movements go back millions of years. Today, the existence of a small, stubborn, ancient plant on the banks of the Saint John River is the most immediate reminder of the role of ice in the ecosystem. The Furbish lousewort, a pretty, spiky perennial with tubular yellow flowers, depends on the yearly breakup of the river ice to maintain its foothold as a unique species to this valley. This member of the snapdragon family is found only on the upper stretch of the Saint John River and nowhere else on earth. It simply does not deserve its ugly name. It is very picky about its habitat, demanding a northern or northwest exposure, at the foot of sloping, shaded riverbanks.

It was named for Kate Furbish, the Maine naturalist and botanical artist who discovered it in 1880, and declared "probably extinct" in a 1975 American report on its status. In 1976, researchers conducting an environmental impact study in the area were surprised to find it alive and well. Recent estimates say there are fewer than 1,000 of the plants within the area between the Canada-U.S. border above Grand Falls and the mouth of the Aroostook River. There are also a few thousand plants in the area between Big Black River and Fort Kent, Maine.

Not only is the Furbish lousewort fussy about sunlight, shade and moisture, but it also wants to be the only belle at the ball, and it allows just one kind of bumblebee, *Bombus vegans*, to pollinate it. It only grows in areas that are subject to flooding, ice-scouring or "slumping" of earth, trees and brush that get rid of its competition and clear new areas for it to colonize. Meanwhile, its deep roots anchor it firmly to the riverbank, ensuring that it survives when the other vegetation is torn away. If only it were called the yellow dreamflower, its chances of attracting environmental supporters would be so much greater.

We made our way through Nova Scotia to the magnificent Bras d'Or Lakes in Cape Breton, Canada's largest inland sea. Here is where Alexander Graham Bell built his beloved Beinn Bhreagh (Gaelic for "beautiful mountain"), his summer refuge and favourite home, where he and his wife Mabel chose to be buried. Since the building of the Canso Causeway between the mainland and Cape Breton in 1955 obstructed the flow of the water, there has been an ice bridge used by wildlife to go back and forth every winter. The last ice cap retreated from Cape Breton just 9,000 years ago, in the area now occupied by the Chéticamp Reservoir, but parts of the island, such as the North Mountain, show no trace of glaciation. The experts think Cape Breton is at the conjunction of four separate tectonic plates, and therefore the factors influencing it are complex.

Sea levels around Cape Breton are still rising at the rate of about 30 centimetres a century, and the western part of the island may be sinking at about twice that rate, for reasons that do not seem to be fully understood. It is entirely possible that in the future, the highlands of Cape Breton will become a chain of islands, but that could only enhance the rugged beauty that Alexander Graham Bell loved so much.

The largest town on the island, Sydney, is also the departure point for the ferries to Newfoundland. Even Canadians forget how large our country is. On the map, Newfoundland appears much more manageable than it is, and of course a map does not tell you how much of it is still gorgeous wilderness. Once you have spent 6 hours on a ferry from Cape Breton, you still have 905 kilometres of driving on the Trans-Canada Highway ahead of you to get to St. John's, on the other side of the island.

Newfoundland and Labrador may be the most ice-affected province in Canada—and that is truly saying something! The island of Newfoundland is the northeastern-most extension of the Appalachian mountain system in North America, formed from three parts of the earth's crust brought together about 400 million years ago by continental drift. Central Newfoundland is actually the remains of a 500-million-year-old ocean floor that lay between North America and Africa; its east coast, my destination, was once part of southwestern Europe or North Africa.

While Newfoundland is still mountainous and rugged, for the last 200 million years it has mostly been eroding under the assault of water and ice. For two million years, until the last glacial maximum 18,000 years ago, the great ice sheets advanced and retreated across Newfoundland and Labrador many times. The tip of the Northern Peninsula was the only part of the island overrun by the Laurentide Ice Sheet (you can watch the retreat from its dominance of North America to remnants hugging Hudson Bay and Greenland on the website of the Illinois State Museum).[7] The rest of the island was covered by its own dome-shaped ice cap, from the uplands towards the coast. In Central Newfoundland, to this day, you can catch glimpses of twisted knobs of rock, all that is left of higher landscapes that have almost disappeared through erosion. In true Newfoundland fashion, they have an original name: they are called "tolts." There are also "erratics," large pieces of rock that are geological strangers to their present home, just dumped there unceremoniously by a retreating ice sheet.

The passage of the glaciers is visible everywhere on the island. The landscape has been smoothed, polished, carved, and later flooded to create magnificent deep fjords in the coastal areas. With the melting of the glaciers, the ice retreated, covering inland areas with till and gravel. The ice sheets had weighed the land down and squeezed it out towards their margins. With melting, the land rebounded, so that areas that had been beaches, deltas and home to marine animals when the ice weighed it down, are now on much higher ground.

St. John's Harbour is truly breathtaking—such an obvious natural seaport, it has been used for shipping and fishing since the latter days of the Italian Renaissance at the beginning of the sixteenth century. Water Street in downtown St. John's is North America's oldest commercial street north of Mexico. Signal Hill, overlooking the harbour, is a national historic park with spectacular views and a place in history as the birthplace of wireless communications. In 1897, Newfoundland celebrated the four hundredth anniversary of its discovery by John Cabot (or rather, Giovanni Caboto) and his son by erecting Cabot Tower on Signal Hill, to commemorate Queen Victoria's Diamond Jubilee. In 1901, this is where Guglielmo Marconi inaugurated the electronic age as he stood to receive the first transatlantic wireless message, the letter s in Morse code, from a transmitter in Cornwall, England.

Newfoundland was an independent Dominion of the British Crown until 1949, when it joined Canada in a tight vote that remains controversial to this day. Arguably, the proximity of the dangerous sea and ice conditions make life here both more precious and more reckless. There is nothing like a huge berg sitting right in the middle of the Narrows, the entrance to the harbour in St. John's, as an eloquent reminder of the inescapable presence of the North Atlantic ice that has such a profound influence on the life of the city. This is the home of the 1982 Ocean Ranger disaster, when eighty-four men were lost from an oilrig off the coast near St. John's. While the ice did not cause the capsizing of the wreck, it made the rescue operations infinitely more difficult, and played a role in their failure.

St. John's is also home to Memorial University, the National

Research Council's Institute for Ocean Technology (IOT) and the Centre for Cold Ocean Research Engineering (C-CORE)—taken together, a mecca of ice research for oceans, and increasingly, a partner in developing the knowledge needed for space exploration. In the summer of 2002, it was also going to be home for a few days to 140 of the world's top experts in the physics and chemistry of ice. As a layperson attending the conference, I wanted to listen and learn, and make the most of my opportunity to meet some remarkable masters of the ice.

Among those attending were Victor Petrenko, a Russian physicist now based at Dartmouth College in New Hampshire; George Ewing, Chancellor's Professor Emeritus of Chemistry at Indiana University at Bloomington, who could have been a poet; Dr. Ian Jordaan, a research professor and engineer originally from South Africa and one of the hosts of the conference; Dr. Edwin R. Fitzgerald, Professor Emeritus of Johns Hopkins University, a distinguished mechanical engineer fascinated with ice; as well as young, emerging scientists like Jason Donev, a twenty-six-year-old doctoral candidate from Seattle whose expertise is the weird and wonderful study of amorphous ice (with a little philosophy and rock music on the side), and Dr. Robert Pappalardo, from the Department of Astrophysical and Planetary Sciences at the University of Colorado in Boulder, whose work is totally focused on extraterrestrial ice.

Because I had never been to a scientific conference, I did not realize at the time how extraordinary it was that scientists would gather to make common cause across so many disciplinary boundaries. I was about to find out just how broad and deep a subject ice would turn out to be.

CHAPTER TWO

"White men always think of ice as frozen water,
but Eskimos think of water as melted ice . . ."
—Jerry Kobalenko in *The Horizontal Everest*

THE ROCK THAT FLOATS

It's no wonder that the conference in St. John's attracted chemists, geologists, engineers, crystallographers, climatologists, physicists, mineralogists and even closet artists (I never did find out who made the ice-sculpted fish that dripped noisily through the opening ceremonies). There are so many different ways to look at ice, with an impact on everything from health and pleasure to weather and space travel. The ice and snow cover influences global climate. Falling snow and ice crystals "scavenge" pollution right out of the air. Ice clouds in the stratosphere play a role in ozone destruction. Frost-heave damages roads, buildings and crops. Ice cubes sublimate and leap out of their trays in self-defrosting refrigerators without ever turning to water. So many mysteries . . .

Ice is actually a mineral, di-hydrogen oxide. Minerals are chemically homogeneous, with an organized structure of natural, inorganic origin. Ice fits this description perfectly: it has a consistent recipe (H_2O); it is organized in a symmetrical hexagonal structure; it is formed naturally and inorganically.

Interestingly, mineralogists do not think of *water* as a mineral, because it does not have the crystal structure of ice. While it may also feel strange to think of ice as a rock, it really is—though it is made up of a single type of molecule, and most rocks combine different elements. This explains why many geologists are interested in ice, one of the very few known rocks able to float.[1]

Almost every substance known to man becomes denser, and therefore heavier by volume, as it moves along the continuum from gas to liquid to solid. From gas—water vapour, or steam—to liquid, H_2O plays by the rules. But in the transition from liquid to solid ice, it reverses those rules almost completely. As many may remember from high school chemistry classes, when water freezes, its molecules jump to attention at each angle of a hexagonal crystal, which then floats on its originating liquid. This increases the volume of frozen water by 9 percent over liquid water at "normal" atmospheric pressure. Because of this, H_2O's freezing process is often considered a destructive force: it makes water pipes and glass bottles burst, and destroys road surfaces during freeze-thaw cycles.

But this rare trait also allows life to flourish on our planet. Imagine, for a moment, a world in which the oceans froze from the bottom up instead of the top down. What food source could grow and prosper there? How would higher-order animals have evolved? Many scientists think such a world would not support the kind of life we have on earth today. This gives us an insight as to why so much effort and money goes into searching for ice on other planets.

Why Does Ice Float?

So why does ice float? Dr. Paul Barrette, one of the organizers of the Newfoundland conference, is a geologist who works on ice mechanics and applied engineering research. He was the first person to show me a model of an ice crystal. He showed how the melting process loosens the molecular bonds in most solids, making the resulting liquid less dense than the originating solid. When liquid becomes a gas, the bonds are loosened yet again, and the gas is generally far less dense than either the solid or the liquid. As we have already seen, H_2O is different.[2]

The hydrogen bonds in H_2O have some unique properties. If you think of each water molecule as a little round man with outstretched hands and feet, his body would be the oxygen atom, and his feet would be the hydrogen atoms (he would always keep his legs apart at an angle of 104.5 degrees, giving him the look of a perpetual cheerleader). Each of his outstretched hands would be a lone pair of electrons coming off the oxygen atom. The little man's hands and feet (the hydrogen atoms and the electrons) would form a kind of tetrahedral structure that is key to understanding the behaviour of the water molecule.

Philip Ball, a prolific and imaginative science writer with a grounding in both science and the arts, has captured the imagination of other ice scientists with his representation of the structure of ice crystals as an infinite network of little men holding each other by the hands and feet. I first found this illustration in Jason Donev's doctoral thesis.

When H_2O is in liquid form, the little men are doing a vast, intimate and disordered dance, with hands grabbing feet, and moving on to some mysterious music.[3] The formidable Linus Pauling, Nobel Prize winner both for chemistry and for peace, first identified the entropy, or disorderly nature of water, in 1935. This was a major contribution to the understanding of water chemistry, and remains fundamental to all progress on the topic since.

The extraordinary flexibility of the hydrogen bonds allows the molecules to change partners a billion times a second. When the temperature drops to the freezing point, however, the little man becomes rigid (who can blame him?), stretching his arms and legs straight out, transfixed into a lattice where hydrogen feet grip electron hands in an endless sequence. This also fixes the spaces between the atoms, and takes up 9 percent more room than the dance of the liquid, making it less dense than water. Voilà— ice floats.

Crystal Beauty

The frozen little men are at the molecular level, and we cannot see them with the naked eye. More familiar to us are snowflakes, six-point ice crystals with unique lacy patterns. Aristotle was the first person in recorded history to try to understand the crystal structure of snow, which is a flat crystal lattice of ice. In 1611, Johannes Kepler noticed that snowflakes had six corners and were flat, but chemistry was not advanced enough at that time to explain why, since no one had yet articulated the concept of atoms.

Although the French philosopher and mathematician René

Descartes left us the first detailed account of snow crystal structure in 1637, it was not until W.A. Bentley, a Vermont farmer and fanatically devoted photographer, began his study of snowflakes early in the twentieth century that people began to understand there is a virtually infinite variety of these ornate works of nature. Bentley's mother had been a schoolteacher. She taught him at home until he was fourteen; when he was fifteen, she gave him a small microscope she had used as a teacher in her classroom. It was this that allowed him to undertake his life-long study of snowflakes. At first he drew them, but he found this an entirely inadequate way to record their intricacy and their beauty. Although Bentley's father thought this obsession with snow was nonsense, Bentley and his mother were eventually able to persuade him to buy a bellows camera for his son, to rig with the microscope. During a snowstorm on January 15, 1885, and just before his twentieth birthday, Bentley was able to produce his first—in fact, the world's first—photomicrographs ever taken of an ice crystal. Later, he said: "The day that I developed the first negative made by this method, and found it good, I felt almost like falling on my knees beside that apparatus and worshipping it! It was the greatest moment of my life."

Bentley was the first to document visually that snow crystals are symmetrical and hexagonal, but each one grows differently.[4] In 1904, he wrote a paper positing that the form of ice crystals was a function of air temperature.[5] He stated that crystal structure could reveal circulation within a storm, and that a single crystal, because of the changes in its form, could bear witness to changes in the temperature of the air through which it had fallen. Such insights were half a century ahead of the meteorological science of his day. It would be thirty to fifty years before other scientists even addressed some of these issues again.

Poorly understood by his neighbours and family, and ignored by the scientists of the day, Bentley did all of his groundbreaking scientific research and writing while contributing his full share of hard labour on the dairy farm he shared with his brother's family. In the 1920s, the media began to pay some attention. In 1922, he wrote a remarkable article about his technique for photographing snowflakes for *Popular Mechanics* magazine. It is humbling to read it today—to capture snowflakes with his primitive set-up he used either a turkey feather or a broom bristle. Over the years, Bentley took more than four thousand remarkable photographs of snowflakes through the microscope attached to his plate camera. Many of these can be seen at http://snowflakebentley.com, a website maintained by Vermont's Jericho Historical Society.[6] In 1925, Wilson "Snowflake" Bentley said of his legacy: "Under the microscope, I found that snowflakes were miracles of beauty; and it seemed a shame that this beauty should not be seen and appreciated by others. Every crystal was a masterpiece of design and no one design was ever repeated. When a snowflake melted, that design was forever lost. Just that much beauty was gone, without leaving any record behind."

Bentley's insights about how snowflakes are formed continue to evolve today, in a place that hasn't seen any snow since 1949: the Caltech campus in Pasadena, California. There, in an experimental cold chamber in a physics lab, Dr. Kenneth Libbrecht, a professor of physics, makes designer snowflakes and studies how they form. Sometimes, he also studies them in nature. He particularly likes the ones he finds in Timmins, Ontario. He is trying to figure out why it is that changes in humidity, wind and temperature result in such different shapes of snowflakes. For example, at just below the freezing point of 32°F, the crystals look like little plates. But just a few degrees below that, they become small columns of ice, like pencils. Then around 5°F, the flakes become the large, ornate plates that fascinate everyone from small children to interior designers.

In collaboration with the Wisconsin-based photographer Patricia Rasmussen (the modern Bentley), Dr. Libbrecht has produced a stunning book called *The Snowflake: Winter's Secret Beauty*. Their photographs are probably the best snowflake images ever published. Dr. Libbrecht promotes the book as a field guide for amateur snow hounds who want to catch these gorgeous ephemerals on a coat sleeve, a window or a cold metal surface, and examine them under the magnifying glass. Such beauty is rarely available so easily. Beauty is an end in itself. But as we shall see, ice crystal formation also contains useful information, for disciplines from weather forecasting to the hardware underpinnings of artificial intelligence and micro-manufacturing.

ICE SHEETS, GLACIERS AND SASTRUGI

When enough snowflakes fall, the land is blanketed with fluffy snow. As snow accumulates over time, it compacts under its own weight, which starts to squeeze out the air between the flakes. At this stage, known as *firn*, it is still separated into individual granules, but it is much firmer than the original snow blanket. The process of compacting, aided by the weight of additional snowfalls on top of the firn, continues to squeeze out air or compress the air that cannot escape. Eventually, the pressure welds the granules into glacier ice. This can take anywhere from fifty years to three thousand. In Antarctica, the firn layer can be more than 100 metres deep. If this process of falling and compacting snow happens in cold places, where melting does not keep up with freezing (as in the very Far North, in Antarctica and at high latitudes), then glaciers form. If the glaciers are on high ground or mountains, their weight gradually pushes them down, and they begin to move, carving the land as they flow like big rivers of ice. Their movement is full of complexity, influenced by the shape of the underlying bedrock, air temperatures, wind velocity and many other factors.

Glaciers in the coldest regions tend to be more stable than those in more temperate zones, stabilized at or around the freezing point, although even in the coldest parts of Antarctica, glaciers can contain fast-moving ice streams that move several times faster than the surrounding body of the glacier. These differences in velocity contribute to the opening up of crevasses that are very dangerous to people travelling on the surface. Glaciers in more temperate zones tend to develop a thin film of pressurized water underneath which propels them to move faster than the more stable, colder glaciers. They can push quite far into populated areas. For example, the Athabasca Glacier is right beside a highway in the Canadian Rockies, and you can easily visit it (see Chapter 12).

If the glaciers are continental, as in Greenland and Antarctica, they are known as ice sheets and they simply spread until they reach the coast and spill over into the ocean. Antarctica is the highest, windiest, driest continent on earth. On its ice sheet are the striking sastrugi, ridges that look like frozen waves on the ocean. Sastrugi are created by the high winds that constantly buffet the surface of the southernmost continent. They are common in Antarctica, and are clearly visible on the upwind face of Antarctica's famous ice megadunes. These amazing formations are so big no one knew they existed until the advent of satellite imagery allowed us to see large-scale patterns on the earth's surface.

The Antarctic winds are so powerful that they can actually carve ice. Dr. Ted Scambos of the National Snow and Ice Data Centre (NSIDC) thinks the megadunes began because the winds were disrupted by peaks in the ice, probably formed by hills and valleys in the underlying bedrock far below the surface. The interplay of cool, moist air and water vapour, rising and descending over the years, triggers a refreezing pattern that sticks to the ice crystals and enlarges them so that they become extremely coarse: each crystal can be up to 2 centimetres across. The images from NASA and Canada's Radarsat suggest that these coarse grains alternate with fine ones, creating alternate rough and smooth surfaces. The radar data make the rough upwind face, which scatters energy, appear bright in the images, while the smooth surface and coarse snow grains on the downwind face absorb more energy, making them look darker.

Ice sheets in extremely cold coastal areas such as Antarctica, Alaska, Greenland and the Canadian Arctic can also develop tongues that extend out over frozen bodies of water. In

Antarctica, for example, as the falling snow thickens and expands the sea ice around the continent, glaciers extend out onto it and create massive coastal ice shelves. The ice around Antarctica grows to twice the size of Australia every winter, and then it shrinks back with warmer weather. Similarly, the Canadian Arctic "land" becomes many times larger in the winter, as land-based glaciers and sea ice come together to join up islands and form huge ice shelves that people and animals can use as bridges and highways for travel. The behaviour of this ice affects the ocean currents, the winds and other forces that interact and eventually influence the weather you and I experience, no matter where we are on the planet.

THE COLOUR OF ICE

People are often intrigued by the colour of ice and snow. The idea that snow and ice are white is really a perception based on the extraordinary reflectivity of the multifaceted crystals. Ted Scampos suggests that hard candy is a useful proxy. No matter what colour the candy is, if you smash it into tiny pieces, the pieces look white.[7] "That's because the light we see is bouncing off the surface of the broken sugar grains rather than penetrating the inside of the sugar where the color is. Snow looks white because of tiny reflective edges, but ice looks blue because the light travels through the crystals for a longer distance before it comes back to you."

Light particles, or photons, come in different wavelengths, which the human eye sees as different colours. Short photon waves look violet to blue, while longer ones look redder. When the waves hit an object, they can bounce back, (reflection); they can bounce in several directions (scattering); they can pass right through (transmission) or they can give up their energy crashing into molecules inside the object, and die (absorption). Photons of different wavelengths react differently to various kinds of molecules. An apple mostly bounces back the longer-wavelength red photons and absorbs the other ones, thus appearing red to us.

Snow is full of air and reflective surfaces—rather like diamond-dusted whipped cream. But by the time it turns to solid ice, much of the air is gone. What remains in the form of embedded air bubbles causes light to scatter, so that in nature, ice appears mostly white. In old glacier ice, the air is either gone or extremely compressed, so that the ice is clear and the light penetrates much more deeply. The deeper the light goes, the more the red wavelengths are absorbed. Blue wavelengths can go 24 metres into the ice before they are absorbed. At any place closer to the surface than that, you can see glowing blue light. When you look into the ice, it looks bluest from the inside. This is because the light has filtered through until only the blue wavelengths remain. Sometimes you can also see violet, green and dark grey, from the related spectrums.

Truly cold glaciers never thaw, and they are made up of the purest, most beautiful ice on earth, with an astounding range of colours. In addition to the blues, violets, greys and greens that result from the way ice molecules interact with light, the glaciers also pick up dirt, rocks and minerals on their travels. These incidental additions can add black, brown and yellow streaks. There is even an occasional algae bloom that creates a rosy-red blush on some glaciers. Apparently, this algae is safe to eat and tastes like watermelon, but most of us are unlikely ever to try it!

It is these very cold freshwater glaciers, weakened by the wave action lapping beneath them when they reach beyond the shore, that calve into the ocean in spectacular crashes, producing the floating glaciers we call icebergs.

MY FIRST ICEBERG

At the conference in St. John's, Jeanine Daigle showed her magnificent photos of icebergs. She was the first person I met who actually made a living from icebergs, although she wasn't the last (see www.imageinspired.com for Daigle's work). The year 2002 was one of the years when warmth and ocean currents had conspired to shorten the season when it is possible to see icebergs in the Narrows, the mouth of St. John's Harbour. By July, that was good for shipping and fishing, but it wasn't good for me.

We headed out after the conference across the island and up the northern peninsula to L'Anse aux Meadows, a UNESCO World Heritage site that marks the only known remnants of a Viking settlement in North America. From there, we went on to Iceberg Alley headquarters, St. Anthony's Bight. There, at last, I would see a sight I will never forget: my first iceberg from sea level, close up. I had often seen icebergs from the air, while flying over the North Atlantic. I had seen hundreds, if not thousands, of iceberg pictures in my pursuit of ice. Now, as we boarded the 15-metre *Gaffer III* with skipper Paul Alcock, I could barely contain my anticipation. Paul's family owns Northland Tours, which operates iceberg, whale-watching and fishing trips out of St. Anthony's. Their enthusiasm to share their knowledge of this unique environment is unflagging.[8]

The excursion was an odd combination of rich lecture and good ol' boy party. At one point, one of the Alcock brothers dipped a fishnet into the water and scooped out chunks of iceberg for us to handle, or put into our drinks (the drinks fizzed gently as the ancient compressed air escaped from the ice). For part of the trip, there was rousing Newfoundland music and singing, but there was also a quiet, contemplative time as we approached the clear brilliant aqua base of the berg and people became absorbed with taking pictures. Many simply couldn't speak as they looked up at it.

In my mind was Jeanine Daigle's image of an arched iceberg looking like the Snow Queen's Palace at Sea, far more impressive than this first iceberg I was seeing "in the flesh," so to speak. I no longer cared: the sight and smell of cool freshness around it, the excitement of being up close, the luminosity of the colours in the July sun more than made up for the relative modesty of this particular berg. It was grounded in 55 metres of water, and parts of it towered as much as 25 metres above the ocean. The locals told us it had been three times as large when it first grounded, and they considered it medium-sized.[9] Along this coast, icebergs are often 46 to 60 metres tall, and 15 to 23 metres wide. The tallest arctic iceberg ever seen in these parts, in 1967, was some 168 metres above the surface of the ocean, or about a third the height of the CN Tower.

The base of the medium-sized iceberg grounded in a little sheltered bay near St. Anthony's Bight was visible below the surface and dangerously and deceptively foreshortened by the clear water, shimmering brilliant aquamarine. While most people know that only the tip of an iceberg is above water, about one-eighth or one-ninth of its mass, that doesn't usually mean that the depth the berg reaches below water is seven or nine times what you see above. While icebergs come in many shapes, most often the bulk below water is a large mass that extends around its above-water tip, frequently only 20 or 30 percent deeper below than above. Experienced sailors know better than to come in too close around this base.

Up close, this berg's surface was marbled with thousands of bright blue, turquoise and green veins. My glaciologist friends had explained that as the mother glaciers to these icebergs heave and move over the rocks beneath, they crack and open up crevasses that can swallow up hikers and skiers. As meltwater rushes into these cracks, it refreezes quickly from the outside in, with very few air bubbles in comparison to the rest of the glacier. In the larger veins, it was easy to see where the meltwater had crystallized inwards because it had formed a visible seam, a tiny vertical line of air bubbles at the centre of each vein, where the freezing surfaces had touched and sealed off the crevasse.

Sun, wind and water had carved the berg into idiosyncratic shapes. A small flock of birds was exploring one end of it, while the waves lapped away at its underside. You could see that as the water wormed away, it would eventually change the shape of the iceberg, and from there, its centre of gravity and its balance. At the same time, the part of the ice that was exposed to the sun and the air was melting faster than the part that was sitting in the water (the water temperature, at 3°C, was significantly cooler than the air). Icebergs that change shape due to melting can become deadly to hovering boats.

As we circled this berg from the observation deck of the

Gaffer III, each of its surfaces glistened with a different light and colour. I could have circled it for hours. That was the only berg in St. Anthony's Bight the day I was there. Most of the ones that reach the North Atlantic come from the one hundred major glaciers in Greenland and a few more in northern Ellesmere Island. Of forty thousand icebergs a year that drift south from the Arctic, ten to fifteen thousand of them calve from twenty major glaciers between the Jacobshaven and Humboldt Glaciers in West Greenland. This group provides the vast majority, some 85 percent, of the bergs that reach the "latitudes of melt" off the Newfoundland and Labrador coast known as Iceberg Alley (roughly between 51° and 46° North).[10]

From Greenland or Ellesmere, travelling at speeds of up to 2 knots an hour (half as fast as you can walk), the glaciers make their way slowly southward into the North Atlantic. Often, they spend a year or two frozen into the pack ice around Baffin Island in the High Arctic, or they grind to a halt on the ocean floor until they have melted enough to continue their stately progress. Canadian author Will Ferguson is fascinated with this process: "Translucent marble, Matterhorns on the move, they roll under the waves, they grind along the bottom of bays, they lurch to a dead stop, they melt themselves free."[11]

A Closer Look

A scientist I met at the conference, Dr. Victor Petrenko, an engineer and physicist at Dartmouth College in Hanover, New Hampshire, studies the microsurfaces and behaviour of ice crystals. Dr. Petrenko is a rarity in his field, a pure research scientist who also thinks constantly about practical applications for his findings. He loves the unusual transparency of ice, although he is careful to position this as his human, emotional response. "It is, perhaps, the most transparent material we know. With pure ice in Antarctica, you can see clearly for hundreds of metres, much farther than in water. It is an intrinsic property of the material. Any material can be transparent within a certain range of frequencies, but ice has an unusually wide window of transparency."

Dr. Paul Barrette was one of the scientists who had encouraged me to come to the highly technical conference in Newfoundland in the first place. Though a geologist, he was also susceptible to the unscientific romance of ice. In preparation for the sessions, and to give me some background, he invited me to work with him in a laboratory cold room to understand what glacier ice is like up close.

First, using a pointy hammer, he chipped off a triangular chunk from a piece of fifteen-thousand-year-old ice—about the size of a big flowerpot. Kept in the lab freezer, the piece was from an iceberg calved at least two years earlier from a Greenland glacier and harvested for Dr. Barrette in Iceberg Alley. "If you listen carefully, you'll hear a crackling sound. It's little air bubbles, so pleased to escape from their prison under pressure, to be free at last," he joked as he held the freezer door open.[12] The air escaping from our chunk had been locked into the Greenland ice sheet for at least ten or fifteen thousand years, which is why people believe it to be very pure. This is largely true, but as we shall see, the ice also contains a record of past environmental conditions—which were not always as pure as we might think.

Paul Barrette and his colleagues rely on "iceberg cowboys" to lasso samples of this valuable ice for their research purposes. Working from small boats, many of these cowboys are former fishermen, displaced by the disappearance of the northern cod off the Grand Banks of Newfoundland. Equipped with the same tools and weapons their forefathers used in whaling and sealing, these entrepreneurial adventurers also use guns to help them break off chunks of icebergs. Sometimes they work with smaller berg pieces, known as "growlers" or "bergy bits."[13] Growlers range from the size of a small car to the size of a large house, while bergy bits are even smaller. They are no less dangerous for shipping, though, because they lie low in the waves and are very difficult to detect. A ship ploughing ahead at full speed can experience a nasty shock when hitting one.

When the iceberg cowboys have pieces of a manageable size, they lasso them or haul them in with fishnets, while hoping the process will not destabilize the massive bergs and cause them to shift suddenly, or overturn. If that happens, they can be in real trouble, because the sheer size of the underwater portion of a berg is guaranteed to create massive swells, or possibly even crush their boats. These cowboys are initially hired by vodka and glacier-water bottling companies; donations for research purposes can come from either the men themselves or the companies who buy their "bounty."

In July 2004, the iceberg cowboys ran into some controversy. Tourists in the town of Bonavista were shocked when a crew from the Canadian Iceberg Vodka Corporation showed up to hack away at an iceberg they were watching and photographing. The tourists decided to cut their visit short in protest. The mayor of Bonavista, Betty Fitzgerald, promptly asked the provincial government to protect the icebergs as a valuable tourist resource.

Dr. Barrette, on the other hand, was grateful for the cowboys who donated the iceberg ice for his research. Wearing insulated gloves, he stuffed our beautiful triangular piece unceremoniously into a felt boot liner (somehow I was little shocked at this), and we made our way across the street to the cold room at the National Research Council of Canada's Institute for Ocean Technology (IOT).

In the anteroom, we suited up until I felt like a polar bear— Gore-Tex overalls, parkas, heavy gloves, insulated snow boots with felt liners. We had no choice about the gear, since the temperature in the cold room is kept at just –15°C at all times. Flip-flopping in my big boots (the engineering facility had no women-sized boots), I followed Paul Barrette into the airlock and then into the cold room. He had brought a very heavy and very sharp high-carbon knife blade in with him. He fitted the blade into a bench-mounted microtome, or precision machine. With a large and noisy slant saw, just as if the hunk of ice were a piece of wood, he carved out a piece, 10 centimetres square and 3 centimetres thick. It looked smooth to the naked eye, but it was not nearly smooth enough for our purposes. We were going to make a thin sample, the format used in research on the structure and behaviour of ice.

With a drop of water from a Thermos in which the water was kept above freezing in the cold room, we welded one side of the sample to a glass slide. It was the lowest-temperature and most unorthodox welding I had ever seen. (I have since learned that all ice carvers use this technique, including chefs doing wedding set-ups in Miami.) He began to shave away at this slice of glacier ice, first 50 microns at a time, then 20 microns, then 10, then 5, and then 2. A micron is only one one-thousandth of a millimetre, and yet the ice shavings curled up off the sample like lavish silver ribbons. The cold room kept the ice shavings intact, so Dr. Barrette needed to brush them away with an incongruously large paintbrush from time to time.

After hundreds of passes (a few done by me, under his guidance), when we had one perfectly smooth surface, he used a utility knife to disengage the rough side of the sample from the glass. Again taking drops of water from the Thermos, he welded the edge of the perfect side to a smooth piece of glass, taking care not to allow the ice weld to infiltrate between the glass and the surface we had so painstakingly prepared. We repeated the process on the other side, and eventually, we had a thin sample of just 0.6 millimetres.

Using polarized filters, Dr. Barrette photographed the thin sample. And what a revelation! The six-sided crystals, under the weight of fifteen thousand years of ice, reminded me of nothing so much as Edvard Munch's painting *The Scream*. They appeared to be moaning silently with the pressure—not just of the weight of the ice, but of a force called *shear*, which deforms and distorts as the glacier grinds against the bedrock, sliding slowly, inexorably, over thousands of years, into the sea and towards the vodka man's boat.

The crystal shapes were astounding enough, but what Dr. Barrette did next was completely unexpected to a layperson. The thin slice of ice was translucent in the cold room light. Explaining that he was using a technique common in observing rocks and minerals, Barrette took out two polarizing filters. First, he laid them over the sample at 90-degree angles, and everything looked black. But then, keeping one on top of the sample, he put the other underneath, and a riot of colour emerged.

Although we seldom think about it, all colour is refracted light. Without the filters, the many tiny surfaces in the ice reflected the whole spectrum of light very efficiently, and made it appear white. The filters caused refractions in the sample to look like a 1960s fractal painting: magenta, forest green, mustard yellow, midnight black and royal blue. There was no longer anything silvery and virginal about our sample. And when Dr. Barrette shed horizontal light across the slide, you could see tiny pits and imperfections that had been invisible a moment before. These, he explained, were air pockets that had been pressured and squeezed for fifteen thousand years. *See colour photo insert.*

I was awed to see the ice up close in this privileged way. Now, I wanted to step back and learn more about the big picture.

CHAPTER THREE

"Water is the most fundamental of finite resources."
—American Association for the Advancement of Science

THE INFLUENCE OF ICE

The earthly cryosphere is made up of all the different kinds of ice we have on the planet, whether it is in the ground, as part of the permafrost; in the air, as snow, hail or condensation trails hanging in the sky in the wake of jet aircraft; on land or on water. Even though the cryosphere represents only a fraction of the volume of the amount of water on the planet, it has a major influence on the regulation of climate and weather. We can say where a given planet in our solar system will be in nine months, ten days, three hours and ten seconds, but we cannot predict the weather where we live accurately, even a week from today. This is because the physics of our atmosphere are extremely complex, much more so than the movement of planets. The factors that determine climate and weather: the planet's hydrology (the entire water system), plate tectonics and geology, ocean currents and wind systems, cloud formations and sunspot activity: all these interact with, influence or are influenced by, the various forms of ice.

In order to learn about how ice influences global climate and weather, we need to examine the overall role of water here on our blue planet. It is not pretty. Water has the potential to be the single most divisive issue of the twenty-first century, overtaking oil and religion as a source of conflict among the earth's peoples.

Of all the water on earth, almost 98 percent is salt water.[1] Just over 2 percent of it is fresh water, and more than *three-quarters* of that amount is locked in the cryosphere, frozen deep in the ice sheets, primarily over Antarctica and Greenland, and in mountain glaciers across the continents, inaccessible to humans, animals and plant life. Only 0.00003 percent of all the world's surface water (from lakes and streams) is clean, or potable. The balance of available fresh water has been polluted, and needs to be treated before humans and animals can use it. This explains why water is such a precious resource.[2] According to UNESCO, "When you know that nothing on Earth can live without fresh water, that a human can't survive after three days without it, you see how precious this resource is—and how much we need to protect it."[3]

In fact, fresh water is "the most fundamental of finite resources" according to the American Association for the Advancement of Science (AAAS). There is simply no substitute for it, and it is not always where we need it, when we need it, in the amount and quality required. Of the world's easily accessible fresh water, we already use more than half.

There is also a severe mismatch between where that fresh water is, and where it is needed. The Amazon River Basin generates 15 percent of global runoff, but has only 0.4 percent of global population.[4] Asia, with 60 percent of the world's population, is unable to capitalize on the 36 percent of global runoff it receives, which comes mostly in the intense rains of the short monsoon season, when it cannot all be easily captured for use. Canada has more than 30 times the amount of fresh water per person as China, but that is misleading: despite its vast size and wealth of fresh water, Canada's population is so concentrated that in urban areas like Toronto, the water table is overloaded and fragile. At the dawn of the twenty-first century, we humans face a situation where 1.1 billion of the world's people do not have enough clean water to drink, and 2.5 billion do not have enough to meet basic sanitation standards.[5]

Water respects no boundaries, but that has never stopped humans from trying to retain it. Bordering jurisdictions around the world behave unilaterally, beggaring their neighbours by damming rivers so people downstream have no water. Many of the world's great rivers no longer even reach the oceans. Mostly, they are diverted to irrigate crops (60 percent of the world's water usage), or sometimes to frivolous purposes, such as watering golf courses in deserts.

Some countries, like Libya, pump most or all of their water from underground. This water is often called "fossil" water, because like fossil fuels, it is not renewable in the sense that it cannot be replenished quickly enough by rainfall. Every year, Libya pumps seven times its annual rainfall volume from deep beneath the Sahara Desert to irrigate its crops. India pumps at twice the recharge rate, and some water tables there are falling by 1 to 3 metres a year, leading to land collapses in areas where the water table is badly depleted. This poses a real dilemma. The AAAS Atlas of Population and Environment estimates that if India gave up groundwater "mining," its grain production could fall by 25 percent. How, then, would India feed its people? And yet, this use of fossil water resources is clearly unsustainable.

THE HYDROLOGICAL CYCLE

On average, a drop of water stays in a river about sixteen days before reaching the sea, and in the atmosphere about eight days before falling as precipitation. But if that drop of water freezes into a glacier, as we have seen, it can stay there for thousands of years.

A major river like the Ganges moves millions of tons of water a day, but freshwater bodies in the ground (known as aquifers) move very slowly, over tens, even hundreds of thousands of years. Only the shallowest of these tend to be tapped for human use, as it is difficult to drill down to reach the majority of aquifers. It *is* possible for these freshwater resources to be supplemented by precipitation, meltwater from glaciers, dew, fog drip, reservoirs created by dams, and artificial recharging of aquifers—however the extreme slowness of groundwater cycles remains. For one thing, aquifers can only absorb water very slowly, which is why the speed of glacial melting from mountain glaciers and ice sheets is relevant to this dilemma: if the melting happens too fast, the ground cannot absorb the fresh water, and it simply runs off to the ocean. This is why it is ultimately so serious for humans when an aquifer is "tapped out," or used up faster than it can be replenished.

With population growth and careless use of the existing water supply, the amount of water actually available per capita is falling, and its quality is deteriorating. In 1970, global run-off of fresh water was 12,900 cubic metres per capita.[6] By 1995, partly driven by population growth, that amount had dropped to 7,600 cubic metres per person per year. With such intensive use of the planet's resources, it is hardly surprising that water quality is suffering.

THE CRYOSPHERE

Given this situation, the cryosphere, which is the sum of all the frozen earth and water on the planet, becomes crucially important to our future. This holding tank for more than three-quarters of the global freshwater reserves contributes to the regulation of climate through its influence on ocean currents. The cryosphere slows down global warming by reflecting the sun's energy back out into space, instead of absorbing it as open water does. The technical term for this reflectiveness is *albedo*.

The cryosphere affects the surface energy, water cycle and atmospheric circulation, as ice on the ground influences the temperature of the air and wind patterns.[7] Greenland, for example, is still experiencing the remains of the Wisconsin Ice Age. The ice cap is so bulky—2,400 kilometres long, 725 kilometres wide and up to 3,350 metres thick—that it weighs down the land. The middle of the world's largest island is actually concave—360 metres below sea level! The sheer size of the ice sheets in Greenland and Antarctica—entire mountain ranges are buried beneath them—creates gravitational pull that affects sea levels for great distances around them.

The cryosphere provokes so many complex interactions that it is difficult to predict the future of climate, or even whether or not a dock at your cottage will be left high and dry in any given summer. But the fact remains that the food we eat, and the way we live, work and play are all affected by this pervasive and mysterious global system. We have good reason to try to understand what is going on: the global system is now changing at unprecedented speed, and a growing number of scientists believe that we may be approaching a tipping point, where each and every one of us will be profoundly affected by the consequences.

I have come to think of the cryosphere as a kind of icy crust that moves constantly over the earth's surface, expanding and contracting, making waves, giving life and taking it away with equal aplomb.

SEA ICE

The cryosphere is primarily made up of land-based ice, glaciers, ice sheets and permafrost. But what many people do not realize is that all ice crystals, even sea ice, are fresh water. In order to form into crystals, water has to expel salt molecules. It takes a long time to do this with sea water. So sea ice begins its life as a fragile, barely-there network of slushy potential ice called *frazil* or grease ice. If the water is calm, it quickly congeals into a silky-thin, elastic crust called *nilas* that rides the waves and shatters like glass. If the water is rough, the frazil eventually congeals into *pancake ice* with upturned edges—it really does look like pancakes in a frying pan.

Nilas eventually hardens into something that looks like Swiss cheese. The holes in this young sea ice are filled with increasingly salty brine, as the hardening process expels more salt. It takes a year or two for hard, solid ice to form from sea water, and closer to three years and more before an Inuit hunter can safely melt it to drink. Sea ice can be wildly beautiful. It forms very differently from glacier ice, or even freshwater ice found on lakes and rivers. It is not at all homogeneous, and in fact is quite different from top to bottom. In the Far North and in the Antarctic Ocean, where sea ice often survives the summer, it goes through a heating, cooling and hardening process called *annealing* that rejects the salts entirely and makes the ice much stronger.[8]

In the Arctic Ocean, sea ice is very mobile under the influence of currents and winds, so it crashes together, pulls apart and refreezes. This ends up creating a landscape of huge ridges, sharp jagged peaks of monocrystalline rock, all of which makes surface navigation to the North Pole a logistical nightmare. Many have called it a jigsaw puzzle that just never fits together. To make matters worse, the whole mass moves. American explorer Dr. Frederick A. Cooke described the sensation of being there in his controversial 1908 book *My Attainment of the Pole:*

> *There was about us no land. No fixed point. Absolutely nothing upon which to rest the eye to give the sense of location, or to judge distance. Here everything moves. The sea breathes, and lifts the crust of ice which the wind stirs. The pack ever drifts in response to the pull of the air and the drive of the water.*

The conference at Memorial devoted many presentations and workshops to sea ice, in part because of its crucial importance in world climate.

PERMAFROST

Permafrost is part of the cryosphere, but it is actually permanently frozen rock or soil, which may or may not have a crystalline growth pattern that behaves like ice.[9] There is permafrost under parts of the Arctic that were never under the glaciers, and in some places, such as the area east of the Taimyr Peninsula (a part of central Siberia that juts into the Arctic Ocean), it can reach a depth of 1,900 feet. Permafrost lies beneath as much as a quarter of all the world's land surface, including all of Antarctica and virtually all of the Arctic, but also in high elevations such as the Tibetan Plateau, the Himalayas and the Rocky Mountains. There is even permafrost at the equator, on Mount Cayambe, a 5,775-metre summit in Ecuador.

Researchers are still learning fundamental things about permafrost. Historically, they assumed that ground temperature and air temperature were always equal, but that is far from the case. Iceland and Scandinavia, northern cold-climate countries that border on large bodies of water, have little permafrost. There are boreal forests on much of the northern hemisphere's permafrost, but no one knows what will happen if there is a sudden melting. The Arctic contains almost a third of the earth's stored soil carbon. If melting permafrost were to release this, no one knows whether it would be reabsorbed by wildly growing new plant life, or whether it would simply stoke the fires of rapid global warming. Because there is so much of it, this carbon issue is watched very closely by all kinds of people who care about the global environment. But anyone who wants to build a road or a building in a very cold region has to pay close attention to permafrost itself as well.

Ice-rich permafrost can hold twice as much H_2O as unfrozen ground. Oddly, then, even if this ground is full of frozen water, it is stubbornly impermeable to liquid water, so that in areas where permafrost exists, the water table is very high and the soil poorly aerated. For plants trying to grow on permafrost, it might as well be bedrock: there is no way for them to drive deep roots into the ground, or to grow very high. Even if the frozen ground has a high water content, the plants on it will suffer from drought. This explains why exquisite arctic plants husband their strength, sometimes taking years to produce a single flower. A two-inch moss campion plant may be fifty years old. This is why it is so devastating when such an environment is despoiled: it needs such long periods of time to renew itself.

The frozen ground can contain wedges and lenses, frost cracks called "patterned ground" and frost boils, called "pingos." Walking on it feels like stepping on a stiff sponge. It has its own subtle beauty. As you head north (or up into mountains if they are high enough, even in tropical zones) you eventually encounter what is called the tree line, the limit to where trees can grow. This line is often surprisingly dramatic—here there are trees, and beyond here not a single one, as if the mountain had been shaved down to there. The trees that do survive in shallow ground above permafrost need to spread their roots to survive. They hug the ground for stability, to stay close to the reflected heat and to shelter from the wind.

When spring comes, the surface layer of ground above the permafrost can become very unstable. The trees can begin to lean "every which way," which is why the northern trees are sometimes called "drunken pines." The instability makes it very hard to build reliable roads and solid buildings; it causes existing infrastructure to fall apart suddenly. This layer above the permafrost is also very vulnerable. It can sustain permanent damage from building, driving, or even walking on it. Humans and heavy equipment moving over permafrost can leave tracks that last for many years, and permanently alter the habitat of native animal and plant species.

This is one reason why there has been so much tension over prospective oil drilling in Alaska's Arctic National Wildlife Refuge. Some economically stressed Northern communities want the jobs and investment that will come with the oil industry, while others fear for the fragile arctic environment. They argue that the thin soils over the permafrost have taken thousands of years to accumulate a thickness that can support plant life, and can be scattered to the winds by a heavy vehicle in no time flat.

The same phenomenon that makes damage to permafrost areas so long-lasting also makes High Arctic historical sites a treasure trove for archaeologists. Whereas sites in temperate and tropical zones would break down, rot or disappear, the cold temperatures and ice preserve artefacts and sites that are hundreds, and sometimes thousands of years old in the Arctic and the Antarctic. It has been possible to learn a great deal about failed polar expeditions and mountain cultures from thousands of years ago because they have been preserved in this way.

For example, we know about a group of Thule people, prehistoric seafaring hunters who settled beside a small freshwater lake in the High Arctic about a thousand years ago.

There were fifty or sixty people in the group. They systematically slaughtered bowhead whales in large numbers. They used the meat and the blubber for food, fuel and clothing; the bones they used as beams for their shelters. The refuse from this killing polluted the little lake and its environs, turning it into a slimy, moss-choked waste disposal site. Their actions altered the ecology of the lake *to this day.*[10] The findings have startled those who have thought of the High Arctic as pristine; researchers say this is the earliest record of human impact on an arctic aquatic ecosystem—a history that continues to evolve faster than we can record it.

EXOTIC ICE FORMS

In addition to being an icy crust on the surface of the earth, the cryosphere includes ice in the atmosphere, such as the crystals that make up clouds, and contrails, the ice crystals that are suspended as condensation in jet aircraft exhaust. That is the specialty of Professor Jean Suzanne, a distinguished French researcher from Marseilles. Most of us would not be able to imagine a connection between the state of ice research and the tragedy of September 11, 2001. And yet, as I learned at the conference in St. John's, the unique circumstances around 9/11 did provide an opportunity to study something that would never have occurred otherwise.

When all civil aviation was halted in the three days following September 11, 2001, Professor Suzanne and his team benefited from an unprecedented research opportunity. Never since the dawn of the aviation age had North American skies been free of airplanes for three days. This three-day period without a trace of contrails in the sky allowed his researchers to make comparative measurements. They discovered something startling: the ice hanging in the sky on a normal day—in other words, the normal number of airplane contrails above North America—is directly related to higher temperatures on the ground, up to and exceeding 3°C higher. They now believe that contrails behave much like cirrus clouds in insulating the earth from the cooler portion of the atmosphere above. This very significant impact was unexpected to most specialists in the field, and raised interest in pursuing this research further.

Another venerable professor, Dr. Greg Dash, a physicist from the University of Washington in Seattle, outlined a controversial theory.[11] He suggested that ice-on-ice collisions in the atmosphere could be shown to transfer an electric charge and to cause lightning. This theory set off an uproar among the scientists of various disciplines in attendance. Despite Dr. Dash's significant and lengthy credentials, several much younger scientists obviously considered him a bit of a rebel. One of them confessed to me that this kind of intellectual "electric charge" was part of the attraction of such a multidisciplinary conference, and hugely entertaining. Certainly, the idea of little ice balls crashing into each other to make lightning was counterintuitive, and kind of fun.

FIRE AND ICE

If there was an even hotter ticket item at the conference, it was *clathrates*, ice cages sometimes known as "flammable ice." Presentation after presentation took a run at explaining these ice crystals that form around gas molecules. Under certain conditions of high pressure and low temperature, the ice cages trap gases within the lattice structure. The cages may contain flammable or inert gases; hydrocarbon clathrates are a nuisance when they form inside gas pipelines in the Arctic, for example. Clathrates are believed to be present on other planets in large quantities, and possibly at the heart of comets. They are therefore of great interest in space exploration.

Clathrates are also found in ocean beds and permafrost all over the world. The theory is that methane gas migrates up from the earth through tectonic geological faults, getting trapped in the ice cages when it hits the icy bed in the cold ocean. The cold, high-pressure conditions keep the ice cages submerged and very stable. An estimated twenty times the amount of known natural gas reserves is contained down there—to some people's minds, ripe for exploitation by an energy-hungry world.

There is just one big problem: when you try to exploit them, the clathrates can decompress and release damaging greenhouse gases into the air, or they can catch fire and burn off the energy you were trying to harvest in the first place. The Japanese, who are desperate for energy and have little access to a fossil fuel supply of their own, are working hard to solve this problem. But in the meantime, clathrates are bubbling up out of the permafrost, accelerating the warming of the arctic air. Some scientists think sudden releases of methane clathrates may have caused rapid climate change in the distant past. Others are advancing the idea that clathrates may help to solve warming problems in the future. They think it might be possible to trap rogue greenhouse gases in these clathrate ice cages, and bury them deep in the ocean floor. This might hold the promise—or perhaps the illusion—that humans can use the ice to adapt the planet to their needs.

AMORPHOUS WATER ICES

Most of the ice we will ever see on earth has the crystalline structure we have been describing. But some scientists are pre-occupied with amorphous ices, meaning ice whose atoms are arranged in no particular order. This is true of solids like common glass, which is cooled so fast from the molten stage that the atoms just don't have time to get into an orderly structure. But why would this happen with ice, which most people would experience with a definite crystal structure?

If you can imagine water molecules almost too cold to freeze, that would be amorphous water ice. If water molecules are little men, when it gets extremely cold—let's say, 120 Kelvin (−153.1°C)—the little men get too tired to fight their way through the square-dancing liquid crowd to be in the thick of the action. They just want to slink along the edge of the gathering, and try to join the pack without spending too much energy.

This is the image Jason Donev evoked for me. He has worked with a $650,000 atomic force microscope that has a vibrating tip (300,000 times a second) like an old-fashioned record player gone mad. The whole thing is about the width of a human hair. This instrument provides the only way scientists have found to measure the atomic structure of amorphous water ice: using remote controls, they bring the vibrating tip so close to the surface of the material that the vibrations bounce off the molecule; they then use a laser to measure it.

The reason this instrument is essential is that at a molecular level, amorphous water ice can only be felt tactically, it cannot be viewed graphically—a strange concept for most of us. This is because the conditions required to create pure amorphous ice on earth are so stringent and difficult that it has to be created in incredibly tiny amounts in a laboratory. The atomic force microscope does this work under the "ultra-high vacuum conditions" required. The chamber has to have a pressure of less than one-trillionth of normal atmospheric pressure. Just getting the air out of such a chamber is complicated. As Dr. Donev explains, the chamber is about the size of a vending machine, in stainless steel. In order for the water not to sublimate away entirely under so little pressure, it has be kept extremely cold (the forementioned 120 Kelvin, or −153.1°C). At that temperature, you are working with amorphous solid water.

This is fundamental scientific work, learning about the behaviour of surfaces, and it may appear highly esoteric. Why do we need to know the diffusion rate of solid amorphous water? It is something that can only exist in remote places like comets or the rings and moons of Saturn, so what practical use is it? Says Donev, "Water mediates a lot of chemical reactions, like in the ocean. We think it's possible that amorphous solid water is actually mediating chemical reactions in space, on the surface of various particles of planetary rings. There are chemical reactions there that we see in the infrared spectrum. And we think that those chemical reactions take place over a much longer period of time than they would if they were just in water."

If this still sounds esoteric, space exploration is not the only application for knowledge of amorphous materials. Increasingly, and as we reach the limits of miniaturization in information processing hardware, researchers are looking to materials such as amorphous silicon to build the next generation of micro-processors. For example, some photovoltaic cells in solar power panels are made with amorphous silicon because it absorbs solar radiation 40 times more efficiently than single-crystal silicon. Miniature processors using amorphous materials could potentially overcome the problems of overheating that tiny metal circuits are now encountering.

The problem with developing new products based on these amorphous structures is the dearth of existing computer models to explain what is happening. Only experiments can lay the foundation to do the required modelling. There may not always be funding to do such fundamental scientific work, but some-times, as in this case, a commercial reason can be found to justi-fy the effort. So Jason Donev, a brilliant young low-temperature condensed-matter experimental ultrahigh-vacuum technology physicist (and pretty good rock musician), may end up studying these concepts, not to advance our basic knowledge of ice, but to help some commercial enterprise manufacture a better memory device by growing tiny little hemispherical brains within the amorphous silicone. Which just goes to show, ice can lead to anything, including other planets.

■ ■ ■

One of the world's reigning experts on the moons of Jupiter is Dr. Robert T. Pappalardo, from the Laboratory for Atmospheric and Space Physics at the University of Colorado in Boulder. Dr. Pappalardo looks more like a young ballet choreographer than an astrophysicist, and he is certainly an elegant presenter. He had been given one of the most prestigious spots at the St. John's conference, and he took full advantage of it. His pictures of the surface of the Jovian moon Europa were breathtaking—and so was his ability to explain the images.

Think lava-lamp, he told us, an icy version of the old hippy "must-have" decor item. Europa's ice is warmer closer to its core; this warmer ice keeps rising to the surface through the colder ice, in an kind of ice convection that is much like the 1970s gadgets that made a return to fashion in the late 1990s. Europa's orbit revolves around its immense master planet Jupiter, which projects its forces of gravity and tidal friction to keep this lava-lamp effect going. On Dr. Pappalardo's "icy moons" website, the little virtual lava lamps are in perpetual motion, just like the insatiable curiosity of the men and women who work on this leading edge of ice science.[12]

CHAPTER FOUR

"If all the beasts were gone, man would die from a great loneliness
of spirit. For whatever happens to the beasts soon happens to man.
All things are interconnected. This we know."
—Chief Seattle, 1854

THE ICE-ADAPTED BIOSPHERE

In 1997, researchers funded by the U.S. National Science
Foundation (NSF) excavated a cave on Prince of Wales Island
in Alaska. There, they uncovered parts of a human jaw and
pelvis between 9,200 and 9,800 years old—the oldest human
bones ever found in Alaska. European explorers venturing into
the Arctic from the sixteenth century on found it extremely
difficult to survive in the regions of ice and perpetual winter
night. The humans who lived in those Alaskan caves would
have had to be highly skilled at living on and with the ice—
just as a few aboriginal peoples and some species of animals are
today. In Chapter 5, we will look more closely at how humans
have adapted to living with ice, but here, we will look at the
rest of the biosphere—plants and animals.

Extreme cold and ice are powerful forces of nature: if they
do not kill living things, they compel them to adapt. Plants,
microorganisms, animals and humans all face do-or-die conditions that separate the survivors from the pack. Every spring in

the Arctic, the creatures and plants in the layer beneath the snow start waking up when the sun begins to reach them through the snow. This early sunlight, and the insulation from the cold air, gives them a jump on the season. Purple saxifrage, an ice-adapted plant that nourishes musk oxen, for example, immediately flowers under the snow, and starts attracting insects to pollinate it.

Many ice-adapted plants and creatures, from the lousewort to bumblebees and woolly bear caterpillars, trap heat in woolly growths or body hair. The layer of fine down closest to the body on a musk ox has ensured the shaggy animal's survival since pre-historic times. Known as *qiviuk*, it is softer, finer and lighter than cashmere and eight times warmer than wool. This warmth and lightness have convinced the fashion industry that it is worth paying a premium to make the world's most expensive sweaters out of qiviuk, obtained from both wild and domesti-cated musk oxen when the animals are moulting, and therefore without harming them.

Flowers such as the Arctic poppy adapt by turning to follow the sun, and holding their petals to focus its warmth on their seeds. The Arctic poppy is able to give itself the equivalent of 25 percent more sun time by using this technique to increase the temperature inside its parabolic shape by 10 percent in rela-tion to the outside air. Another flower, the bell-shaped Arctic heath, traps warm air from the ground by facing down.

■ ■ ■

Humans have adapted to the ice in even more dramatic ways, if William H. Calvin is right. He believes that if we can plan

ahead, speak articulately or pitch a ball accurately, it has something to do with human adaptation to the ice ages. Dr. Calvin
is a theoretical neurophysiologist at the University of
Washington School of Medicine. In his provocative book *The
Ascent of Mind: Ice Age Climates and the Evolution of Intelligence*,
he proposes that four ice ages, over two and a half million years,
forced humans to adapt by rapidly enlarging their brains. He
thinks the abrupt climate changes that occurred within the life-
times of single individuals would have "promoted the incre-
mental accumulation of new mental abilities that conferred
greater behavioural flexibility." Among these skills, he includes
the capacity for human language, the ability to plan ahead, and
the ability to perform complex rapid movements such as throwing. Each sudden climate change, or "population bottleneck,"
he proposes, led to the survival of those people who were able
to adapt quickly and to learn the new skills required. He links
this directly to parts of the human brain that research has told
us made sudden gains during these very same historical periods
of sudden climate change.

Calvin's gift for conveying impossibly complex scientific
information with a light touch and original thought make him
a joy to read. His theory of human adaptation forced by the ice
ages rests on rapid behavioural adaptation, something that
would have become easier for humans than for animals, once
that big brain had begun to evolve.

■ ■ ■

The animals that survive today in the Arctic—and to a lesser
extent the Antarctic—have all learned behaviours and adjusted

their biology to live with the ice. Caribou, polar bears and dall sheep have hollow hairs that channel sunlight to the skin and preserve warmth. As winter approaches, lemmings grow extra claws to dig their burrows through the ice; they wear them out by the summer. Many animals hibernate during the time when food is more difficult to find, or change colour, like Arctic foxes, between the arctic summer and winter. Ptarmigans do both.

Others adapt in amazingly sophisticated ways. Seals, for example, give birth on ice floes and have a delayed implantation mechanism for eggs in their wombs; this allows them to time the birth of their pups to coincide with the breakup of their winter ice habitat into floes. The seal pups have a better chance to survive being eaten by polar bears this way, as the hungry bears (*Ursus maritimus* is a sea mammal) are forced to swim between the floes. On open ice, the bears could snap up the baby seals by the dozen.

Seals have bodies designed for swimming and for energy conservation, with blubber to insulate them and two layers of hair, guard hair and underfur, to keep them war. They use their flippers to regulate heat through an arterio-venous shunt that prevents heat loss when it is cold. When it is warm, you may see them fan their flipper "fingers" to shed body heat. When you see a seal basking on a rock, he is recovering from a period of shutting down oxygen to his organs while underwater, and taking the time to digest.

Elephant seals have an extraordinary capacity to stay under water for up to two hours, as far down as 1,150 metres. They can slow their heart rate down from 130 beats a minute to 25 or less when they are diving, restricting blood flow to their brains and muscles only, and shutting down everything else. Life on the ice is hard and unstable: male seals fight to stay with one cow but try to have as many offspring as possible, while females try to have just a few and make sure they survive. The seal pups have a high mortality rate, so mothers try to feed their newborns intensely, drawing on their blubber to produce a rich, high-fat milk. As soon as possible, they jettison the pups. This is only realistic, since ice floes are dangerous places, where the mother and the pup can easily be separated: the sooner they are independent, the higher their chances of survival.

Polar bears, in order to be efficient hunters, rely on a remarkable sense of smell that is one hundred times better than yours and mine. If you want to photograph a polar bear sleeping on an ice floe, you will need very good eyes. Your heat-sensitive camera won't help you find one because the variable blubber layer that protects polar bears from heat loss works so well that they "disappear" from the heat-sensitive radar. The naked eye might not work that well either: their fur is not actually white; it is transparent, made of hollow individual hairs that reflect as white to the human eye. These hollow hairs carry the sun's short-wavelength energy to the bear's black skin, an element in the polar bear's unique and sophisticated heat-exchange and management system that can keep the skin 15 degrees warmer than its surroundings. This complex and intriguing system has evolved specifically for living on the ice, and for constant movement in and out of frigid waters.[1]

The bears go through enormous weight fluctuations, hundreds of pounds every year, in order to ensure their own survival and that of their young. They can live off their blubber for months, turning down their metabolisms like a thermostat and waiting for the right time to emerge. Females den for a long time when they are pregnant, needing only a mouthful of snow from time to time. They have extraordinary skills, building dens out of ice and snow that are models of architecture and design, regulating ventilation and temperatures to meet their needs, and those of their helpless, tiny cubs (they are only the size of rats at birth), until they are able to fend for themselves sufficiently to come outside. The knowledge and skills required to build these dens are astonishingly close to those of humans who have evolved igloos as the best-adapted way to live on the ice.

One startling sight in a floating ice habitat is a huge killer walrus (males often weigh more than 1,300 kilograms) fast asleep, his tusks dug into the edge of an ice floe, floating in the frigid water, thanks to air sacs under his throat. Among themselves, walruses are the party animals of the ice, piling up sometimes one hundred at a time, socializing and snout-kissing. But their long ivory tusks and their foul tempers make them the most dangerous ice-mammal to humans, and experienced ice adventurers know better than to be fooled by their playfulness.

The Arctic cod (*Boreogadus saida*)[2] has adapted well to living with the ice, nuzzling into crevices of sea ice to look for nutrients even during the brief polar summer, when the sea ice fragments. Its role in the arctic food chain is considered so crucial that despite numbers in the 100,000-tonne range (sufficient in theory to attract the attention of industry), scientists discourage any thought of exploiting it commercially. The Arctic cod leaves its icy shelter only to grasp prey—and no wonder. The pack ice shelters a hanging forest of diatomaceous algae that attracts the small planktonic creatures that anchor a whole food chain. What the Arctic cod has not adapted to is human innovations: when icebreaker ships are in the vicinity, they overturn the pack ice and the nutrients, leaving the fish exposed. Separated from their submarine shelters, the cod are soon eaten by marine birds, such as kittiwakes, which have learned that there are good things in the wake of these ships. Clever kittiwakes always trail icebreakers and icebergs, both disturbers of the underwater habitat, knowing food will turn up right around their wakes, sooner or later.

But the most interesting ice adaptation in the animal kingdom, to me, is among the creatures that have internalized ice and befriended it, robbing it of its capacity to kill them.

INTERNAL ICE
HOW IS IT POSSIBLE?

I first learned of this elusive animal capacity to make internal ice from the documentary filmmaker Gail Singer. It is an incredible story. Singer once attended a cottage party with a group of friends. She promised to cook them frog legs, but admitted she was squeamish. She would only do it if the men in the party agreed to hunt for the frogs and kill them when the time came. They found plenty of frogs, which they loaded into the freezer to kill them. Once the frogs were frozen, Singer cut off the legs for cooking, throwing the frog bodies into a large green garbage bag, which she set down by the door. To her horror, as she was cooking the frogs' legs, the green garbage bag began to move. At the time, she had no knowledge of the fascinating history of the wood frog *Rana sylvatica*.

As far back as May of 1747, Captain Francis Smith stepped off his ship, the *California*, touching land near the Arctic Circle. His travel-log notes an astonishing phenomenon: the emergence of "an infinite Number of Frogs, with a great croaking" after wintering frozen in holes in the ground: "A remarkable experiment is to take the Earth in which the Frog is so froze, and to break that Earth in Pieces without thawing it, the Frog will then break with it as short as a Piece of Glass. But . . . lay that Earth at a small Distance from the Fire, so as to thaw it, and the Frog will recover his Summer Activity, and leap as usual."

This is the earliest record I have found of the paradoxical ability of extreme cold to be a lifesaver as well as a killer. The frogs are among a handful of freeze-tolerant animals that have somehow evolved the ability to use ice rather than letting it go on a cellular rampage to destroy their bodies. They lower their body temperatures and metabolisms and increase the ability of their organs to survive without oxygen, so that they can live for months as if clinically dead. They also have refined damage-repair mechanisms, so that they can halt bleeding or start healing right away upon thawing, if they are injured while frozen.

Modern researchers want *Rana sylvatica* to help them advance the science of organ transplants. Although not unique in the animal world, its ability to endure the actual formation of ice within its body has attracted close attention. Woolly bear caterpillars can live fourteen years at winter temperatures as low as −94°C on Ellesmere Island in the Canadian High Arctic.

Periwinkles, mussels and barnacles can freeze and thaw themselves twice a day as the tide pops them in and out of extreme frigid air. Box turtles, spring peepers, chorus frogs and grey tree frogs can also survive freezing.

Rana sylvatica is a remnant of the last ice age, the only frog found north of the Arctic Circle, farther north than any other North American reptile or amphibian. Its presence seems to track, roughly, the retreat of the glaciers: from northern Georgia and in isolated colonies in the central highlands, in the eastern to central parts of Alabama, up through the northeastern United States, and all the way across Canada into Alaska. It lives in forest, muskeg and tundra, hiding under stones and stumps in winter, and it breeds in wood ponds in the spring.

Wood frogs spend two to three months frozen over the winter, in shallow pockets of dead vegetation. While this kind of hideaway may not be as secure as the recesses of a lake, it does give them an edge over aquatic frogs that have to wait under the ice surface of the lakes where they winter before becoming active in the spring. The wood frog can leap into action, breeding a month or more earlier than the leopard frog—a definite advantage in an environment with short summers.

Captain Francis noted its distinctive voice, variously described as hoarse clacking, quacking like a duck, or sometimes "lots of chuckling." Perhaps it does have something to chuckle about. It sounds like a pretty silly and promiscuous creature. Male wood frogs hop around embracing any other wood frog they can find, certainly not influenced by modern body image propaganda. If on squeezing, they find a female fat with eggs, they are interested. If she is thin, they let her go, since it means she has already spawned.[3] If the squeezee is another male, he lets out a loud croak, and there are no hard feelings.

This ordinary-looking frog has smooth skin, is up to 7 centimetres long and can camouflage itself in various shades of brown, tan, rust or green. Sometimes, it has dark spots on its back; usually it has a black bandito mask, almost like a little raccoon. It mates in April in the more northerly habitats, earlier in the south, and takes four years to develop into adulthood (if males who go around embracing everybody in sight can ever be considered mature adults).

The wood frog's uncanny ability to survive frozen contradicts much of what we know about the effect of ice on living things. When ice forms inside living cells, it becomes a deadly, rampaging force. As ice crystals take shape in the water that is everywhere in living bodies, the crystals push and deform cellular walls; their sharp branches puncture small blood vessels and scramble the microarchitecture of the cells themselves, so that when they thaw, the damage is severe. If the ice forms inside the cells, it can rupture them; if it forms externally, it sucks the water out of the cells and leaves them dehydrated and shrunken. If the cell walls collapse beyond a certain point, they remain folded and can never regain their original shape.

In the blood, the freezing process shuts down the delivery system so that oxygen and nutrients do not reach the organs, and the metabolism is interrupted. Humans cannot tolerate this process at all; neither can organs harvested for transplant. This remains one of the greatest challenges of transplant medicine, since it means organs must be used within hours of being harvested. Solving this problem could revolutionize organ transplants by alleviating the chronic mismatch between supply and demand for transplant organs. It would save many lives, and greatly improve the quality of life for many more.

The received wisdom—based on tragic experience with the frostbite and gangrene that sets in with cell destruction—is that living tissues such as an organ harvested for transplantation can only survive by completely avoiding the formation of ice crystals. This is why researchers such as Dr. Kenneth Storey at Carleton University in Ottawa and Dr. Boris Rubinsky at the University of California at Berkeley are fascinated by freeze tolerance in the animal world.

Kenneth and Janet Storey were determined to get to the bottom of the wood frog's secret: "One day they are no more than frogsicles; the next they are too nimble and squirmy for us to catch. How do they do it?"[4] Dr. Storey often keeps the "frogsicles" in plastic Tupperware containers in his laboratory fridge. While frozen, they have no heartbeat, brain activity or breath.

Typically, animals that can tolerate ice crystals in their bodies do two things that humans cannot do: first, they avoid freezing inside the cell structures, and grow the ice in spaces between the cells in their bodies. They do not wait for the ice to invade them; they are actually proactive in the freezing process. When the temperature hits $0°C$, they release special chemicals that start the crystallization process, called *ice nucleators*. This actively triggers the ice formation, but in a slow, controlled way that gives the animal time to make the metabolic adjustments it needs to survive. These nucleators can come from bacteria on the skin or in the animal's digestive system, or sometimes in the form of ice nucleating proteins released into its blood. The second mechanism to survive freezing involves building up high concentrations of sugars or sugar alcohols inside the cells to act as a kind of antifreeze. When ice forms all around the outside of the organs, sucking out their water, these sugars form a syrup that does not freeze, and protects the architecture and integrity of the cells from the inside.

Some of the adaptive mechanisms evolved because the frogs had to be able to survive dehydration caused by wild fluctuations in the water available to them. Many frogs can handle fluctuations of more than 50 percent of their total body water. No other vertebrate—certainly not humans—can do this. These frogs simply do not differentiate between losing water into the environment, or adjusting to abdominal ice. The ice accumulates in the abdominal cavity, where it is not damaging delicate blood vessels or expanding beyond the ability of cells or organs to hold it.

Kenneth and Janet Storey, both biochemists, have described what they find: "When we dissect frozen frogs in our lab, we invariably find lots of flat ice crystals sandwiched between the skin and muscle layers of their legs. A huge mass of ice—relatively speaking—also fills the abdominal cavity and encases all the internal organs. The ice contains not only the water that was in those spaces originally, but also water that was sucked out of the frog's organs. Indeed, the liver may be dehydrated by as much as 25 percent, and it is visibly wizened. The reason for the disproportion is clear: by sucking some of the water out of its organs—though not too much, otherwise its cells will collapse—the frog keeps the blood vessels in the organs from bursting as they fill with ice."[5]

This striking description shows that the frog is freezing selectively. This is because ice crystals can only form out of pure water. As they form, they expel whatever else is in the water, and it becomes more concentrated in whatever other compounds or liquids are there. In the case of the wood frog, it is expelling carbohydrate antifreeze. At a certain point, the process reaches an equilibrium that prevents any more water from being drawn out of the cells. Generally, the frog generates just enough antifreeze to allow 65 percent of its body to turn to ice at between 3 and 4°C.

Using genetic-sequencing technology, Dr. Storey has identified genes for three previously unknown proteins that protect the frog cells from rupturing during freezing. This also works to ensure cellular survival in mammal cells—even without concentrated glucose, which Dr. Storey had earlier identified as a cryoprotectant, or antifreeze for living cells to prevent the formation of ice crystals. He had already shown the importance of slow cooling to the survival of the wood frog before Dr. Rubinsky began working with cryoprotectants for liver transplants. Rubinsky was investigating other, more traditional techniques for organ preservation, but by 1990 the wood frog's success had piqued his interest as an alternative method. Rubinsky and Storey experimented with freezing wood frog liver tissue and taking Magnetic Resonance Images (MRI) of it.

They found that at about −7°C, the cells would shrink to as little as half their original size through partial dehydration, while blood vessels expanded to accommodate the ice crystals.

The tissue could tolerate this amount of freezing. Once they froze the tissue to −20°C, however, the cell membranes shrivelled and collapsed and the expanding ice crystals ruptured the blood vessels.

Rubinsky and Storey came to understand that successful freezing depended on a kind of osmotic balance between the cell and the tissues around it. The cells in the wood frog's body can lose up to 60 percent of their water and still rehydrate and find their original shape when they are thawed. But beyond that, the cells are too badly damaged to regain their original shape. This is exactly what happens to humans when they get frostbite. If human tissues are exposed to extreme cold, the skin first turns white (this is called frostnip) and can be brought back to health if treated promptly. This can be very painful, as the nerves awaken from cold to warmth. But under continued exposure to extreme cold, the tissue loses its blood, turns black and dies. This is the indication that the body's water has turned into ice crystals that have ripped apart the cells and the blood vessels. When left untreated, the condition turns gangrenous and requires amputation of the affected body part. Historically, the outcome has often been extreme misery, and death.

We may be able to learn more about preventing ice from damaging human tissues from other species besides the wood frog. Some fish and insects (beetles and spiders in particular) can also survive freezing. The winter flounder, a polar fish, manufactures an "ice blocker" protein that prevents tiny ice crystals from getting bigger by latching onto them and preventing more water molecules from joining to make them bigger. The crystals are never allowed to get big enough to do any real damage.

Freeze-tolerant insects tend to use sugar alcohol (glycerol) as a cellular antifreeze, while the frogs use glucose, the same blood sugar as humans have. But whereas human diabetics suffer massive internal injuries when their blood sugar doubles or goes even higher, the frogs can easily raise their blood sugar by 100 times or more without a problem. Studying how the frogs prevent the glucose from damaging their proteins could lead to treatments that help human diabetics better manage their disease.

On the basis of his work with the wood frog, Dr. Rubinsky (a professor of bioengineering and mechanical engineering) has designed a pilot protocol to freeze donor organs for long-term storage before transplantation into a recipient. He intends to mimic the wood frog's glucose saturation process using a computer-controlled pump. The cocktail's temperature is decreased by two degrees per minute until freezing. The key is to get the cocktail into the entire organ as fast as possible, which is why it makes sense to experiment with the blood vessel–rich liver. He has been having good success with rat livers, although he has revealed that finding a surgeon who was able and willing to do liver transplants on such tiny patients was not easy. The next step will be human trials.

For half a century, doctors have been successfully preserving small pieces of human tissue. Human sperm and embryos have been frozen in liquid nitrogen and revived, as well as skin and corneas. But larger organs pose a problem because so far, they cannot be rapidly and evenly infused with the protective solutions needed to control ice growth, and so they cannot be preserved through freezing. A human heart can live only eight hours outside the body, even when it is kept chilled. But its chemical processes are different than a liver's, and would need different antifreezes and different approaches to cold preservation. As long as we cannot safely freeze human organs, this means that transplants will remain a race against the clock, and people will die because the right match cannot be made on time.

Health Canada says that more than 3,700 Canadians are now on waiting lists for organ transplants for kidneys, hearts, lungs and livers. Thousands more need organ and tissue donations of corneas, heart valves, bone grafts and skin. Every day in the United States, twelve people die because they cannot get transplant organs on time. Worldwide demand is growing by 15 percent per year. There is a burgeoning organ transplant tourism business in the developing world, where desperate poor people donate organs to wealthy people for money. Researchers hope that they can learn to apply the ice secrets of the wood frog to human needs to save lives instead.

Hope springs eternal, however. For some, it is not enough to think about organ transplants. They want to use cryopreservation to attain life after death. For years, rumours have circulated that Walt Disney was obsessed with cryonics, and that his body is kept frozen in a tower at Disneyland, etc. These rumours have been roundly discredited, but when baseball legend and Hall-of-Famer Ted Williams died in the summer of 2002, it was no secret: he had himself frozen in the hope of coming back some day when the state of knowledge is more advanced than it is now. His corpse is in a stainless-steel vat of liquid nitrogen kept at −195°C at the Alcor Life Extension Foundation in Scottsdale, Arizona. Alcor is only one of several

U.S. cryonics organizations. The company claims to have custody of the bodies of almost half of the hundred-odd people who have died expressing the wish (and putting up the funds, no doubt) to be cryogenically frozen so far, and to have signed up several hundred more for the treatment. Dr. Storey is not buying it, at least for the far foreseeable future. He does not think our progress in working with ice crystals inside cells will bring back Ted Williams to pitch a game again anytime soon.

Instead, we will be much more enlightened by what the humans who have actually lived on the ice for thousands of years have to teach us.

CHAPTER FIVE

"Being Eskimo,
In the Arctic,
We always knew
We could walk the wind
And it would carry us
Back home."

—Fred Bigjim, Inupiant Eskimo poet, Alaskan,
Harvard graduate, from his poem "Walk the Wind"

THE ARCTIC AS HUMAN HABITAT

Just for a moment, take the time to look at the Arctic Ocean from above the globe, as if it were a northern and much larger Mediterranean, surrounded by different lands and different peoples whose long and fascinating history most of us never learned in school. This perspective is not the usual one.

A satellite photo of the Arctic Ocean looks very different in summer and in winter: it is hard to believe you are looking at the same place. The ice cover grows so large in the winter that it is as if the continents expanded. It becomes possible to travel across the ocean as if it were very rough land, a kind of arctic highway made up of huge, stable shelves of ice moored to the land, or floating on the ocean. This large and deep body of water (12,000 feet deep at the North Pole) makes all the difference in the human capacity to live in the Arctic.

There are huge differences between the two polar zones, which explains why the Arctic has been inhabited for at least the last 20,000 years, while the Antarctic is the only big piece of land in the world that has never been inhabited by indigenous peoples, and is not even legally owned by any country. In the Antarctic, a continent surrounded by oceans, the warmth from the ocean currents never influences the land enough to stimulate melting, and geothermal heat from the earth's crust just cannot penetrate enough to make a difference. As a result, the ice sheet has built up to 2,150 metres there, and the average year-round temperature is a blistering −51°C. In combination with Antarctica's long distance from anywhere inhabited by humans, this explains why the only people who have ever lived there have been scientists in internationally sanctioned research stations.

There are glaciers throughout the Canadian and Russian archipelagos, but the only permanent ice sheet in the Arctic, on Greenland, is just one-eighth the size of the Antarctic one. The average thickness of the Arctic ice pack is only 3 to 6 metres, and year-round average temperatures hover around −18°C. The 15 million people who live around the Arctic Ocean speak fifty different languages; the ice is their familiar habitat for most of the year, and they understand exactly how to live on, and with it. Unlike in Antarctica, they also experience beautiful summer vegetation and flowers. For those who depend heavily on hunting seals, walruses and whales, the ice actually makes it easier to reach the game, and to hunt.

This "ice road" is by far the best way to travel, as long as it is frozen hard. But from the moment that daylight returns in the spring, the ice cover begins to erode and shift, becoming far more dangerous. The aboriginal peoples of the Arctic have learned to navigate these dangerous periods, but modern adventurers do so at their peril, and few attempt it without good reason.

Archaeologists have found evidence that modern humans or Neanderthals using stone tools lived in the frigid Far North of Russia thirty thousand years ago. Not much is known about how they would have survived the ice age, but other experts say that Palaeolithic art died out about twenty thousand years ago, when the big ice sheets still covered most of the top third of the globe. Until 7500 BC, when a period of warming melted enough of the ice sheet to submerge it, there was a land bridge across the Bering Strait. Knud Rasmussen, the half-Inuit, half-Danish explorer, interpreter, translator and chronicler of the North, was probably the first to say, in his 1927 book *Across*, that this is how most North American indigenous peoples came from Asia to North America. Today, his theory is universally accepted by experts in the field. Twelve thousand years ago or more, travellers migrated from northeast Asia via Beringia, a vast plain area, now submerged, that once connected Alaska to their original homeland. There are different theories about how they made their way south from there. Some scientists espouse the theory that they came through what is now Yukon, then headed south as the great ice sheets parted along the eastern side of the Rockies. Others suggest that they may have used boats along the southern margin of Beringia and moved south along the northwest coast of North America. This would have allowed them to bypass the difficulties of travelling on the continental ice sheet, and could explain their progress into regions much farther south, as far as Peru and Chile, subsisting on a marine diet, during the last ice age.

These early immigrants would have been people who used whalebones and skins to build houses and boats. The earliest Paleo-Eskimos moved across Canada to Greenland, living in skin tents and eating land mammals, birds and eggs. Their tradition is known as the Arctic Small Tool Tradition and goes back forty-five hundred years. Each adult had to be highly skilled at making surprisingly sophisticated stone tools and sewing implements such as spear points, microblades and scrapers.

Somehow, their fine skills were lost over time. The Dorset from three thousand years ago made tools that were larger and cruder, but still had some resemblance to the Small Tool Tradition. But by fifteen hundred years ago, the Late Dorset phase, the tools had become simpler and the shamans had taken over. They believed in the helping spirit of the polar bear, and left behind many bear-shaped items such as carvings and amulets. The Late Dorset lived in longhouses grouping six to eight tents, which they pitched near polynyas, areas of water that remain ice-free in the winter. The Dorset did have the skills to mine rocks in northeast Newfoundland for use in making bowls and lamps.

From AD 900 to 1100, the Dorset were the dominant force in Greenland, but by AD 1300, they had been replaced by the more innovative Thule Inuit. The Thule came from the Bering Sea area and followed the same route as their predecessors, but they were whalers. They made half-buried sod houses and slept on early versions of what we now think of as a captain's bed, a clever use of space: a platform with storage capacity underneath it. For roofs, they used bullhead-whale jawbones and ribs with a layer of skins, topped by sod. The Thule made many fine tools and expressed themselves artistically with carvings, decorative elements and toys for their children. They discovered ways to drill holes quickly, and how to use dogs to speed them across the ice—a great liberation from the Dorset habit of laborious walking with heavy packs.

The Thule were also creative businesspeople: they traded throughout the Arctic and even farther afield: reindeer and ivory from Siberia, caribou and sea mammals from Alaska, copper from Ontario or the Bay of Fundy, soapstone and chert from Labrador and across the Arctic. As they moved across the Arctic, they had to adapt, because they could not rely on the same sources of food and tools in different places. For example, the need to hunt on the sea ice drove them to make more tailored clothing.

The Norse artefacts that have been found in the Canadian High Arctic and in Greenland show that they farmed sheep five hundred years ago, much as some of the Greenland Inuit do today, although for many of the intervening years it has been too cold to do so. Much of the subsequent contact between indigenous peoples and Europeans has been far less benign than this transmission of farming practices.

WHO ARE THE ARCTIC PEOPLES TODAY?

Although nearly all of the Arctic has been colonized and is now legally part of the territory claimed by one of the eight countries that border on the Arctic Ocean, the indigenous peoples of these territories, in many cases, beg to differ.[1] In their view, the entire territory of ice, permafrost, tundra and taiga belongs to them and has been their home since time immemorial. Since the United Nation's Year of Indigenous Peoples in 1993, there has been growing global awareness of this idea.

Since 1989, there has been an internationally accepted definition of indigenous peoples,[2] which applies to those: "who are regarded as indigenous on account of their descent from the populations which inhabited a country, or a geographical region to which the country belongs, at the time of conquest or colonisation or the establishment of present state boundaries and who, irrespective of their legal status, retain some or all of their own social, economic, cultural and political institutions. . . . Self-identification as indigenous or tribal shall be regarded as a fundamental criterion for determining the groups to which the provisions of the Convention apply."[3]

You have to be paying attention, because you can easily offend some of the groups that are affected by these measures. Just choosing the right words to use in describing them can be a minefield. In Alaska, the collective indigenous peoples are known mostly as Natives, although this includes Eskimos (Inupiat and Yupiit), the Aleut (from the Aleutian Island Chain), the Alutiiq-Aleut (Prince William Sound and Kodiak Island), the Athabascan Indians of the interior and the Southeast Coastal Indians who are also known as Pacific Indians (Tlingit, Haida and Tsimshian, also present in Canada). The Gwich'in and the Inuvialuit have cross-border relations between homes in Canada and northern Alaska.

Only the Eskimos and the Athabascans are, strictly speaking, within the geographic Arctic, but Alaska does not generally make that distinction. Native Alaskans used to form the majority in the state, but are now reduced to about 15 percent of the population, concentrated mostly in two hundred small villages rather than Alaska's larger communities.

In Canada, the Arctic Region covers Yukon, the Northwest Territories, northern Quebec and the eastern part of Labrador, which is part of Newfoundland and Labrador. Those generally considered as Arctic-Canadian indigenous peoples are the First Nations in Yukon, the First Nations, Metis, Inuvialuit and Inuit of the Northwest Territories, the Inuit and Cree of Quebec and the First Nations and Inuit on the coast of Labrador. The word *Eskimo* is considered pejorative by Canadian Inuit. Although the Inuit and the Cree are a tiny (but politically significant) minority in Quebec, they form the majority of the population in northern Quebec, which is known as Nunavik.

Recently, the Canadian government reached a much-awaited and eagerly followed agreement with some of the indigenous peoples to carve a new territory called Nunavut out of the Northwest Territories (population 12,000). The Inuit are a majority in Nunavut, and so have negotiated regional self-government. The Dene, as a First Nations minority in the west, prefer a political structure that guarantees them specific ethnic rights.

People all around the circumpolar region are watching the evolution of these governance models very closely, particularly in Nunavut, as it is truly a new development that may provide inspiration for other countries wishing to move forward in their relationships with their indigenous peoples. In the Arctic Region, all governments, business and non-indigenous peoples are trying to figure out how to manage these relationships better; in some cases they are dealing with multiple levels of legal agreements, court cases, negotiations and trial by media. Historical complexities have made some of these discussions painful for all concerned.

Greenland has just under 50,000 indigenous Greenlanders and just over 8,000 Danes. The Saami are the only indigenous group in Norway (40,000–50,000), Sweden (17,000) and Finland (5,700). About half of Finnish Saami are reindeer herders (reindeer are domesticated caribou). The biggest numbers are in Russia, which has twenty-six different groups of distinct indigenous peoples, not all of them Arctic, but all counted together. The largest are the Yakut and the Komi, who enjoy special status because they have their own autonomous republics. In 1989, there were 382,000 Yakuts, 344,500 Komi, 150,000 Kareliens, 18,000 Kamchadals, 2,000 Saamis and a handful of Veps and Izhors. These populations have experienced much upheaval.

After Russia's 1917 Communist Revolution, ethnic Russians were either forced or encouraged to move into the indigenous peoples' territories, which were mined and developed primarily for economic reasons. Since the collapse of the Soviet Union, there has been an exodus of many of these "immigrants," leaving a shortage of doctors and engineers. It is hard to tell what this will mean, but to add to their difficulties, the indigenous groups have been separated and moved around so that they are no longer concentrated geographically, and seem to have lost control of their destiny as a coherent group.

These Russian indigenous peoples speak many languages and, with the exception of the Komi and the Yakuts (which tend to dominate the smaller groups) no one group makes up the majority of the population anywhere. Mostly, these indigenous people receive no special consideration when it comes to giving them jobs in the industries that have moved into their territory. To compound their problems, Russia continues to exploit its fragile northern environment in ways that most developed countries would consider reckless: heavy vehicles trample the taiga all summer; chemicals that have long been banned in continental Europe and North America are still in use without widely accepted precautions. While the disenfranchised Russian indigenous peoples are paying the heaviest direct price, these practices affect millions of others, as the resulting environmental degradation affects air, soil and water quality for thousands of miles around.

In many cases, groups such as the northeastern Siberian Eskimos and the ones on St. Lawrence Island, Alaska, have relatives across national boundaries. These particular Eskimos are still celebrating the fact that they can now see each other regularly, something that was forbidden from World War II until recently.

An Unhappy History

The history of encounters between Arctic peoples and Europeans is not a happy one, by and large. With few exceptions, the

Europeans missed the boat at every opportunity to learn from the experts how to live with the ice. In many instances, the explorers behaved cruelly and with impunity. For example, in 1897, Admiral Peary brought six hapless Inuit from Greenland, including a small boy named Minik, and put them on display at the American Museum of Natural History in New York. Thirty thousand people paid 25 cents each to see them, but within a few months, four of them had died of pneumonia or tuberculosis, including Minik's father.

One adult survivor returned to Greenland, but seven-year-old Minik was left behind. He was adopted by the museum's janitor, but never recovered from a feeling of profound betrayal after learning that the museum had faked his father's funeral and put the skeleton on display for the public. Although he returned to Greenland in his late teens, he was not able to adapt there either, and later died of the Spanish flu in a New Hampshire mining camp. Minik's story has been the subject of a book recently reissued with a foreword by Kevin Spacey (*Give Me My Father's Body: The Life of Minik, The New York Eskimo* by Kenn Harper), a theatrical play, and is currently being developed as an opera by the Tapestry New Opera Company in Toronto. It has certainly captured public attention; even though it is difficult to imagine such a thing happening, it took almost a century—until 1993—before the museum returned the bones of the four dead Inuit to their families in Greenland.

One exception to the attitude typified by Peary was Vílhjalmur Stefánsson, (1879–1962). His stories of living and learning in the Arctic mark a striking departure from those who preceded him. Stefánsson was an anthropologist raised in

Winnipeg, Manitoba, in an Icelandic immigrant family. He moved to the U.S. to make his fortune as a very young man, and had been working for the very same American Museum of Natural History when he first went to the Arctic.

Stefánsson, who had an illustrious career, primarily as an author and lecturer, was a sunny optimist in many ways, in marked contrast to other Arctic explorers whose writings emphasized the hardships and difficulties. He was a brilliant and complex figure of groundbreaking insight, but also an enigma. From 1906 on, when he began travelling to the Arctic, he was torn between two keen and warring realities: his love of life with the northern peoples and his ambitions for celebrity in the Lower 48. One assumes he was sincere in his own notebooks, published in 2001:

> *They took me into their houses and treated me hospitably and courteously, but exactly as if I were one of them. They gave me clothes to wear and food to eat, I helped them in their work and joined in their games, until they finally forgot that I was not one of them, and began to live their lives before my eyes as if I were not there. This gave me a rare opportunity to know them as they are.*[4]

He knew them very well: he had a child, Alex Stefánsson, with his Inuit seamstress Fannie Pannigabluk (at the time, a seamstress was absolutely vital to a person's survival in the Arctic). But despite his admiration for the Arctic peoples, and his willingness to credit Fannie with help in the field, he never acknowledged his Inuit family and did not communicate with his son after childhood. Even his six grandchildren, who all live in Greenland, to this day are torn between anger at his callous behaviour and pride in his remarkable legacy.

THE STAGES OF ARCTIC EXPLORATION ACCORDING TO VÍLHJALMUR STEFÁNSSON

- **FIRST STAGE:** Scandinavian Eskimos and other Mongoloid people spread slowly northwards into Europe, North America and Asia to occupy richer hunting grounds, adapting slowly. For Stefánsson, this is not true exploration, which by his definition must link adventure and heroic endeavour.
- **SECOND STAGE:** Explorers such as Edward Parry sit in their ships or huddle in shelters on shore until winter is over. Stefánsson views this as primitive exploration, but says disapprovingly: "The battle with frost and storm . . . was a form of trench warfare."
- **THIRD STAGE:** Parry has a breakthrough: he understands that it is possible to organize expeditions on the hard ice pack beginning in January and February; in fact, that it is safer before the first thaw, in April.
- **FOURTH STAGE:** In his 1913–18 expedition, Stefánsson seeks to demonstrate that it is possible to survive in the Arctic by hunting and eating as the indigenous peoples did, living only on meat and blubber from the polar sea. He writes: "When the polar regions are once understood to be friendly and fruitful, men will quickly and easily penetrate their deepest recesses." Why? Because "the northern people do not abhor the North."

Canada's Governor-General and head of state, Adrienne Clarkson, gave the 2003 Stefánsson Memorial Lecture in Akureyri, Iceland, the home of the Stefánsson Arctic Institute, on the occasion of the Institute's fifth anniversary. In her remarks, she told her audience about Stefánsson's first encounter with the Copper Eskimos of the Western Arctic, whom he called the Blond Eskimos:

> *As Stefánsson made his way across the ice and snow, he saw figures in the distance approaching him. Not wanting to frighten them or invite hostility, Stefánsson set down his rifle and his pack on the ice and stretched his empty arms toward them. They responded by putting down their staves and harpoons. And thus the two worlds met, with arms open in peace, in respect, in a true willingness to embrace and learn about the other.*

However imperfect Stefánsson was, this sentiment inspired Ms. Clarkson to look forward to a time when we might achieve a fifth stage of exploration: dissolving the notions of centre and periphery that prevailed in the past; honouring and including the world's indigenous people, and learning from them the remarkable lessons they have to share. This is more than rhetoric, as we are finding out in so many ways.

DEEP UNDERSTANDING OF LIGHT, SPACE AND TIME

The Inuit in particular have a remarkable artistic tradition that has now been recognized by collectors for at least forty years. Their deep understanding of space and light, developed from generations of living on the ice, has resulted in a body of work that resonates for people around the world. As with many indigenous peoples, they do not recognize the notion that artists are somehow different or separate from other people. Life and art are beautifully intertwined and give meaning to each other.

In the United States and Canada, at least, there are signs that other disciplines are beginning to recognize the value of indigenous knowledge and wisdom. For example, the Sea Ice Knowledge Exchange, funded by the U.S. National Science Foundation, relies on Inupiat and Inuit contributors to clarify and give depth to scientific findings about sea ice. Ilkoo Anguikjuak and Geela Tigullaraq, an Inuit from Clyde River, Nunavut, are among a group of indigenous people working with the NSF scientists to interpret observations in sea ice that are extremely important to understanding climate change. Their long experience with sea ice, and with animal behaviour, is greatly enriching the ways in which the scientists record and understand the complex changes that are going on. A big benefit of the exchange between Nunavut and Barrow was a sharing of skills and knowledge. The people of Barrow were amazed to see Tigullaraq's children speaking fluent Inuktitut when she showed them her home videos: "There was a big crowd behind me," she told the *Nunatsiaq News*. "Everybody kept on saying, 'Come see, little kids speaking Eskimo!'" Meanwhile, Angutikjuak shared the Baffin method of seal-skinning at a conference in Barrow, teaching Inupiat youth how he did it.

There is much more than language and seal-skinning to share, however. Just as the scientists have realized that indigenous peoples have a valuable body of knowledge that can enrich their work, others are discovering yet another dimension: indigenous peoples have a tradition of thinking in much longer timeframes than most of us. This has proven to be a real eye-opener for Canada's Nuclear Waste Management Organization (NWMO), charged with finding a way to manage the long-term storage of the country's used nuclear fuel from power production. As part of its sophisticated public consultation process, the NWMO is mandated by its founding legislation to make a special effort to consult indigenous peoples on the issue.

When the organization began to do this, a very interesting thing happened. The timeframe for managing used nuclear fuel is so long (it will still be radioactive 100,000 years from now), that ice ages enter into the considerations of where to put it and what to do with it. It also turns out that no one has ever designed and built something to last 100,000 years.

When the NWMO held consultations with indigenous peoples, it discovered that their thinking began, as a matter of course, with a timeframe of seven generations, or about 175 years, and their "institutional" memory took into account the kind of massive changes that an ice age could create. For example, local First Nations have named a rare white bear (the offspring of two black bears, each with a recessive gene that produces the white bear) found only off the rain coast of British Columbia, the Spirit Bear. Their legend says that the Creator made every tenth bear white to remind his people always of the ice age. How many of us can refer casually to a story handed down from the ice age?

This seven-generation period that comes as a matter of course in indigenous wisdom corresponds exactly to the first phase of implementation that the NWMO is contemplating for its recommended way to manage the high-level nuclear wastes. It also corresponds to the maximum number of generations one person might be fortunate enough to know, in one lifetime, from great-grandparent to great-grandchild. Traditional aboriginal knowledge and wisdom have become crucial components in finding the best way to manage problems created by one of the world's most advanced industrial processes: it is humbling to realize that the indigenous peoples already think in ice time.

CHAPTER SIX

"All maps are selections from all that is known,
bent to the mapmaker's purpose."
—Ward L. Kaiser and Dennis Wood in
Seeing Through Maps: The Power of Images to Shape our World View

THE EARLY EXPLORERS AND CARTOGRAPHERS
THE NORTH OF THE IMAGINATION

Because the Antarctic is so much farther away from human populations, the story of ice exploration begins in the Arctic. Until half a millennium ago, the Arctic was simply a white hole on European maps. Mapmakers in ancient Greece, China, Russia, the Arab World and Europe imagined the North in all kinds of ways: as an open ocean, as a frozen continent, as a polar mountain with rivers flowing from it. Early Norse maps showed Greenland as a peninsula that reached from Northern Europe to North America. Even modern flat maps are misleading in a sense: they present the world to us as a flat array of continents with oceans in between them.

We don't tend to pay much attention to the top and bottom of the map. The top, with the exception of a distorted Greenland, looks mostly blue, and the bottom looks mostly white. As a result, and because we rarely look at the globe from above, most of us still do not truly grasp what the Arctic is: an ice-covered ocean twice the size of the Mediterranean Sea, but like it, ringed by land—continents, in fact. If you were to draw a line linking all the points that experience temperatures of 10°C in July (the July isotherm), it would roughly define the Arctic—far more relevantly than the Arctic Circle itself, at 66°30′N. The July isotherm also corresponds roughly to the tree line, or the northernmost point where trees can grow. It meanders up and down across the Arctic Circle. The region known as "the Arctic," or circumpolar region (around the pole) includes the Arctic Ocean; the northern reaches of Canada, Alaska, Russia, Norway, and the Atlantic Ocean; Svalbard; most of Iceland; Greenland; and the Bering Sea. The North Pole itself is impossible to mark, a place of rough waters and eternally shifting ice floes.

We know that now. But for hundreds of years, people across Europe shared a belief in the existence of some Hyperborean paradise, to the west or to the north of Europe. The vision was surprisingly consistent, from Greece to Scandinavia and points in between, but they had different names for it: Isles of the Blessed, Vineland, the Elysian Fields, the Hesperides, Avalon, El Dorado, Irish Brasil. Whatever it was called, people believed that in this paradise, cattle would fatten quickly and effortlessly, vines would burst into fruit once a month, and wheat would pump out delicious ready-cooked loaves without bothering to produce grain. People there would live in perfect peace. Pindar wrote of them: "With shining laurel wreaths about their locks (of hair), they hold feasts out of sheer joy. Illnesses cannot touch them, nor is death foreordained for this exalted race." Here indeed was an incentive to try and find the Hyperborean paradise, but there was just one hitch: there was a hell of ice to cross before you could get there.

Many of the earliest explorers were fortified in their struggles by the idea that they would find this land of milk and honey beyond—if they could only make it past the ice. The curiosity and yearning for a better life overcame their fear, and perhaps their common sense much of the time.

Pytheas was a Greek sailor who actually did find a land of milk and honey—just this side of the ice—and gave it a name that still resonates today. He set sail from the Phoenician city of Massilia, what is now Marseilles, in 330 BC. He was looking for tin and amber, commodities that had great value in the ancient world (amber was used for everything from high fashion to quack medicine). In the course of a six-year odyssey, he circumnavigated the British Isles, discovering the Orkneys and something he named Thule, which may have been the north coast of Norway or Iceland.

Pytheas wrote a book about his travels, called *On the Ocean*, of which only excerpts quoted by others survive. When he reached the place he called Thule (it may also have been the Shetlands or the Faroe Islands), he said the night was only two or three hours long there.[1] He found the farmers of Thule sophisticated: they threshed their grain in barns, for example, at a time when such buildings were unknown in southern Europe. They also ate fruits and drank milk, as well as a brew made from grain and honey—perhaps a cross between beer and mead.

"Ultima Thule" has come to have many meanings, among them a remote goal or ideal. This meaning probably descends from the idea of the Elysian Fields, forever inaccessible beyond the ice barrier. Knud Rasmussen also gave the name Thule to the ancient culture that spread to Canada and Greenland from Alaska around AD 1000. No one knows for sure, but Pytheas situated his Thule six days' sail north of Britain. Although the Romans did not like Pytheas, and would not give him much credit for his achievements (it was they, after all, who wrote the history), most Western accounts suggest that he was the first Arctic explorer in recorded history.

Certainly, Pytheas made the Greco-Roman world much bigger by bringing back the first descriptions of the midnight sun, the aurora borealis (northern lights) and polar ice—real observations, rather than the pie-in-the-sky notion of the Elysian Fields. His description of a "congealed sea" one day farther north than Thule was handed down to us by Pliny the Elder, and by the early first-century geographer Strabo:[2] "Pytheas also speaks of the waters around Thule and of those places where land properly speaking no longer exists, nor sea nor air, but a mixture of these things, like a 'marine lung,' in which it is said that earth and water and all things are in suspension as if this something was a link between all these elements, on which one can neither walk nor sail."[3]

This *marine lung* was a term for a jellyfish; Pytheas was probably grasping for a familiar image to describe something he was seeing for the very first time: pancake ice, with turned-up edges as a result of banging together while it is freezing. We can only try to imagine how someone from the sunny blue Mediterranean would have viewed the frigid, silvery world at the edge of the drift ice, where slate-coloured sea, slush and sea ice meld with the bone-chilling fog to reduce visibility to nil.

The notion of an ideal world beyond the ice continued to be a very powerful draw. Iceland, first settled by Irish monks and then by Norsemen in the ninth century BC, may owe something to this ideal. It is now the world's oldest democracy, with a legislature, the Althingi, that dates from 930. Despite its name, only about 11.5 percent of Iceland's land mass is permanently ice-covered. It sits on geological faults where hot springs bubble up out of the ground (these springs are tapped to heat many of its buildings), and its climate is greatly tempered by the heat released from the North Atlantic current. Nevertheless, it has 11,650 square kilometres of glaciers, including the huge Vatna Glacier. One of its southern outlets shears off, or calves, into the North Atlantic. At 8,400 square kilometres and a depth of 900 metres, Vatna contains more ice than all the glaciers on the European continent put together—on an island slightly smaller than the state of Virginia.

Iceland has always provided abundant food for its own needs, from fresh fish and seafood to all kinds of meat and rye grains. The warm Gulf current that enables this must have seemed miraculous to early explorers growing terrified of impassable ice and storms on the open ocean. It is not hard to understand, then, that ice-battered Norsemen, looking for a home, would have found Iceland a congenial refuge—often from the rough arm of Viking justice, since the sagas show they were always killing each other in drunken brawls. The adventures continued as the groups split up and moved on to Greenland, and eventually, to

Newfoundland (Vinland), reaching North America five hundred years before Christopher Columbus.

The search for a new, safe home is certainly part of the exploration story, for Europeans as well as for the aboriginal peoples of the circumpolar region. For the aboriginal peoples, it was a matter of survival, escaping harsh climatic conditions and seeking food. But there are other motives for exploration: mapping new territory is fundamental, because all future progress depends upon it. Another very common thread in the early European exploration narrative is the pursuit of lucre. Someone always thought that if only they could reach the far shore, the distant land, the Northwest Passage, the Northeast Passage, Cathay or India—there would be untold wealth at the end of the struggle through the ice.

GREENLAND
AT THE EDGE OF THE MAP

The story of human settlement in Greenland closely follows the advance and retreat of the ice: it was a relatively hospitable place when Eric the Red first showed up there. He had been banished from Iceland for three years in 982, for killing two people "without reason." His three years up, he decided that Greenland would make a good new colony; he organized a convoy of twenty-five big Viking ships to return to there. Five hundred of these people arrived at what is now called Erik's Fiord and founded the Eastern Settlement. The climate was much milder than it was later, when the English explorers showed up: the ice was sufficiently at bay that it was possible for them to live off the land, building stone and turf houses with turf roofs.

In 1001, Erik's son Lief founded a settlement at what is now l'Anse-aux-Meadows, Newfoundland—five hundred years before Columbus arrived in the New World. The area was attractive to the settlers for its relatively ice-free, mild climate at that time, but perhaps because of repeated conflict with the locals, whom they called Skraelings, they stayed only a few years before their return to Greenland, bringing valuable lumber and, legend has it, grapes.

For a while, the Greenland Norsemen did well, sending walrus ivory and gyrfalcons (prized for hunting), hides and sealskins to Bergen on the Norwegian coast, in exchange for metals, foods and manufactured tools. The ships from Bergen would reach Greenland every two to three years, and as long as the weather held, the little colony prospered. At that time, Southern Europe remained blissfully unaware of the Norse legacy.

The Norwegian Vikings sailed north and west; the Danes went south and west (King Canute was a Dane who ended up ruling Britain) and the Swedes pushed east, conquering everybody from the Gulf of Finland, down the river systems of what is now Russia, and all the way to Constantinople. Overall, the Vikings dominated the far northern latitudes for centuries.[4]

In 1261, after coming under Norwegian rule, political and economic factors shoved the Greenland colonies out of sight, out of mind, and they died out. Some scholars think that they were affected by an increasingly cold climate (the Little Ice Age); others that they simply intermarried with the aboriginal population. Whatever happened, their disappearance shrank the map of the world from the European perspective. Iceland became the outer limit of most maps.

MAPPING AN ICE-BOUND WORLD

The European perspective was far from the only one. Even today, no one map of the world does a perfect job of conveying all the information you need to know to understand where everything is, how big it is, how long it takes to get from here to there, and what is the best route. The earliest surviving record of a scholar asserting that the world is round dates back to Pythagoras, in the sixth century BC; he was followed by Parmenides, who argued in favour of this idea in the following century. Aristotle, who lived around 350 BC, made six arguments to prove that the earth is spherical, and from then on scholars generally accepted this idea.

Around 250 BC, Eratosthenes measured the circumference of the earth quite accurately. Ptolemy, the Greek astronomer and geographer, had great methodology, but his results reflected the poverty of his data.[5] Ptolemy mapped the known world in about AD 140 in his eight-volume *Guide to Geography*. It elaborated the geocentric theory that would prevail for the next fourteen hundred years in Europe. If only he had used the measurements set out by Eratosthenes, he would have been pretty much bang on; as it was, and despite his skills at calculating correctly, he missed a number of locations by a wide margin. The Romans didn't contribute much in this area despite their great road-making skills. They just weren't strong enough at the math required to figure out how the entire world worked.

On the whole, Europe was well behind the Arab world when it came to cartography: "At a time when Europe firmly believed in the flatness of the Earth," writes the Arab historian Ameer Ali (1849–1928), "and was ready to burn any foolhardy person who thought otherwise, the Arabs taught geography by globes." Ptolemy was translated and distributed in the Arab world by the ninth century, and immediately, Arab scholars began building on his knowledge. Shortly after the turn of the first millennium AD (1000), Al-Biruni had figured out how to use triangulation to measure the earth. His calculation that the radius of the earth was 6339.6 kilometres was not duplicated in the West until the sixteenth century. There is also evidence that the great Arab mariners reached the West Indies, investigated the interconnection of the earth's oceans as far as the Bering Strait, and that they understood the great ocean system long before it was even posited in the west.

Whatever the Arabs were doing, even the Europeans were beginning to find Ptolemy's view of the world too limited by the mid-fifteenth century. Many began to question Iceland's position as the edge of the known universe. The Fra Mauro map of 1459, for example, shows that Greenland was again being drawn onto maps, albeit still as a peninsula extending across from Norway. Alternatively, it was drawn as an extension of Asia. Once the Europeans started using the magnetic compass, they began depicting the North Pole either as a separate continent, or as a big black mountain rising out of nothing.

THE MERCATOR PROJECTION
EUROCENTRIC SPIN OR SAILOR'S BEST FRIEND?

Most people think of Gerhardus Mercator (Gerhard Kremer), a German/Flemish cartographer, as the author of the first true atlas with maps (although his younger colleague, Abraham Ortel, known as Ortelius, actually published a comprehensive atlas first). Mercator's projection of the earth as a whole is still widely used. If this is surprising, given the problems it creates, we have to remember its original purpose. He titled his map "A New and Enlarged Description of the Earth with Corrections for Use in Navigation," and that is a very helpful description. The big advantage of Mercator's map has always been that it allows sailors to take compass bearings and sail in a straight line. This is especially useful at the poles, where the meridians of longitude begin to converge, but parallels of latitude do not.

Since it is impossible to represent a spherical object on a flat plane with total accuracy, Mercator's map, by keeping the meridians of longitude in a straight line to facilitate navigation, exaggerates the size of land masses near the poles, and minimizes the size of land masses near the equator. It makes Europe look bigger than South America when the opposite is true. It makes Greenland look larger than the whole African continent, which is patently ridiculous (it is only one-fifteenth the size of Africa). In developing countries, many people still think of the tissue of assumptions that have resulted from the Mercator projection as a sign of some kind of imperialist conspiracy.

In 1974, Arno Peters tackled the ingrained perceptions that had resulted from hundreds of years of using the Mercator projection map. He published his own projection, which brings home how much larger Africa is than North America, and South America than Europe. Since mapping the spherical world on a flat surface is so problematic and will always require sacrificing something, Peters obtains the right size proportions at the expense of shape. Mercator, while sizes are out of whack, does a better job of shape. Both generalize because it is impossible to account for every specific small detail on a large-scale map.

On a Mercator map, Mexico and Alaska are each the right shape, but because of the size distortion introduced by its projection, their different relative sizes means that North America, overall, is not exactly the right shape. So the closer in you get, the more accurate the Mercator projection is. Neither projection is much use for local travel. For that, you need regional charts and maps with a high degree of accuracy.

The period of early cartography and exploration was a time of great ignorance, but avidity for a good story. There were genuine scientists and explorers at work, but often they were just plain wrong. Sometimes, this was because they were missing essential tools or knowledge keys that did not yet exist. From the Low Countries in the 1500s and 1600s, leadership in cartography passed to France in the 1700s, because a French national survey based on trigonometric techniques led to new levels of accuracy. But it was not possible to have a true map of the world until, eventually and inevitably, countries began cooperating and overcoming the politics of things such as the starting points of measurement systems. The biggest breakthrough happened at an 1884 conference of twenty-six countries in Washington, DC. Those present agreed that the 0 meridian of latitude would go through Greenwich, England (after it had been moved around among the cities of Paris, Cadiz, Naples, Pulkova, Stockholm and London). In the following years, this and the use of the equator as the 0 degree parallel of latitude were gradually accepted internationally, and it became possible to have internationally accepted maps of the whole world. This would make it much easier for explorers to penetrate the ice of the polar extremes.

■ ■ ■

Cartographers were essential to progress, but they had to compete frequently with charlatans and con men who could wheedle money out of sovereigns and investors, in the hopes of reaching the fabled riches of Cathay or India. In 1497, John Cabot (actually Giovanni Caboto, from Genoa) sailed from Bristol under the patronage of Henry VII of England. Like other freelance explorers of the time, he took his money where he could find it. Nobody in England was very interested in his discovery of Newfoundland in 1497, but it did spark European interest in the possibility of a Northwest Passage to Cathay north of the island. Historians now think that European fishermen, probably including the men of Bristol, had been fishing the Grand Banks for years, but had simply never raised the issue of ownership. The English attitude began to change, as they realized that the French were financing expeditions led by Verrazano (a Tuscan) and Cartier, and the Spanish were funding Columbus (another Genoese).

The Spanish already had jurisdiction over the Caribbean, and the Portuguese over the ocean around Africa. By the end of the fifteenth century, the English had come to fear that the Spaniards might block their trade with continental Europe. There was big money at stake. The players who were funding the various expeditions were most concerned about opening up a trade route to Cathay under their own control. There were many hypotheses to be verified: Cabot's New Founded Isle might be the furthest east coast of Asia. Perhaps it was a continent of its own, or it might just be a big island among many western lands; either way, it would have to be circumvented, either from the north or the south.

WILLOUGHBY TACKLES THE NORTHEAST PASSAGE

The English had known about a possible northeast passage, a White Sea around the top of Norway, since Ottar and his Norse companions had filed a report on it in the year 880 and Alfred the Great had transcribed it. But no other record of attempts to conquer it has been found until the year 1553, when Sir Hugh Willoughby, an English businessman with no naval experience, set sail from London to find a Northeast Passage to China, on the recommendation of Sebastian Cabot (then the Pilot Major of England). Cabot had long served the Spanish Throne, and was highly knowledgeable about world geography.

The Willoughby expedition was the first—and the last—of something ambitiously and charmingly titled the *Mystery and Company of Merchant Adventurers for the Discovery of Regions, Dominions, Islands, and Places Unknown.* Sir Hugh's ship, the *Bona Esperanza*, proved untrue to her hopeful name. He and his men, all sixty-six of them, died after getting stuck in the pack ice near Murmansk. The speculation is that they were the first of a long line of explorers to die from carbon monoxide poisoning, after building fires in shelters tightly sealed from the blistering cold. Only Willoughby's second-in-command, Richard Chancellor, survived the winter on the Kola Peninsula to establish new trade arrangements with the Czar of Russia, Ivan the Terrible. This led to the formation of the Muscovy Company, so that the London merchants who had backed the expedition did eventually get some return on their investment. Chancellor's luck ran out in 1556, when he was shipwrecked and drowned while pursuing his exploration of the Northeast Passage.

THE ARCTIC MISADVENTURES OF MICHAEL LOK AND MARTIN FROBISHER

Another syndicate of London merchants, headed by Michael Lok, funded an expedition under the command of Martin Frobisher, a professional seaman who also appears to have been a bit of a rogue and an adventurer. The expedition spared no expense on navigational instruments, maps and other tools. But the largest of the three little ships under Frobisher's command was only half the size of the ones Columbus had taken to Hispanola more than half a century before (the *Santa Maria* had measured 26 metres in length).

The *Gabriel*, the *Michael*, and a tiny pinnace with a four-man crew that was lost near Iceland early in the trip, were not nearly as robust as later Arctic expedition ships. It must have been excruciatingly scary to sail them in dangerous, ice-ridden waters. Their first experience of real ice off the coast of Greenland was memorable. Michael Lok gathered eyewitness accounts and reported that on July 11 "they had sight of land unknowne to them, for they could not come to set fote theron for the marveilous haboundance of monstrous great ilands of ise which lay dryving all alonst the coast thereof. . . . And bearing in nerer to discover the same, they found yt marveilous high, and full of high ragged roks all along by the coast, and some of the ilands of ise were nere yt of such height as the clowds hanged about the tops of them, and the byrds that flew about them were owt of sight."[6]

The experience was, in fact, hair-raising. It was foggy and the visibility was very limited. It was like guiding an eggshell blindly through a giant pinball machine, with suddenly looming reefs and loose rocks eddying around with the current and the winds. Even those who had been on the Muscovy Company ships to Arkhangelsk, where ships had frozen into the pack ice for the winter, had never seen anything like the giant icebergs breaking off the impassable coast of Greenland.[7] The *Michael*, separated from the *Gabriel* during the storm that had sunk the pinnace, scurried back to London, making it by September 1.

Frobisher may have been a bit of a con man, skilled at convincing rich men (and even the Queen of England, who was to become one of his backers) to part with their money. But he was also a superb sailor. He saved the *Gabriel* more than once through quick and masterful action. On July 14, she was knocked on her side and flooded, her rigging ripped apart, but he managed with his men to right her, and with a tiny foresail intact, they were able to keep going until the weather calmed enough that they could repair the ship.

HAIR-RAISING ADVENTURES

Frobisher Bay is about 300 kilometres long and reaches widths of 50 kilometres. At its mouth, it is buffeted by 3-metre tides; at least nine months of the year, it is choked with ice. Not exactly your hospitable little port, but neither is it the passage to Asia that Frobisher was convinced he had found. It is possible that he thought any passage between the Atlantic and the Pacific across the top of the continent would resemble the tortuous and winding way between South America and Tierra del Fuego, discovered by Magellan fifty years before. It may have been a foggy day when Frobisher and his navigator, Christopher Hall, climbed to the top of a hill on the shore to look around, so that they could not see the land curving inward about 19 miles away, at the bottom of the bay. Or he might have been indulging in some wishful thinking, and thinking of what to tell his investors. He had to get more money out of them . . .

After losing five sailors to shore and kidnapping an Inuit to take home (no one knows what really happened, but it poisoned the relationship with the Baffin Island Inuit for all three Frobisher expeditions). Frobisher headed home, arriving in London on October 9, 1576. The staged fuss about his supposed find of a Northwest Passage died quickly. A bigger fuss then erupted about a piece of black stone from an Arctic beach[8]— and it was to leave Michael Lok wishing he had never heard of Martin Frobisher.

Good Money after Bad
BISOGNA SAPERE ADULATARE LA NATURA

We can pinpoint the moment where all the Queen's money and many of the Queen's men started out towards a disastrous destiny in the High Arctic ice west of Greenland. It was when Giovanni Battista Agnello, a rather louche Venetian assayer, told Michael Lok that he, and he alone, knew how to extract gold from the black stone. Three other reputable assayers, including the official one in the Tower of London, had said the stone was worthless. But desire is a very powerful thing: the Queen and her investors desperately wanted to believe that England was at last going to catch up to its rival powers who were already extracting fabulous wealth (or rumoured to be) from the Americas. Caution was thrown to the winds. Agnello said his secret was "*Bisogna sapere adulatare la natura.*" He knew how to flatter nature all right—and Lok, these results in hand, knew how to flatter the Queen.

Elizabeth was already a passive investor in the first venture. But with a purported gold find, everything changed. Frobisher was no longer a privateer who had a deal with a few investors: he was a senior naval officer in the Queen's service, and the investors were participating in her project. This certainly made it easier to raise money and obtain men and resources. But it also greatly complicated the politics of the situation. Despite early misgivings ("Battista dyd but play the alchemist") even the Queen's down-to-earth secretary of state, Sir Francis Walsingham, threw in a couple of hundred pounds. Queen Elizabeth herself put in £1,000, mostly in the form of a good 200-ton ship, the *Aid*, with a crew of 65. This was a huge improvement over the first attempt: Frobisher was now the head of a fleet of three ships (the *Gabriel* and the *Michael* were back) and 120 men, including 30 miners and assayers who were to dig out the gold ore and bring it back to England. The Queen's money also bought some heavier apparel than the flimsy threads in which the men of the first expedition had shivered—and they had not even experienced a real Arctic winter.

With government participation comes regulation, and Frobisher's instructions were much more explicit than the first time. The first beneficiaries of this were a bunch of convicts the expedition had originally been told to maroon on the Greenland coast, but since their presence would have exceeded the number of men allowed, they were put back ashore—one imagines, to their great relief.

These were early days in exploration, and the sight of three ships with 120 men on board lying offshore was enough to send whole populations scrambling from their villages. The people of Orkney were sufficiently alarmed to abandon their homes when they saw the Frobisher fleet, but eventually they were persuaded to exchange fresh food for used clothing and shoes, and the expedition was off to find the gold at the mouth of Frobisher Bay. In later years, the Orkneys would prove a valuable recruiting station for the Hudson's Bay Company, which found the Orkney men to be more reliable than others, particularly those from the cities.

After a difficult trip through the icebergs and pack ice around Greenland, the assayers struck out at Little Hall Island, the source of the original black stone. Other islands around had plenty of ore, so the next step was the ritual claiming of the new discoveries and any riches they might generate for England. The scene of Frobisher planting a cross and claiming the land for Elizabeth was to be played out repeatedly all over the Arctic, and eventually the Antarctic. As long as the land was not already claimed by another Christian monarch, this was considered legitimate and sacred. The native peoples who already lived in these places probably thought it was ridiculous or offensive mumbo-jumbo, just as we might today, but the practice was to lead to one of the broadest legacies of all time: from wars, extinctions and unnecessary deaths to the most noble principles of freedom and democracy in the founding of the New World.

Frobisher, however, was involved in an early version of a tawdry drama that has played itself out repeatedly ever since: the massive gold fraud. There was no gold, and despite a third expedition to look for it, there never would be. Michael Lok, who had been a prosperous and highly reputed merchant, was ruined for life and suffered the indignity of debtor's prison in his old age. Some of the black ore from the third Frobisher expedition ended up being used as building materials in Dartford, England, where the assays finally proved its uselessness. More was abandoned on a beach at Smerwick Harbour on the Irish coast, where the *Emanuel of Bridgwater*, one of the ships in the 1578 expedition, barely made it to shore after a horrendous battering in the ice of the North Atlantic. Subsequently, the black, virtually gold-free rock was used to build a large retaining wall. Now, hundreds of years later, it is at last disintegrating into the sea upon which it was transported there at such great cost.

OFF TO A BAD START

Frobisher did redeem himself with the Queen (although it is not clear why he was given the opportunity to do so) by his bravery and leadership in the war against the Spanish Armada.

There is no contesting the skill and bravery with which he and his men battled terrible ice conditions. Time and again, the expeditions were threatened by storms and ice floes with strong winds behind them, coming at the ships like rock sculptures of Formula 1 race cars. It must have been absolutely terrifying. But there is also no question that his handling of relations with the Inuit was ignorant and brutal, the problems compounded by a language barrier and profoundly different assumptions.

At a place that they named Bloody Point, the Frobisher party killed five or six Inuit with their guns, while in return they wounded just one Englishman with their arrows. Robert McGhee, an Arctic archaeologist, says:

> They seem to have viewed the Inuit as we might observe a previously unknown species of strange, dangerous, and potentially entertaining animal. They were continually surprised by the human emotions and conduct exhibited by their prisoners, and found it difficult to understand these as attributes shared by all peoples, rather than only by those whose character had been formed by European society and the Christian religion.[9]

Frobisher was just one of a number of Arctic explorers, not all of them English, to kill natives relentlessly, or to take them prisoner and parade them back home like circus animals. Usually, they did not survive the terrible sea voyage, the strange diet and the unfamiliar viruses; most such prisoners died an early death in captivity.

The attitude behind this behaviour, shared by most of the European explorers, was to cost them dearly. Hundreds of lives were lost as European explorers remained blind to the beautifully adapted technologies and social structures the Inuit had created over thousands of years. Not until John Rae in the late nineteenth century, Knud Rasmussen and Vílhjalmur Stefánsson, at the beginning of the twentieth, would Inuit approaches be recognized as valuable and essential to survival on the ice.

FILLING IN THE BLANKS

Strange theories abounded as the pioneering naval explorers tried to put their maps together. In 1772, a Swiss polymath named Samuel Engel was promoting the idea that ice could only form from fresh water (since ice expels salt, he was onto something, but his conclusion was wrong). He thought, therefore, that if a ship kept away from land with rivers pouring fresh water into the ocean, ice would not form. Many tried to sail over the top of the earth, continuing to believe in the legend of an ice-free polar ocean. Another theory, that the Artic's twenty-four-hour summer daylight would melt the ice, was also proven wrong.

Slowly, the explorers began to come to terms with the idea that it would take small boats and sledges, not ships, to go over the polar ice pack. The image of the evil north took on new life: they spoke of the ice as a prison, as if it were an adversary, alive and determined to prevent them from conquering the pole. And they were determined to complete the map of the world because they understood its potential.

CHAPTER SEVEN

"Exploration is the physical expression of an intellectual passion."
—Aspley Cherry-Garrard, author of *The Worst Journey in the World*

"I am assured these seas will forever prevent discovery being made."
—Captain James Phipps of *Racehorse and Carcass*, 1773

ENCOUNTERS WITH BIG EYEBROWS

Eight years after Martin Frobisher's third expedition to Baffin Island limped and straggled home cross the North Atlantic to bitter recriminations and disgrace, John Davis came ashore in Cumberland Sound. Here, about 200 kilometres north of Frobisher's useless, abandoned mine on Countess Warwick Island, he found an Inuit sled "made of firre, spruce and oaken boards sawn like inch boords." The sawn boards were very likely good English wood left behind in a trenchful of goods abandoned when Frobisher's party had escaped with their lives before the oncoming winter storms and freeze-up. To people who relied on whale bones and preciously conserved pieces of driftwood to meet their needs, this wood (originally intended to build a shelter for the colony Frobisher never founded), would have represented a store of buried treasure. Along with the nails and other things left behind, it would have been traded across the High Arctic by travelling Inuit.

The place where the treasure was found was named Qadlunaat Island by the Inuit, for the strange "white men with the big eyebrows" who had stashed it there. Three hundred years later, the name would be transcribed by the American journalist Charles Francis Hall as "Kodlunarn Island," the name you will find on modern maps. Hall had gone to a great deal of trouble to learn the Inuit language, and was at that time exploring the faint possibility that members of the lost Franklin expedition might still be alive in the High Arctic fifteen years after its disappearance in 1845. Robert McGhee found Hall's original diaries in a cupboard at the Smithsonian Institution's Armed Forces History Collections and read them, marvelling at Hall's writing habits:

> *Turning the water-stained pages and attempting to decipher the cramped writing in smudged black ink, I found it difficult to conceive the discipline and will required to write several words every day under the conditions of nineteenth-century Arctic travel. After I had become accustomed to reading the misspelled but spare and vivid prose of Elizabethan adventurers, Hall's florid and self-conscious Victorian style, even in these rough journals, felt like wading through syrup.*

What fascinated Hall was a startling discovery, which McGhee describes as follows:

> *While he travelled in Frobisher Bay, Hall's Inuit companions told him stories about five qadlunaat who had been marooned in the area, had lived with the Inuit over a winter, and had*

*then built a ship and sailed away. He was also told about qadlu-
naat who came to the area in several ships, constructed a stone
house, dug a trench as a reservoir on a small island, and built a
ship there. . . . At first he thought that he had found clues to the
missing Franklin expedition, but the geographical location was
wrong and the stories related to events that had occurred far
longer ago than the fifteen years since Franklin was last seen.
Eventually he concluded that the oral traditions of the Inuit
referred to an episode that had taken place almost three centuries
earlier, the Frobisher expeditions to what was then known as
Frobisher's Straits.*

It is interesting that this three-hundred-year-old story was
still very fresh for Hall's Inuit friends. The story of the five men
left behind during Frobisher's first expeditions, as well as the
exact location of his mines, had been lost for three centuries by
the time of Hall (who figures again later in this story), but
many other explorers had braved the ice, and the Inuit people
had seen a lot of big eyebrows during that time.

Time Reveals All
BEER AS ESSENTIAL ARTIC FUEL

The notion of time is very different in the Arctic. Just as the
Inuit carry stories for a very long time, the earth preserves the
mark of human activities. Another century later, in 1991, a team
of archaeologists found that little had changed over four hundred years.[1] For example, they identified a barren area where the
fragile, slow-growing vegetation had probably been pressed into
service for insulation of the Elizabethan habitations during the

Frobisher expedition. The Arctic's isolation and cold preserve artefacts and sites in a way that is difficult to imagine in more populated and more temperate zones. This points to the vulnerability of the arctic environment to human intervention, but it has also proven a great advantage to historians and archaeologists—as well as to Inuit in search of wood and metal to make harpoon tips.

The 1991 research team found four-hundred-year-old ship's biscuit (the Inuit were not as interested in it as in the wood and metal) in the mine left behind by Frobisher when he made a rare wise decision not to leave a colony on the ice of Countess Warwick Island. Amusingly enough, one of the reasons the colony did not get built was the absolute importance of beer as a food group at the time. The miners on the island were each getting a gallon of beer a day, as a matter of course.

The Frobisher fleet left England carrying 84 tons of beer, but for various reasons (ships sank, the beer leaked when heavy stuff was piled on top of it, and some of the men misbehaved and drank too much on the way out) this was down to 24 tons by the time they had to make a decision about staying for the winter. There was rebellion in the ranks: 24 tons of beer just would not be enough, and this played a role in the eventual decision to return home. The shipboard accounts of the day complain bitterly that they had to drink water on the return voyage. One explanation for these complaints could be that water was often foul and dangerous to drink at the time, whereas turning it into beer made it much safer.

In England, the beverage had not quite achieved the sacred status that it already had in Belgium. (This was due to the fact that the monk Arnold and his brewer fellows survived the plague by only drinking beer, while telling the public they were messengers from God. Thus was Catholicism solidly implanted in Belgium. Father Arnold became St. Arnold and the Confederation of Brewers still has its Guildhall on the Grande Place in Brussels, the only one of the original guildhall buildings left standing in this prominent location.) Beer is full of B vitamins and carbohydrates, and would have been considered essential by all classes of the population at the time. During Lenten fasting, the beer was made stronger and sweeter to sustain them during the period when they were not eating. In 1576, English beer would have been a dark, heavy, nutrient-rich brew. It was not until Bass created its rich, amber red beer in 1778 that lighter-coloured beers came to England; all others were dark like Guinness.

Beer was consumed copiously; everyone drank heavily and some people were paid in beer. Armies fought on beer, and it may have been the bulkiest part of any cargo. According to Master Brewer Bill White of Oland Specialty Beers, a knowledgeable beer historian, the Pilgrims would probably have kept going south to warmer climes had they not needed to land at Plymouth Rock to get a grain crop going because they had run out of beer. So many destinies have been forged because of beer. Brewmaster White says he was told in New Zealand that the famous Captain Cook was one of the first to recognize the health benefits of beer, and that while crew members often had to be forced to eat sour lemons and limes to prevent scurvy, "He never had to flog anybody to get them to drink up." Captain Cook claimed to have lost only one seaman to illness throughout his illustrious naval career.

FOR KING AND COUNTRY

Until the end of the nineteenth century and even into the early twentieth, the bulk of the ice exploration that captures the imagination was the work of the English. This is not because they were particularly capable, but for different reasons: first, they were late into empire-building, and therefore had to push farther north and farther south to find new possessions. And second, they managed to create a mythology of heroism and sacrifice that, ridiculous though it may appear to today's cynical audiences, held a powerful allure for many. This included talented men not born into the right class or family. Given the British class system, it was very difficult to get expeditions funded if their leaders did not have the right military or aristocratic credentials.

When we look back with today's eyes and think of the abominable conditions under which the men on these expeditions lived and travelled, the attraction of this powerful mythology is intriguing, to say the least. Mostly Navy men, they came by ship to seek their fortunes and to find the Northwest Passage. Inevitably, the ships would be locked into the ice for the winter; often, they would be crushed. In his journal, George DeLong[2] describes this frightening experience: "At 6:10 A.M. awakened by the trembling and cracking of the ship. The ice was again in motion, grinding and crushing. I know of no sound on shore that can compare with it."

Expeditions set sail loaded down with live animals for food, and rats to prey on everyone and everything aboard; water in wooden casks that would be full of maggots in short order, atrocious and unhealthy food and vast amounts of beer and spirits, usually Navy rum.

In fact, as authors Peter McFarlane and Wayne Haimila put it in their book *Ancient Land, Ancient Sky: Following Canada's Native Canoe Routes*:

> *Below deck the stench—ripe and acrid from rat droppings mixed with mildew, rot and the odours of never-washed bodies—was so strong that scientists of the day speculated that it was a violent explosion of these shipboard vapours that created ball lightning.*[3]

Being cooped up in the close quarters required to stay warm in the polar ice pack, whether on the ice-bound ship or in a makeshift shelter, made basic hygiene fiendishly difficult. While the link between hygiene and good health was little understood, keeping the explorers and their crews healthy enough to survive the winter (especially in the years before they understood how to prevent scurvy) was probably the single biggest challenge of the time.

THE INFATUATION WITH THE POLES

It is hard to reconcile this disgusting picture with the romantic polar infatuation that swept the British Isles from the eighteenth to the twentieth centuries, and arguably, continues somewhat today (although Gore-Tex, satellite phones and sophisticated portable equipment have really changed the nature of the interest). It might have started sooner, but for a surprisingly influential (at the time) and since-forgotten 1633 voyage narrative called "The Strange and Dangerous Voyage of Captain Thomas James," the subject of a doctoral thesis by Colleen Franklin of Ottawa.

James was searching in 1661 for a route to Cathay on behalf of the merchants of Bristol.[4] Within a few weeks of his departure, Luke Foxe[5] undertook the same mission on behalf of the merchants of London. Although both men had harrowing experiences, returning to England with crews suffering from scurvy, their attitudes could not have been more different—and this presaged a transition in eras.

James reacted with medieval superstition, viewing the wind, snow and ice as evil entities, while Foxe took pleasure in a modern scientific curiosity, making frequent notes about his sightings of birds, animals and vegetation. Franklin says church and secular writings of the medieval and early Renaissance periods often suggest that Lucifer's throne is in the north. From the Bible to Chaucer, "it works its way through the popular culture so that you find jokes about it in the *Canterbury Tales*, where it is used to suggest evil." Ironically, then, because James was more educated than his crew, he brought this idea that evil is northern to his writing; they would not have read enough to know about it. The James account achieved lurid popularity in London, and may have inspired Milton's description of hell as a barren, icy place in *Paradise Lost*.

This irony—that the educated man's book based on medieval fear crowded out the open, curious man's far more modern view of the icy north—influenced the course of events in the Arctic for a long time: James turned off potential British explorers for almost a century after his account became a best-seller. Foxe's account, with all its helpful noting of flora and fauna—and its wonder at the sheer beauty and tenacious life of the north—was frozen out until it was finally republished in 1898.

For a century after James, there was very little interest in the Northwest Passage. In the nineteenth century, Edmond Burke's articulation of the sublime as the great but terrible, began to invest the north with a spiritual presence. Nineteenth-century portrayals of this sublime presence were often evil. Paintings and cartoons from *Punch* from the era feminize the north as a cold and evil temptress, luring men to their deaths. This melodramatic imagery was persistent. Even when the missions into the ice were serving political and economic purposes, the rhetoric was almost purely scientific, and public-spirited.

The presumed nobility of purpose in the naval expeditions to the Arctic created a strange situation: those who knew the most about the Arctic, and had adopted the best methods and technologies for survival there, were the least likely to find favour with financial backers in England. On the contrary, the code ensured that right into the twentieth century it was often the least suitable candidates who were deemed worthy of leading expeditions.

Polar Exploration Timeline

Year	Arctic Exploration	Global Exploration	Antarctic Exploration
330 BC	The Greek sailor Pytheas of Massilia sets off on a six-year exploration of Britain and the waters north of Scotland. He describes Thule, which may have been the Faroes.		
AD ca. 870	The Norseman Floki Vilgerdarson discovers Iceland.		
983	Erik Thorvaldsson, named Erik the Red because of his flaming red hair, reaches Iceland.		
1000	The Viking Leif Eriksson settles in Newfoundland.		
1492		Christopher Columbus lands in Hispanola and discovers "the New World."	

1497	Vasco De Gama sails from Portugal to India via the West coast of Africa and the Cape of Good Hope.
1594–97	The Dutch explorer Willem Barents discovers Spitzbergen
1599	Dirk Gerritsz of Holland spots the South Shetland Islands when the wind forces him off course while rounding Cape Horn.
1607–10	The Englishman Henry Hudson makes voyages to Hudson Bay, Hudson River, Greenland, Spitzbergen and Jan Mayer.
1615–16	Englishmen William Baffin and Robert Bylot make two voyages to Baffin and Hudson Bay and discover the Jones, Lancaster and Smith Straits (named after three patrons of their voyages).
1725–42	Czar Peter the Great sends Vitus Bering, Dmitri Laptev and Vasily Chelyuskin on the Great Northern expedition where they explore the Bering Sea and Arctic Siberia

YEAR	ARCTIC EXPLORATION	GLOBAL EXPLORATION	ANTARCTIC EXPLORATION
1768–72			The British Captain James Cook leads two voyages during the course of which he discovers New Zealand and removes Terra Australis from tropical and temperate latitudes.
1772–75			On this second voyage, Captain Cook sets off to discover the Antarctic continent and unwittingly circumvents it. He discovers the South Sandwich Islands and South Georgia Island. His diaries tell of seal and whale populations; this drives whalers to continue exploring the Arctic.
1778	Captain Cook goes to Alaska and establishes the separation between the American and Asian continents when the sails trough the Bering straight.		
1800			Sealers begin hunting the New Zealand fur seals of the Antipodes Islands.
1806			Sealers begin exploiting the New Zealand fur seals of the Auckland Islands.

This NASA image of the earth shows the extent of the ice cover on Antarctica and the surrounding ocean. Clouds also appear as white—but then, they are made of ice crystals too. This starkly beautiful image shows how thin the atmosphere is that sustains life on earth. *(Astronaut photo, Apollo 17)*

The earth is seen here from above the Arctic, an ocean rimmed with continents. The sea ice and the Greenland ice cap are clearly visible. The image is centred on the North Pole, in the middle of the Ocean. It is a composite of true colour images from several NASA sensors assembled in 2000. *(Courtesy of NASA)*

This image of the Illecillowaet Glacier in British Columbia was taken in 1913.
(Courtesy of the Earth Sciences Information Centre, Natural Resources Canada)

Daniel McCarthy, Associate Professor of Earth Sciences at Brock University, has plotted the retreat of the Illecillowaet Glacier over the last century and has provided this image. What was ice covered in 1913 is now mostly bare rock.

Sastrugi are wind-sculpted snow and ice dunes. They are most common on wide-open plains in Antarctica, but they can also be seen in the High Arctic, for example, on Ellesmere Island. These are at South Pole Station in Antarctica. *(Mr. Fred Walton, NOAA)*

The Bennington Glacier in British Columbia is on the boundary between Mount Robson Park and Jasper National Park. You can see a medial moraine and large lateral moraines on the bottom left and bottom right. The sandy, well-lit feature nearest the lake is an ice-cored esker (a very rare thing to see at an alpine glacier). *(Daniel McCarthy, Department of Earth Sciences, Brock University)*

This kettle hole was created when a mass of leftover glacier ice was trapped in glacial deposits. This one in Norway's beautiful Lysefjord was once used as a giant bathtub by the region's zinc miners. *(Pauline Couture)*

The houses of Gamla Stan, an island that forms the old part of Stockholm, are very high maintenance. They were built on wooden pilings that have lasted for centuries, as long as they were deep in the wet earth. Since the end of the last ice age, when the earth here was relieved of the weight of the ice, the land has been rising at a rate of 4.6 millimetres a year. As it rises, the pilings are exposed to oxygen and start to rot. This ice-age legacy keeps the Stockholm construction industry employed year after year repairing the pilings, propping up the houses and resettling them—until the land rises far enough to start the process over again. *(Pauline Couture)*

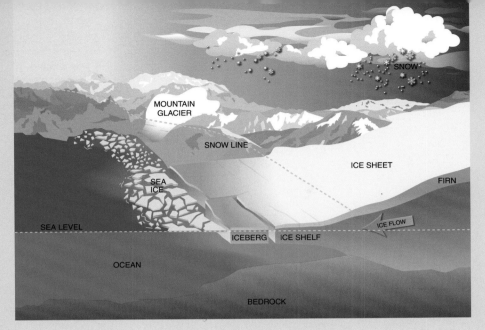

This NASA image explains the basic of ice movement through the cryosphere.

The Larsen B ice shelf in Antarctica shattered and separated from the continent in 2002, forming a plume of thousands of huge icebergs in the Weddell Sea. It is now about 40 percent of the size it was for the past four hundred years, and possibly as long as twelve thousand years. Ted Scambos and his team have determined that ice-shelf collapses are accelerated by meltwater infiltrating into cracks in the ice. The shelf also acted like a stopper for higher glacier ice on the continent, which is now flowing many times faster than before. You can watch an animation of the Larsen B ice-shelf collapse at http://nsidc.org/iceshelves/larsenb2002/animation.html.
(Image courtesy of Ted Scambos, National Snow and Ice Data Center, University of Colorado, Boulder, based on data from MODIS)

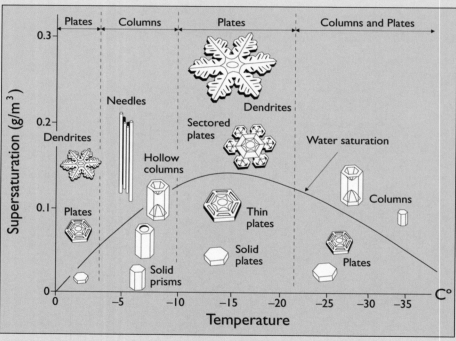

In general, when it's warmer at ground level (0 to −5°C) and a bit colder in the clouds, you see mostly needlelike crystals (#3) with what Kenneth G. Libbrecht calls "lots of gloppy bits." He is the CalTech physicist who produced these wonderful micro-photos of snow crystals and the morphology chart (above). These crystals are usually partly melted and not very well-formed. Some plates (like #2) form at −2°C, but the temperature is rarely stable enough to see well-formed plates (except in Dr. Libbrecht's lab, of course). These also tend to melt quickly when it's that warm. As it gets colder, say −10°C to −15°C on the ground, platelike crystals (#2) appear, including stellar dendrites (#1). When it gets even colder, around −15°C to −20°C, you find smaller platelike crystals with exceptionally nice facets and symmetry. Much colder and it doesn't snow, and the crystals are small when it does. If Dr. Libbrecht wants to study snow crystals in nature, he tends to go to Timmins, Ontario; otherwise, he has to grow them in the lab. *(Snowflake images and chart courtesy of Dr. Kenneth G. Libbrecht, Professor of Physics and Physics Executive Officer, Caltech, Pasadena, CA)*

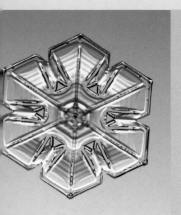  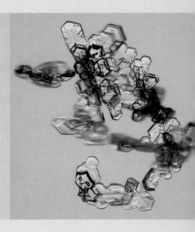

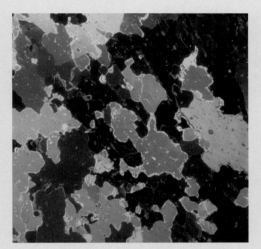

#4 – Very small, hollow stubby columnar crystals typically form around −10°C.
#5 – At −15°C, the stubby column may become a capped column.
#6 – The most common snowflake form, a jumbled mess of plate-like branches.

After careful preparation of a thin sample of 10,000-year-old glacier ice, Dr. Paul Barrette arranged it between two polarized filters. Lo and behold, a riot of colours emerged as the light refracted from the complex crystal structure. The ice came from a Greenland glacier whose weight changed the shape of the crystals as it grew heavier and larger.

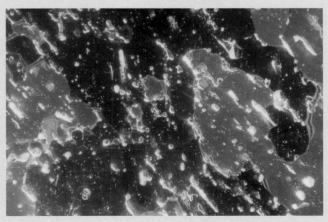

The same thin sample as above, illuminated from the side. The light shows up all the cracks and imperfections in the ice created by its long journey from snow falling on a Greenland glacier, to iceberg in the north Atlantic before being harvested by a Newfoundland ice cowboy.
See page 38. (Images courtesy of Dr. Paul Barrette)

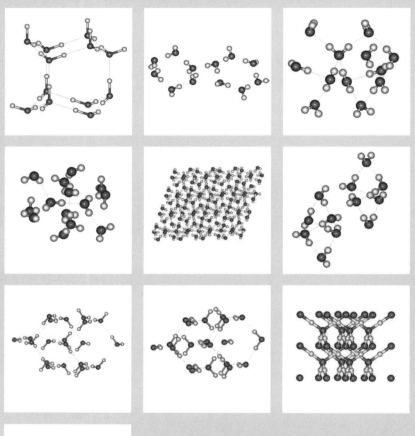

Some of the phases of ice as its cystals form at various temperatures and pressures. Most of us would ever only see hexagonal ice I. The other forms are useful to the understanding of extreme conditions in laboratories and in space exploration.

1819–1920	British explorer William Edward Parry makes his first voyage and seeks out the Northwestern Passages. He discovers Melville Island and names the Barrow straight. John Franklin sets out on his first expedition to find the Northwest Passage; eleven of his crewmen do not make it back.	British William Smith discovers the South Shetland Islands; credit for discovering the Antarctic Continent discovery remains disputed to this day.
1821		An American sealer named John Davis lands at Hughes Bay and becomes the first person to set foot on the Antarctic Continent.
1821–23	William Edward Parry makes his second voyage in search of the Northwest Passage. He reaches the straights of Fury and Hecla from Hudson Bay.	A British sealer named James Weddell reaches the farthest southern point anyone had reached to date.
1824–25	William Edward Parry makes his third voyage in search of the Northwest Passage. One of his vessels shipwrecks on Fury Beach Somerset Island.	
1825–27	John Franklin makes his second land and canoe voyage to the Arctic seacoast, where his crew explores and maps out over a thousand miles of coastline from Coronation Gulf to Prudhoe Bay, Alaska.	

YEAR	ARCTIC EXPLORATION	GLOBAL EXPLORATION	ANTARCTIC EXPLORATION
1827	William Edward Parry tries to reach the North Pole via Spitzbergen. In doing so, he reaches the farthest northern point anyone had reached to date and that anyone will reach for another fifty years.		
1831	James Clark Ross is the first to locate the Northern Magnetic Pole in what is now the Canadian High Arctic.		
1837–39	Peter Dease and Thomas Simpson set off on an overland and canoe expedition on behalf of the Hudson's Bay Company to fill the gaps left on the Franklin map.		
1838			John Balleny discovers the Balleny Islands and the Sabrina Coast of Antarctica while in search of new sealing grounds to exploit.

1840	Jules Dumont d'Urville discovers and names Adélie Land south of Australian and makes measurements of the earth's magnetic field in nearby waters. He also makes his own maps of the Southern Shetland Islands and some of certain sections from the Arctic Peninsula.
	Lieutenant Charles Wilkes from the U.S. Navy leads the first American scientific voyage to the Antarctic where he proves once and for all that Antarctica is not an agglomeration of ice islands, but a bona fide continent.
1841	British explorer James Clark Ross sets out to find the Southern Magnetic Pole but finds the Ross Ice Shelf and Mount Erebus (an active Antarctic volcano) instead.
1845–49	Sir John Franklin sets out on an expedition to find the Northwest Passage, never to be seen alive again.

YEAR	ARCTIC EXPLORATION	GLOBAL EXPLORATION	ANTARCTIC EXPLORATION
1848–62	Several expeditions are sent out to search for Franklin and his crewmen, some privately financed by Lady Franklin. The fate of the expedition is only discovered in 1859 and a final expedition is sent to search for survivors in 1860–62.		
1871–73	Charles Hall mans a third expedition in search of the North Pole but dies early on during the voyage. Upon their return home, half of his crew becomes stranded on an ice floe until they are freed by whalers six months later.		
1875–76	George Nares mans the last expedition the British Navy will send out to explore the Arctic and reach the North Pole.		
1878	Baron Nordenskiald is the first to successfully navigate the Northeast Passage.		

1879–82	Lieutenant George Washington DeLong of the U.S. Navy sets out to search for a quick route to the North Pole via Siberia. DeLong's ship, *Janette*, sinks and DeLong, along with most of his crew, dies of starvation in Siberia. Only a handful of men return home from the expedition.
1881–84	Lieutenant Lockwood of the U.S. Navy reaches the farthest northern point and in doing so, takes a record held by the British for three centuries. Only one-quarter of the men in his expedition survive.
1882–83	The First International Polar Year. Twelve Countries establish fourteen bases in polar regions to study and record the earth's climate and magnetism.
1888	Norwegian Fridtjof Nansen is the first to cross Greenland.
1893–95	Fridtjof Nansen and Otto Sverdrup establish a new record for the farthest northern point reached.

YEAR	ARCTIC EXPLORATION	GLOBAL EXPLORATION	ANTARCTIC EXPLORATION
1898			Carson Borchgrevink and his party are the first men to winter on the Antarctic Continent.
1899–1900	Lieutenant Cagni establishes a new record for farthest northern point reached, a mere 22 miles from the point that had previously been reached by Nansen.		
1901			Robert Falcon Scott, Edward Wilson and Ernest Wilson lead an expedition to Victoria Land. From there on, they voyage towards the South Pole before they are forced to turn back.
Otto von Nordenskjold mans an ill-fated Swedish voyage to the Weddell Sea. His ship sinks when crushed by ice.
1903			A French national expedition led by Jean-Baptiste Charcot produces many important charts of the Antarctic Peninsula.

1903–6	Roald Amundsen, commanding a seven-man crew aboard the little *Gjøa*, becomes the first to lead a successful expedition through the Northwest Passage.
1905–6	Robert Peary's fourth Arctic expedition sets out in attempt to reach the pole. Peary does not reach the pole, but establishes a new record for the farthest northern point reached.
1907–9	Frederick Cook claims that he has successfully reached the North Pole.
1908–9	Robert Peary claims he has successfully reached the North Pole.
1910	Roald Amundsen and Robert Falcon Scott both set out to reach the South Pole.
1911	Roald Amundsen succeeds in reaching the pole before Scott.
1912	Scott reaches the pole but he and his four companions perish on the return trip.

YEAR	ARCTIC EXPLORATION	GLOBAL EXPLORATION	ANTARCTIC EXPLORATION
1914–16			Ernest Shackleton enters the Weddell Sea, but his ship *Endurance* sinks after being trapped in the ice. Shackleton leads his men across the ice with three rowboats; after almost two years, he succeeds in securing a Chilean vessel to rescue them without loss of life.
1921–24	Knud Rasmussen undertakes his fifth Thule expedition, which takes him from Copenhagen to the Pacific across the Arctic. His book, *Across Arctic America*, appears in 1934.		
1925			The British set up a biological station on South Georgia to study Antarctic whales.
1926	Richard E. Byrd flies over the pole in a Fokker trimotor plane.		
1928			Richard E. Byrd arrives at the Bay of Whales with the intention of crossing the South Pole via aircraft.

1928–29	The Australian Sir Hubert Wilkins successfully explores 2,100 kilometres of the Antarctic Peninsula via aircraft.
1929	A group of geologists makes a surprising discovery. They study the interior mountains and realize that they were part of the earth's buckled crust. Richard E. Byrd successfully flies from Little America to a point over the South Pole without stopping.
1932–33	The Second International Polar Year achieves groundbreaking ionospheric measurements useful in radio transmissions during World War II a few years later.
1934–39	Richard E. Byrd returns to the Antarctic on two separate occasions in order to further scientific exploration as well as mapping.
1935	American millionaire Lincoln Ellsworth is the first to fly across the Antarctic.

YEAR	ARCTIC EXPLORATION	GLOBAL EXPLORATION	ANTARCTIC EXPLORATION
1946			The U.S. Navy deploys the largest Antarctic movement to date, known as Operation Highjump: 13 ships, 23 aircraft, an aircraft carrier a submarine and some 4,700 men equipped with icebreakers.
1947–48			Norwegian Finn Ronne leads a new expedition to Marguerite Bay, reoccupying the base he shared with Richard E. Byrd in the 1939 Byrd expedition. Ronne solves one of Antarctica's last scientific mysteries when he finds sufficient evidence to prove that the Antarctic Peninsula is in fact connected to the Antarctic continent.
1957–58			International Geophysical Year: sixty-seven nations collaborate.
1958	Nuclear submarine U.S.S. *Nautilus* passes under the pole. Nuclear submarine U.S.S. *Skate* is the first to surface through the ice at the North Pole.		The first overland transcontinental expedition succeeds led by Vivian Fuchs and Sir Edmund Hillary of the Commonwealth.

1968	With the help of an air support team, Ralph Plaisted reaches the North Pole via snowmobile.
1969	With air support, Wally Herbert leads a dogsled team from Alaska to Svalbard.
1977	Naomi Uemura of Japan successfully completes a one-man overland expedition to the pole.
1986	Paul Schurke, Will Steger and Ann Bancroft lead a dogsled team to the pole without re-supplying. Ann Bancroft is the first woman to achieve such a voyage.
1992	Helen Thayer becomes the first woman to do a solo trek to the pole.
1993	Ranulph Twistleton-Wykeham-Fiennes is knighted for his many exploration accomplishments in both the Arctic and Antarctica. The *Guiness Book of World Records* calls him the greatest explorer in the world. That same year, he and Dr. Mike Stroud make the longest unsupported polar journey ever, dragging 500-lb. sledges for ninety-seven days.

YEAR	ARCTIC EXPLORATION	GLOBAL EXPLORATION	ANTARCTIC EXPLORATION
2000	David Hempleman-Adams completes the Explorers' Grand Slam. He has conquered the North and South Magnetic Poles, becoming the first Briton to walk solo and unsupported to the South Pole, walk solo to the North Geographic Pole and scale the highest mountain in each of the seven continents, including Everest. On 1 June 2000 Hempleman-Adams became the only pilot to fly a balloon to the North Pole. On September 29, 2003, he became the first person to fly a balloon solo with an open wicker basket across the Atlantic from Canada to the United Kingdom.		

THE EASTERN APPROACH

The history of the Northwest Passage is long and difficult because the passage itself is so problematic: choked with ice all year round for hundreds and thousands of years (although not for much longer, as global warming continues) and complicated by a maze of ice-trapping islands and dead-end waterways. The only major river emptying into the Arctic Ocean that would have permitted a substantial approach by land is the Mackenzie River. In contrast, although the Northeast Passage across the top of Russia was less icy, there were many river accesses, so that it was mapped over time by explorers who approached it through the river system, much more efficiently.

Because it was taking so long for anyone to penetrate either passage from one end to the other, explorers, adventurers and military men kept attempting the Arctic and the pole itself from different launching points, many of them along the long stretch of Russian and Siberian coastline on the Arctic Ocean. In 1648, Semen Dezhenev discovered and recorded the existence of a strait between the end of Asia and the beginning of North America, but it was not named until the time of Vitus Bering, in 1728.

On his third voyage, James Cook accurately mapped and established the relationship between Asia and America, a more successful outcome than his aborted Antarctic attempt. With his ships *Resolution* and *Discovery*, Cook reached Bering Strait on his third voyage, in the same year as Bering himself, 1728. Although he had set out with a map that showed Alaska as an island, Cook was able to map and accurately establish the relationship between Asia and America on that trip.

Samuel Hearne had provided the overland perspective to join up with Cook's maps. He was the first European to reach the Arctic Ocean via land. Hearne's contribution to the increased knowledge of the whole continent would have been recognized sooner, but for the fact that the Hudson's Bay Company kept it confidential as "competitive" information until they finally published it after his death.

Still, an overall picture was at last coming together from these isolated bits and pieces. The extraordinarily talented Cook met the ice on August 17, naming the northernmost point reached Icy Cape. He then turned back west, probing the pack with his unstrengthened ship. Cook and his crew went back to winter in Hawaii, where he died at the hands of the natives in February—a great and premature loss to the history of exploration. It was left to his midshipman, George Vancouver, to establish that there was no western entrance to the Northwest Passage on the northwest coast.

Many a Royal Navy man earned his stripes on the ice. The course of history would have been much altered if a minor incident in 1766 had gone differently: encountering a polar bear on the ice pack near Spitzbergen, a fourteen-year-old midshipman named Horatio Nelson was saved from an ugly mauling death by the firing of a gun from the ship. Nelson had tried to kill the bear with the butt of his gun after it misfired, displaying the kind of courage that would later distinguish him at the Battle of Trafalgar.

FRANKLIN AND THE GRIP ON THE ENGLISH IMAGINATION
The European wars with the French had long drained British

resources. With Napoleon safely out of the picture at last, the British began flexing their muscles and feeling the urge to focus outward again. Britain had seven thousand officers at the end of the Napoleonic Wars, and many of them (including William Edward Parry, John Franklin and James Clark Ross) became involved in the renewed search for the Northwest Passage. Since they still believed there was an open polar sea beyond the "ring of ice," they thought they would be able to break through it in short order to reach the Pole. Franklin commanded the *Trent*, one of two ships assigned to sail from Spitzbergen in 1818, and quickly pushed back by the ice on that front.

His 1818 service aboard the *Trent* somehow convinced the authorities that Franklin should lead a land-based expedition from Great Slave Lake to the Arctic Ocean the following year. His mission was to paddle or sail east all the way across the top of the continent to map the Arctic coast, and to rendezvous with Edward Parry, who would be sailing a Royal Navy ship west from the Atlantic side. This would have been a monumental task at any time, despite the support of a large number of French-Canadian voyageurs, Metis and Iroquois Indians who hauled the group's supplies on their backs and in canoes.

Franklin pressed on and on as winter was setting in, despite the growing alarm of his companion and guide, Chief Akaitcho, who believed they should take shelter in a safe place until the warmer weather returned. Franklin's obsessive refusal to take expert advice caused the loss of eleven of his men from cold and starvation on the 1819 expedition. In truth, being reduced to eating scraps of boiled leather was a sign that he did not take advice very well, but the media played up his rugged survival by dubbing him "the man who ate his boots" and from then on, Franklin could write his own ticket in England.

Franklin's early expedition diaries, read with the knowledge of his ultimate fate, are filled with the ominous signs of his tunnel vision and stubbornness—although these traits may have seemed like virtues by the standards of the time. On his second expedition, he did succeed in mapping 1,000 miles of coastline, from Coronation Gulf to Prudhoe Bay, Alaska, and was knighted for his pains. But the most famous, the most romantic and the most tragic effort of his life was the third Franklin expedition.

He was already sixty-one and famous by the time he set off on May 19, 1845, to map the Northwest Passage. His determined, ambitious wife, Lady Jane, screaming with boredom after an honorific posting to Tasmania, encouraged him to go for the greater glory of the Crown. Despite his own dreadful experiences of near starvation on the ice, Franklin was determined to conquer the Northwest Passage and to follow through—at last—on the quests initiated by those long-dead but dashing Elizabethans, Sir Walter Raleigh and Sir Francis Drake.

His ships, the *Terror* and the *Erebus* set sail in the glow of national pride and a huge media hullabaloo, with the finest new innovations money could buy, including 8,000 cans of meat, vegetables and soup—a five-year supply (in sizes of 1, 2, 4, 6 and 8 pounds), a crew of 134 officers and men, and the very latest in technology. Their cabins were heated by hot water piped through the floor—luxury! The ships were reinforced with iron planks to help them break through the ice, and each had a screw propeller, driven by a wheel-less steam locomotive from the London and Greenwich Railway—power!

Two whaling ships, the *Prince of Wales* and the *Enterprise*
reported seeing the *Erebus* and the *Terror* in Baffin Bay near the
end of July 1845, just two and a half months after their departure from England. After that, silence. It was three long years
before Lady Jane could even convince anyone to start looking
for Franklin and his men. No one could believe that such a
well-equipped expedition could have come to harm so quickly.
Lady Jane was persuasive, determined and rich: there were fifty-
seven different attempts to find the members of the Franklin
expedition and their fancy new ships—when she couldn't bully
them into trying, she paid them. The rescue efforts thereafter
cost many lives. The mission and its would-be rescuers have
always fascinated adventurers and scholars, making them the
subject of forensic research well into the late-twentieth century,
when anthropologists from the University of Alberta uncovered
the perfectly preserved ice mummy of twenty-one-year-old
midshipman John Torrington, his head tied up like a child with
mumps.

In the 1987 book *Frozen in Time*, Owen Beattie and John
Geiger say their forensic research shows that the famous
Franklin-expedition food tins were sealed with imperfect lead
solder that tainted the food inside each one.[6] Their hypothesis
that this would have poisoned the members of the expedition
was borne out. The bodies of John Torrington and the two
other crew members found frozen on Beechey Island in the
1980s all showed irrefutable evidence of lead poisoning, as well
as the symptoms of scurvy (bleeding, weight loss, weakness),
tuberculosis and deadly pneumonia.

Torrington's hair, demonstrating recent predeath exposure

to the toxic metal, had 600 ppm of lead, or 120 times the normal amount. Lead poisoning causes a range of debilitating
physical symptoms, from anorexia to anemia and extreme
weakness. But it can also have devastating psychological effects,
such as paranoia and impaired judgment. This might help to
explain the other very odd find: a lifeboat mounted on a sledge,
crammed with bizarre choices for a life-threatening arctic-
survival mission: button polish, silk handkerchiefs, curtain rods
and a writing desk.

Reports came in that in 1850, near the mouth of Great Fish
River, Inuit hunters had discovered the bodies of thirty men
and a number of graves. This report came to England in a letter from Dr. John Rae, the Orkney doctor (whose personal
effects I saw in the museum at Stromness).[7] Rae had adapted
well to the Arctic, but this in itself would have reduced his cred-
ibility back home; his letter added fuel to the fire. Because it
made clear that Franklin's men had resorted to cannibalism,
Rae's letter set off a media firestorm, and elicited indignant
responses from all kinds of people, including Charles Dickens.[8]
The sad remnants of regimental silver and other effects recovered by Dr. Rae are on display at the National Maritime
Museum at Greenwich.

Franklin's death was only confirmed in 1859, when a search
party led by Leopold M'Clintock found a cairn containing
messages to that effect, as well as skeletons of some of the last
survivors. Some of them appeared indeed to have resorted to
cannibalism, a fact that was quickly buried by the admiralty.
Sir John had died early on, when only twenty-four of his men
had predeceased him. All the years of hunting in the ice for the

Franklin party had been in vain; they had all been dead all along. But the sad story in no way diminished the mapping achievements of Franklin's second expedition, the greatest single advance in arctic knowledge to that time.

CHAPTER EIGHT

"The exploration of the Arctic is, as much as anything, a story of
wrecks, and starvation, and thwarted hopes of the Europeans
(I include Americans in this term)."

—Peter Stark, *Ring of Ice, True Tales of Adventure,*
Exploration and Arctic Life

HERO WORSHIP

The legend of Franklin died hard, and to this day he has fans
who continue to see him as a conquering hero. They would
include the German novelist Sten Nadolny, whose book *The
Discovery of Slowness* is based on Franklin's life. It has been an
enduring hit in Europe, arriving to North America in English
many years after its publication in German. In this beautiful
work of fiction, Nadolny focuses on Franklin's extraordinary
determination, discipline and focus . . . his slowness, in fact, as
admirable qualities from the perspective of today's speeded-up
world.

The harsh light of scientific reality has been harder on
Franklin's reputation. Contemplating the dead explorer's
leather mitts and snow goggles at the museum in Greenwich,
and the number of futile missions sent to his rescue, one can be
forgiven for thinking that the tragedy lies in the waste of
human lives.

The career of Robert Falcon Scott, also celebrated as a great hero at the time, has taken on a less positive aura with time as well. Scott, whose name is commemorated in the prestigious Scott Polar Institute at Cambridge, was certainly brave. But he was also foolishly stubborn, insisting on bringing English ponies to Antarctica rather than arctic-trained sled dogs that might have saved his life. Roald Amundsen had no such compulsions, and beat Scott to the pole in 1911, while coming out of Antarctica alive. It is likely no coincidence that Amundsen was the first European explorer to study Inuit clothing and technology carefully, and to use it to succeed in his endeavours. In addition to making it first to the South Pole, Amundsen also became the first explorer to make it through the Northwest Passage—such a challenging accomplishment that even today, fewer than two hundred ships have done it.

Scott and four companions did reach the South Pole thirty-three days after Amundsen, to their bitter disappointment. But they were unable to make it back. Their remains were found in a tent pitched just 11 miles short of one of their food-supply depots.

Scott's companion, Aspley Cherry-Garrard, wrote *The Worst Journey in the World*, one of the greatest exploration narratives ever. He is remembered as a great story-teller, and the most remarkable thing about it was that he never lost his sense of humour: "Polar exploration is at once the cleanest and most isolated way of having a bad time that has yet been devised."

The witty British novelist Nancy Mitford wrote about Cherry-Gerrard's account, fifty years after Scott's death: "Nobody could deny that he and the twenty-four other members of Captain Scott's expedition to the South Pole had a bad time. In fact, all other bad times, embarked on by men of their own free will, pale before it. There is the last of the great classic explorations; their equipment, though they lived in our century, curiously little different from that used by Captain Cook. Vitamin pills would probably have saved the lives of the Polar party, so would a wireless transmitter; an electric torch have mitigated the misery of the Winter Journey. How many things which we take completely as a matter of course had not yet been invented, such a little time ago!" This continues to have the ring of truth today.

The Quality of Leadership

A more modern hero has turned out to be Ernest Shackleton, whose Antarctic expedition failed, but whose leadership is now seen as a beacon of courage for our times. When Shackleton's ship, the *Endurance*, was locked in the ice (in January of 1915) and ultimately crushed (in November of that year), he led his men to safety across the treacherous pack ice of the southern ocean. Leaving them on Elephant Island, he made his way by lifeboat to South Georgia, where he was able to procure the Chilean freighter *Yelcho* to pick them up on August 30, 1916.

Modern admiration for Shackleton stems from his constant ability to inspire his men, so that they always kept up the hope that they would make it, and his fidelity to them above his own ambition to reach the South Pole. His memory is also burnished by the amazing black-and-white photos and film footage that exist of his expedition. He understood the value of public relations, and financed his expedition largely by preselling these images. Despite the dire straits in which they found themselves, he and his expedition photographer managed to preserve a good selection of these images. They are very moving to see today: the men playing cards and making music inside the doomed ship; trying to hack their way through the pack ice with axes, saws and anything else that came to hand; the gallant *Endurance* groaning, shuddering and capsizing while the men watch, helpless, from the ice.

Between the time of Shackleton's departure from England and his return with all his men, the world's attention had been completely hijacked by World War I, and exploring the Antarctic had come to seem much less important. The mid-1990s saw a multiyear flurry of books, television documentaries, a TV movie starring Kenneth Branagh as Shackleton and even a spectacular IMAX film that celebrated his life. Its 50-foot-high close-up images of massive south-ocean icebergs flattened audiences in their seats and took their breath away. Intercut with the expedition's actual original images, it shed new light on Shackleton's achievements. Businessmen began to attend Shackleton leadership seminars to learn how to inspire their troops (no one suggested importing giant icebergs for this purpose). It's hard not to wonder what the charismatic Shackleton would have made of it all. He died of a heart attack on South Georgia, attempting to remount his failed expedition.

■ ■ ■

In the year after Scott's death, 1913, the Canadian government agreed to underwrite the first multidisciplinary scientific expedition to the Canadian Arctic, led by anthropologist Vílhjalmur Stefánsson. It, too, encountered disaster, losing more than half its men and two of its ships. Stefánsson had already been exploring for unknown lands in the Beaufort Sea between 1908 and 1912 (the Stefánsson-Anderson expedition) on behalf of American Museum of Natural History. Canadian Prime Minister Sir Robert Borden was concerned about his country's sovereignty in the Arctic, so he intervened to fund the 1913 expedition.[1]

The former whaler *Karluk* left Victoria, BC, in June 1913, under the command of the legendary Captain Robert Bartlett of the famous Newfoundland seafaring family. Its mission was to map the waters north of Alaska, and was expanded to include zoological and scientific research on the northern mainland, under the command of Dr. R.M. Anderson. Two schooners, the *Alaska* and the *Mary Sachs*, were purchased at Nome, Alaska, to handle the increased volume of activity.[2] But the dual mission was to create insurmountable tensions, and the expedition remains controversial to this day.

The *Karluk* was not up to the job of confronting the severe ice conditions off the coast of Alaska, and soon became trapped in the ice. The ship was crushed and sank, but the two smaller schooners were able to navigate in shallower water. They over-wintered in Collinson Point, Alaska, while Stefánsson took off with sledges across the sea ice. The *Mary Sachs* did reach Banks Island, but between 1914 and the 1930s, she was broken up for fuel and shelter, first by her original crew and then by a motley series of white trappers, Inuvialuit hunters and trappers from Aklavik. Parts of her engines were incorporated into a cairn on the hillside above the town of Sachs Creek in 1967. Elder Persis Gruben remembers that when she and her father arrived at what is now called Mary Sachs picnic ground and hunting spot in 1928, the pilothouse had become a house with round portholes, and polar bears would show up and peep in at them.

Stefánsson, who had been counting on the *Mary Sachs* to pursue his northern expedition, was severely disappointed with the loss of the schooner. But he was no sissy, according to *The Vancouver Province*: "He's the toughest man who ever went into the Arctic," declares Stein, with his eyes shining. "If he started for the North Pole he would make it in six months. . . .When he is on the trail he will mark a straight course for his men to march between points, and will himself make a detour twenty miles back into the country to hunt, arriving back at the camp—and with game—before his men have made the straight line march."[3]

■ ■ ■

Stefánsson's colleagues on the 1913 expedition also found it difficult to forgive him for his self-serving and widely distributed account of the disaster, shoving all the blame off onto them. He was a controversial figure, obviously a brilliant arctic traveller, hunter, showman and communicator. He was also a fine analyst whose insights have prevailed in many ways, proving far ahead of their time. But he was not a good manager or leader of groups, and his men paid the price for this.

In 1977, the last survivor of the Karluk expedition called him "a consummate liar and a cheat." Certainly, Stefánsson escaped the horrible fate of drifting in the wounded carcass of the grossly inadequate *Karluk*, listening to the horrendous sounds of the ice crushing it mercilessly to its end. He also took possession of all the crew accounts of the trip and censored them to make himself look better. If not for the presence of Captain Robert Bartlett, the losses would surely have been even more severe. And yet, both Stefánsson himself in his life's work, and the doomed 1913 expedition as a whole, made a major contribution to the body of knowledge about the Arctic that survives and is in use today.[4]

THE HIGH COST OF LEARNING

In the first millennium of our own era, the Vikings were remarkable sailors. They set out to explore in their sturdy boats, and they camped and lived successfully in areas where the late Victorians found it almost impossible to survive. This is likely because the turn of the first millennium AD was a much warmer time than the coldest part of the Little Ice Age, when Sir John Franklin was trying so hard to maintain the Royal Navy's traditional standards, dragging his regimental silver through the arctic wilderness.

Franklin and his peers were imbued with a strong sense of evolutionary superiority by the groundbreaking work of Charles Darwin, and by their own racial assumptions. Ironically, this attitude of superiority dictated a rigid view of the aboriginal peoples of the Arctic as products of a lower form of evolution than the denizens of industrial Britain. It was difficult for Franklin and his cohorts to accept that these "primitive" people could possess vastly superior and more appropriate knowledge and technology for their environment—and that this could have been the case for hundreds, perhaps thousands, of years. While Franklin did unbend enough to provide his men with sealskin coats and gloves on their ill-fated 1845 expedition, his stubborn refusal to adopt more suitable technologies and approaches was costly. As we have seen, Scott's fatal Antarctic expedition used unsuitable ponies, none of which survived, while the Norwegian Amundsen, sensibly equipped with dog teams, made it to the South Pole.

Some forty-seven explorers and adventurers are known to have died trying to achieve the North Pole over the years "from starvation, scurvy, carbon monoxide poisoning, and murder," according to Jerry Kobalenko.[5] Getting to the poles has always been a huge challenge. For most of recorded polar history, the assumption has been that expeditions had to be a multiyear commitment. When we consider the much shorter life expectancies of the period (comparisons are further exacerbated by today's interminable adolescence), this puts a sobering perspective on the prospects and courage of the men who signed on for these expeditions.

MODERN POLAR EXPEDITIONS
IT'S STILL DANGEROUS

Attaining the North Pole is never easy over the ice. It is only accessible between March and May. Before that, the constant dark is a problem, and after that, the breakup of the ice pack is a constant threat to the life and safety of sledge expeditions. Most people who attempt the pole today either go by ice-fortified ship or on expeditions supported by air so that they can go lightly equipped, and make good time. Supply planes cannot land on the ice in the dark, so that means that expeditions cannot be taken by air to their starting point until there is enough light to land.

One expedition in 1995, the Russian-Canadian Malakhov-Weber expedition, did succeed in leaving earlier by getting a head start from Ward Hunt Island in mid-February. They convinced the charter company to land there using military parachute flares and a powerful nose light on the plane. They ferried their supplies out 72 kilometres, then came back to the island to rest up and dry out before launching in early March. The head start allowed them to travel lighter, with a broken trail and half their gear beyond the worst of the ice. They still had to race back from the pole just ahead of complete breakup in June. The expedition was the first to make it to the pole and back without air support, and could only have been accomplished by athletes of the calibre of Richard Weber and Misha Malakhov, using a combination of backpacks and small sleds.

People continue to die in the attempt. Jerry Kobalenko says the relative lack of technical prowess (compared to ice climbing, say) plays into a kind of myth of accessibility that allows well-meaning amateurs to get themselves into huge trouble. Kobalenko shakes his head at what some people think they will be able to do. In March of 2004, forty-three-year-old Finnish adventurer Dominick Arduin became the twenty-ninth person on record to lose her life in a quest for the pole. Whereas most polar expeditions depart from the Canadian High Arctic, Arduin set out from Mys Arkticheskiy, a cape on an island in the Arctic Ocean some 3,500 kilometres northeast of Moscow, intending to be the first woman to make it to the geographic North Pole alone and unaided.

Kobalenko says this route to the pole can be far more dangerous than the more common one from the Canadian High Arctic. Those using it encounter a lot more open water and thin ice at the beginning, when they are "not into the expedition mindset yet." Arduin heightened the danger she faced by refusing a helicopter lift over the worst of the early hazard (a male colleague attempting the same feat accepted and survived). Kobalenko says few are prepared for the reality of this sea ice off the Russian coast: "That sort of sea ice is a very different experience. It's not brittle like fresh water ice. It's more like a water bed. You can actually see a bow-wave issuing from the tip of your ski; it undulates ahead of you and you're bobbing up and down. It's such an alien environment for those who aren't experienced in it. The only place you get that is the Arctic Ocean. People are pushing the limits and they have no idea what they're pushing. On polar expeditions, you stay safe by fear and trembling: one of the main emotional ingredients of a successful trip is perpetual anxiety."

Today's exploration community is a "dog's breakfast of practitioners—from the supercompetent to those who are closer to Mr. Bean than to Roald Amundsen," says Kobalenko. He is not attracted to the North Pole itself, but he is attracted to travelling in the Arctic. This is because there are so few cold, open spaces left that provide the capacity for long, uninterrupted trips through a world of serene beauty, alone. "No matter how tough or strong you are," he says, "you can't carry more than a month or two of supplies on your back or in a canoe, whereas sledding over smooth, solid ice, I can pull 125 kilometres. It is physically gruelling, but I am able to do it, and it's impossible in any other form of travel." He predicts that many more people will discover his form of sledding—on hard pack ice that reduces friction and makes heavy loads possible—as the only way to escape civilization for weeks and months at a time. And the only place to find that kind of ice is in the High Arctic, or in a few places in Antarctica.

Splendid Isolation

The American scientist/explorer Richard Byrd (1888–1957) described the sensation in *Alone*, his remarkable journal of a winter alone in an underground station in Antarctica:

> *May 12 . . . The silence of this place is as real and solid as sound. More real, in fact, than the occasional creaks of the Barrier and the heavier concussions of snow quakes. . . . It seems to merge in and become part of the indescribable evenness, as do the cold and the dark and the relentless ticking of the clocks. This evenness fills the air with its mood of unchangeableness it sits across from me at the table, and gets into the bunk with me at night. And no thought will wander so far as not eventually to be brought up hard by it. This is timelessness in its ultimate meaning. Very often my mood soars above it; but, when this mood goes, I find myself craving change—a look at trees, a rock, a handful of earth, the sound of foghorns, anything belonging to the world of movement and living things.*

Sten Nadolny's description of the feeling is no less powerful for being fictionalized, and sheds light on the attraction of the ice-bound climes, even for armchair travellers (*The Discovery of Slowness,* translated from the German by Ralph Freedman):

Nobody wanted to sleep. No one was used to thinking of the phenomenon of night being so bright. The low sun shone upon the white sails, the ice sparkled as if it were made of diamond caps and emerald grottoes; a frozen city grew and unfolded in wild figures. Nautical language was almost superfluous: they sailed from the "church" to the "fortress," then, bearing past the "cave," to the "bridge." Ice shimmered below the surface of the water, reflecting light. The sea was cloaked in creamy white; seals swam in it as in luminous milk. The crew hung on the rigging and stared at the sparkling hunks of ice that kept pushing behind the ship's keel as though wanting to catch up with it. The sun sank toward midnight, red and alien: the largest banana in the world. It didn't even actually sink—it only went into hiding for a short time, took a bath, and reappeared to dry itself.

CHAPTER NINE

"You can look at ice crystals in a little microscope and then you can
sort of pull yourself back to a satellite, 800 km out and you almost
have the same sense of things. There you are looking at very large
floes and here you are looking at crystals that are a couple of
millimeters across, and yet there are similar patterns and forms in
those, and a lot of similarities in all the different scales."
—Richard McKenna, Director, Ice Engineering Centre for Cold Ocean
Research Engineering, St. John's, Newfoundland

MAPPING THE ARCTIC

As late as 1869, John Shelden, a British mapmaker and artist
(and indeed, with many early maps, it is hard to know whether
you are looking at a map or a work of art) was drawing images
of the North Pole as a mile-high iron cone sticking out of a
small ice-free ocean, surrounded by an impenetrable ring of ice
barriers.[1] When you see this map drawing, it is amusing to note
that Shelden stuck a full-rigged sailing ship and a rectangular
boat full of rowers inside the ice barrier on his polar ocean. One
wonders how these people were supposed to have gotten their
boats over the mountains of ice he imagined ringing this ice-
free polar ocean.

My favourite book about mapping the Arctic is Derek
Hayes' beautiful *Historical Atlas of the Arctic*. It is a stunning

book, which one reviewer called "the most wide-ranging, visually stunning, and historically grounded collection of Arctic maps ever assembled." Many show ice floes and barriers as if they were fixed geographical features, reflecting the best guesses of the mapmakers of the day. The mapping and surveying of the ice-bound Arctic and Antarctic has been a huge undertaking, as we have already seen. This centuries-long endeavour is the foundation for the scientific work that is underway today to understand the nature of the planet's ice.

THE NORWEGIAN POLAR INSTITUTE AND THE WORLD WILDLIFE FUND

There are so many fascinating ice research projects underway around the world that it will be impossible to list them all in this book. But one which allows me to see the original sea charts of Hugh Willoughby (he of the *Mystery and Company of Merchant Adventurers for the Discovery of Regions, Dominions, Islands, and Places Unknown*) on CD-ROM interests me particularly. This joint project between the Norwegian Polar Institute (NPI) and the World Wildlife Fund (WWF) is making a great contribution to the understanding of the role of sea ice in the global ecosystem. Since 1988, the two organizations have funded and managed a project that integrates all the actual data we have from the Arctic: from five-hundred-year-old logbooks of long-dead explorers, right through to modern satellite data. Although we know from recent studies that global warming has caused sea ice to decrease in the Arctic Ocean over the past thirty years, this greatly expanded data archive (going back as far as the sixteenth century) shows that the trend has actually been underway for much longer—at least 150 years!

The project, known as the Arctic Climate System Study (ACSYS) Historical Ice Chart Archive, has digitized more than six thousand charts that track where explorers encountered sea ice, what kind of weather they encountered, and even when and where they caught whales, dating back as far as 1553. WWF financing enabled the publication of the charts on CD-ROM— an astonishing development. Who knew a doomed sixteenth-century ship's logs would become relevant in the twenty-first century, as researchers urgently seek to understand climate change? The charts record the extent of sea ice from 1553 to 2002 in the Nordic seas, from Greenland in the west to the island of Novaya Zemlya in the east, and cover the entire Barents Sea. Willoughby and Chancellor were the first of a long line of explorers and whalers who left meticulous records of their observations, particularly of sea-ice conditions.

Among the greatest contributors to the database were the flamboyant Norwegian explorer Fridtjof Nansen, who commanded a pioneering scientific expedition to the Arctic, and his quiet, efficient second-in-command, Otto Sverdrup. Nansen had first made his mark by crossing the Greenland ice cap on skis at the age of twenty-seven.

Their ship, the *Fram*, is one of the most famous ever to undertake polar expeditions. A sturdy, round-hulled vessel, it was designed and built in 1892 to survive the pack ice without being crushed. Its design is ingenious: the sides are completely smooth so that ice could not cling to it. The hull is reinforced by a tight network of oak beams and braces on the inside. And the rudder and propeller could be pulled up completely when the ice surrounded the ship. In 1893, Nansen and Sverdrup set sail to prove the existence of the Transpolar Drift Stream, a strong ocean current across the North Pole, moving away from the Siberian coast and through Fram Strait between Greenland and the Norwegian Svalbard archipelago. When it became evident that the ship would not drift over the pole, Nansen left to try and make it there across the frozen ocean with dogs and sleds. Meanwhile, Sverdrup remained on board, plugging away at the research: sea ice, water depth, temperature, salinity and ocean currents.

Sverdrup spent almost *three years* drifting across the Arctic Ocean. Every day, he kept his crew busy taking measurements, charting the Arctic seawaters, the ice, the bottom, the currents, the weather—proving that the Arctic Ocean was more than 11,000 feet deep in some places, and not the shallow basin or even the hidden land paradise that many previous explorers had believed was there. The thoroughness and quality of this work stands up and speaks to us across the centuries, a valuable and highly relevant contribution to our growing understanding of our world. The kind of data it provided was unsurpassed until satellites and nuclear submarines became available to add to the world's body of knowledge about the polar regions.

Worth a Visit

The Fram Museum is one of three remarkable maritime museums in Oslo worth a visit. At the top of a street called Bygdøynesveien, is the Viking Ship Museum, where you can see the Oseberg and Gokstad, both excavated in the late-nineteenth century and considered among the world's great maritime treasures. The lines of the Gokstad are heart-stoppingly beautiful.

At the end of the street, past a row of pretty tile-roofed houses, is a little rocky area that overlooks Oslo Fiord. Three museums surround a turning circle: the big A-frame that contains the *Fram*, the modest little *Gjøa*, in which the great Roald Amundsen first completed the Northwest Passage, and the Institute for Pacific Archaeology and Cultural History, widely known as the Kon-Tiki Museum, the most popular museum in Scandinavia. The ubiquitous Amundsen, whom Norwegians regard as one of their great national treasures, also used the *Fram* on his winning polar expedition to Antarctica. So there is a lot of history here.

Seeing the three museums one after the other, the depth of the Norwegian legacy becomes obvious: this small nation of four and a half million people has made a huge contribution to global knowledge of the oceans, and in particular of the ice-capped polar regions. The graceful Viking ships, masterpieces of design and function, are still in production today in northern Norway. It is not hard to imagine a Viking Queen being paraded in the beautifully carved ceremonial ship on display here.

The spirits of Nansen, Sverdrup and Amundsen seemed very present as I climbed up and down inside the sturdy little *Fram*, inspecting its groundbreaking reinforced hull designed for survival in the ice. It is deeply moving to experience the environment in which they spent years risking their lives to learn the secrets of the ice; to see its galley and its tables with their high edges to prevent the food from flying off them in turbulent seas; the ship surgeon's kit with its menacing saws and scalpels; their fur clothing and boots, hung in their miniscule little cabins. It is sobering to see the tiny size and small draft of the *Gjøa*, and to realize that had it been any larger, Amundsen would likely not have made it through the Northwest Passage's most difficult bottlenecks.

It may not be obvious what the *Fram* and the *Kon-Tiki* have in common. But it is reasonable to assume that Thor Heyerdahl, while organizing his 1947 seagoing archaeological experiment, must have been inspired by the success of the *Fram*'s three-year odyssey in the Arctic ice pack. Fridtjof Nansen's idea of freezing a ship into the ice pack and drifting with it to conduct scientific research was mocked, just like Heyerdahl's 4,000-mile drift in a balsa raft. The difference was that Heyerdahl wanted to prove that humans, animals and plants could have moved from South America to the remote South Pacific over hundreds and thousands of years, while Nansen was primarily interested in surveying the geology and physical aspects of the Arctic Ocean. When Nansen, Sverdrup and their men returned to Norway in 1896 after three years in the ice, they were a press sensation, as if they were returning from the dead. By surviving the 4,000-mile journey, Heyerdahl's *Kon-Tiki* earned a place in Norwegian, and world history, right alongside the *Fram*.

THREE POLAR YEARS

For most of the long, colourful history of polar exploration, scientific work at the poles was only a small part of expeditions driven by other, competitive reasons: commerce, sovereignty or adventure. But three polar years beginning late in the nineteenth century (1882–83, 1932–33 and 1957–58) established that scientists could, and should, work in a climate of international cooperation to collect data about the poles. Such projects require extraordinary efforts of diplomacy and logistical coordination, but are richly rewarding for all.

The first Polar Year (1882–83), shortly after the creation of the International Meteorological Association (IMO), was devoted to data collection about weather patterns, the earth's magnetic force and other polar phenomena that affected navigation and shipping at the icy margins of the world. In an era when commerce and industry were expanding quickly, this was a top priority. There were fifteen scientific polar expeditions that year, twelve to the Arctic and three to the Antarctic. Eleven nations participated, and they established twelve research stations. The year of research established for the first time that it was possible for scientists from a wide range of countries to collaborate in their common interest. Their findings made sailors and passengers safer; their civilized cooperation laid the foundation for the management of Antarctica, one of the world's great successes in global governance.

By the time of the second International Polar Year (1932–33), there were whole fields of science that had not existed previously: ionospheric physics, which looks at the outer layer of the planet's atmosphere, for example. To this day, it is only possible to study the ionosphere from the polar regions. The mysterious and beautiful aurora borealis, or "northern lights," and aurora australis, or "southern lights," intrigued scientists at the time. They wanted to study how this phenomenon related to magnetic variations, cosmic radiation and radio wave disturbances. In the 1930s, radio was increasingly important, and they felt it was important to be able to anticipate, and prevent if possible, the disruptions caused by magnetic storms. They found out that the aurora do produce an electromagnetic signal in the frequency spectrum that is extremely low to very low. It is impossible to hear these radio waves without an audio-frequency ELF-VLF radio receiver. It is interesting to note that some people thought at the time that the advent of radio itself was causing disruptive climate change. That did not turn out to be the case, but there is a growing concern about potential health impacts from the sheer volume of wireless activity going on in the world.

The second Polar Year bequeathed us better weather maps of the northern hemisphere, as well as a better understanding of the effects of magnetic storms on radio waves. Still, there were many pieces missing in the puzzle as the international scientific community struggled to understand how ice, atmosphere, land and oceans formed an interactive and interdependent system.

In the 1940s and 1950s, the invention of rockets, satellites and new instruments dramatically improved the ability to measure events in the remote Arctic and Antarctic. When the world's scientists came together to create the International Geophysical Year (IGY) in 1957, it was possible to explore from the floor of the ocean to the upper atmosphere. This was the Cold War era; nuclear submarines under the ice had long-range capability unknown before then. They were able to obtain exciting new scientific data, but they also carried deadly weapons, as the great powers eyed each other nervously.

It was a productive time. Rocket-launched satellites provided remote geophysical measurements. It became possible to work on polar research projects all year round; international cooperation became more systematic—sixty-seven countries participated in the IGY, including the Americans and the Soviet Union's Cold War enemies. Many civilians were recruited to help with scientific observation, providing scientists with information about their aurora sightings and temperature readings from remote northern and southern locations.

Intelligence concerns, then as now, had to work hand in hand with scientific exploration. That is one reason why NASA and the Office of Naval Research have been engaged in monitoring the world that exists under the ice for decades. The next IGY will take place in 2007, 125 years after the first International Polar Year, and the world's scientific community seems confident that it can cooperate to increase our knowledge much more efficiently than players in many other fields.[2]

THE BEST SOURCES OF INFORMATION

If you have an interest in tracking world weather, climate change or ice movements, you were born at the right time. You would have had to leave home for several years even a hundred years ago, but today you can sit at your computer to go to any number of amazing websites that will share advanced technology, pictures and information with you, free of charge. Some of the best sources of such information, much of it beautifully presented and understandably written are:

▪ NASA's Snow and Ice Data Centre:
– its Earth Observing System (the EOS Terra Satellite) launched in 1999
– its Aqua Satellite launched in the summer of 2002
▪ Ice, Cloud and land Elevation Satellite (ICESat), a kind of 17,000 mile-per-hour, extremely accurate orbiting laser measuring the earth's critical vertical dimension
▪ Environment Canada's Meteorological Service, RADARSAT
▪ Canadian Ice Service (CIS), a division of Environment Canada's Atmospheric Environment Service (www.weatheroffice.ec.gc.ca/canada_e.html), one of the world's most reliable, user-friendly and consistently accurate sources of weather data—for any spot on the planet, not just for Canada.

These organizations and many others work together to monitor and report on all the earth's various geophysical systems, above and beyond the ones directly responsible for weather. The CIS manual (*MANICE*) is ninety pages long and has illustrations to help the untrained eye identify all the different species and subspecies (so to speak) of ice. Germany, France, Italy, Russia, the United States and China are all active in the field as well.

From space, the tracking services follow the development of frazil, new sea ice. They track the movement of pan ice on lakes and rivers, pack ice and icebergs in the oceans, helping scientists predict the amount of water that will result from a seasonal snowmelt. This is not easy. For one thing, it is very difficult to measure the thickness of ice from space. Yet this is essential to figuring out how climate change is affecting the cryosphere. Canada and the United States gather submarine data, which show that sea ice is thinning dramatically in some parts of the world. The European Space Agency's satellites operate a scatterometer, a tool that detects ground freeze and thaw. All these and many more elements must be taken into consideration in computer modelling of ice movements and climate change.

The advent of powerful supercomputers to do this modelling work is the single biggest leap forward in the world's understanding of ice. The sheer mathematical complexity of the calculations required to model the interactions among the earth's spheres made it impossible to accomplish in a timely fashion before the supercomputers became available. Of course, supercomputers also increase the possibility of being spectacularly wrong, if data inputs are incomplete, or based on false assumptions. From Ptolemy to today, it's the old axiom: garbage in, garbage out.

The IGY of 1957–58 was a breakthrough time, because of the growth of this valuable international cooperation—but also because the scientists were increasingly excited about the idea that the poles were natural laboratories enabling them to integrate research about the earth, but also about the "heavens above"—the atmosphere, and space itself.

After the IGY, the twelve countries that had established sixty-odd research stations in Antarctica signed a treaty that stands to this day. The Antarctic Treaty of 1961, known as the Madrid Protocol, resolves that Antarctica will always be a place of peace, devoted to the free exchange of scientific information. Nuclear explosions and the disposal of radioactive waste were strictly forbidden in the original treaty, and these standards have become stricter with the addition of side agreements over time. By 1999, the Antarctic Treaty had forty-four signatories representing two-thirds of the world's population.

SIGNATORIES TO THE ANTARCTIC TREATY

CONSULTATIVE PARTIES (27)

- Argentina
- Australia
- Belgium
- Brazil
- Bulgaria
- Chile
- China
- Ecuador
- Finland
- France
- Germany
- India
- Italy
- Japan
- Korea
- Republic of Netherlands
- New Zealand
- Norway
- Peru
- Poland
- Russian Federation
- South Africa
- Spain
- Sweden
- United Kingdom
- United States
- Uruguay

ACCEDING STATES (17)

- Austria
- Canada
- Colombia
- Cuba
- Czech Republic
- Democratic People's Republic of Korea
- Denmark
- Greece

- Guatemala
- Hungary
- Papua New Guinea
- Romania
- Slovak Republic
- Switzerland
- Turkey
- Ukraine
- Venezuela

SHEBA

This is a place where you have keep your headlamp battery in your armpit if you roam out onto the ice on a winter's day—which is twenty-four hours of darkness. A century after the *Fram*'s polar voyage of discovery, a five-year project called SHEBA (Surface Heat Budget of the Arctic Ocean) brought together scientists from Canada, Russia, the United States and Norway to study "the interaction of the surface energy balance, atmospheric radiation, and clouds over the Arctic Ocean."

The mission employed 170 scientists, lasted seventeen months, cost $20 million and was by far the most ambitious civilian research project ever undertaken in the Arctic. The scientists chose to emulate Sverdrup: freezing a ship into the Arctic ice pack and drifting with it for a full year. What they had not foreseen, however, was how much thinner and weaker that ice pack had become.

The project's home was aboard the hefty Canadian ice-breaker *Desgroseillers* (named for an early French-Canadian explorer who made it into the heart of the continent) and a big ice floe that came to be known as SHEBA Station. A tent pitched on it became SHEBA International Airport. There are many challenges to working in such an environment: the airstrip can suddenly develop a "lead," or crack up and display open water just as a crucial supply plane is about to land. Or the various instruments measuring heat exchange between the lower atmosphere and the ice surface can keep blossoming with rime (condensation ice that appears from vapour without transiting through the liquid phase).

On one memorable occasion, industrious researchers decided to drill themselves a "cold tub" in the ice next to their portable sauna near the ship. They did not anticipate that the weight of the surrounding camp would cause their tub-filling hole to become a major gusher that would set the entire camp afloat! (They named it Moby Dick.) Mostly, the scientists laugh about these things, and report an easy camaraderie. Those who work under isolated and potentially dangerous conditions have a vested interest in grown-up behaviour, and most are up to the challenge.

SHEBA's principal purpose—which it accomplished—was to improve the computer model scientists use to simulate the earth's climate. The thinning arctic pack ice plays a very important role in its evolution. The scientists running the supercomputers needed a better understanding of how it is evolving, exchanging heat with the atmosphere, redistributing that heat (or not) and encouraging or blocking the sun's energy. The findings have been plugged into the models, and continue to reinforce that the planet is indeed undergoing accelerating climate change on an unprecedented scale.

WORLD METEOROLOGICAL ORGANIZATION

In our modern age, observing ice conditions is so important that it is done through a virtually seamless web of international cooperation. This successful working culture has at its roots the intelligent, useful, quiet history of the World Meteorological Organization (WMO), which has worked through thick and thin, through politics and uprisings, through wars and disasters. Founded in 1950, the WMO is an agency of the United Nations and a successor to the IMO founded in 1873.

Based in Geneva, the WMO divides the globe into six regions and then it coordinates all data gathering about the world's weather. Everyone who pilots a boat, a ship, a submarine or an aircraft, and every passenger who rides in one, depends on this system. So do people who use highways in winter, grow crops in temperate to extreme climates, or simply want to know whether or not it is wise to go for a hike that day. Without this competent monitoring of the cryosphere, it would not be possible to attain the level of accuracy that we enjoy in modern weather forecasting, and it would be difficult to warn people in advance of severe storms.

Even at the height of the Cold War, the weather networks kept working smoothly almost all the time, exchanging data around the clock, worldwide, without regard to nationalities, ideologies or personalities. Given that weather is a planetary phenomenon, this is essential; thankfully the organization has always been left largely to scientists and specialists more concerned with learning and the public interest than with territory and power. As we understand the whole planet increasingly as one system, this example of monitoring it together will serve us well.

CHAPTER TEN

"The earth's ocean-atmosphere-biosphere system is reminiscent of
an Old Testament god—lots of rules and no mercy."
—William H. Calvin, *The Ascent of the Mind: Ice Age Climates
and the Evolution of Intelligence*

TIME CAPSULES FROM THE ICE

Shortly after the War in Iraq began in 2003, my mother began
to complain that her eyes were itchy. This was nothing new: no
matter where she is in her house, she can tell when someone
coming into the house, or even standing at the door outside,
has been smoking, or is wearing a perfume or a hair product
that will cause her a problem. She has been a terrible scourge for
two generations of teenage smokers, who cannot argue with the
rapid swelling in her face that sometimes takes us to a hospital
emergency department. In other words, she is hypersensitive to
airborne substances. What was unusual this time, in the early
spring of 2003, was her complaint that this particular reaction
was linked to the start of bombing halfway around the world.

I was polite, but very skeptical. I opened my files and began
to read about ice-core research in Greenland and Antarctica. I
already knew that the North has not been spared the effects of
human activities and environmental change elsewhere on the
planet. There is a disturbing increase in the phenomenon of
hermaphroditic polar bears (females with hormonal imbalances

that result in the growth of male genitals). Despite the lack of industry in the Arctic, Inuit women, even in the remotest areas, have high concentrations of PCBs in their breast milk. The Inuit, who have lived for thousands of years on seal meat and blubber, have been told their traditional fare is bad for them. Some whale carcasses, the historical Inuit source of meat, fuel and bones for tools and building materials, are now classified as toxic waste. The windborne transport of toxins and materials over long distances is intensified by a kind of "hopscotch" phenomenon that concentrates the toxins as they touch down and bounce back up on their way into the vulnerable arctic ecosystem, particularly from the poisonous leavings of the old Communist industrial wastelands just on the other side of the Arctic Ocean.[1] This is not a recent phenomenon: ice cores from deep in the heart of the Greenland ice sheet show evidence of the nuclear meltdown at Chernobyl, the volcanic eruption of Krakatoa in 1886 and the use of lead in ancient Roman foundries.

Was it possible, I wondered, that my mother was on to something? If the lead from the Roman foundries had made its way into the polar ice caps, how would human beings breathing the air avoid whatever is travelling through the atmosphere?

■ ■ ■

Every year, as snow falls on the ice sheet, its weight slowly compresses the firn into ice. The summer melting and refreezing process marks the surface with annual deposits much like the growth rings in trees. The reason the layers show up is that summer snow falls in larger crystals, with higher acidity, than winter snow. Using lasers to measure the concentration of dust particles (spring winds usually blow more dust into the atmosphere than at other times of year), researchers can even tell the seasons within a given year apart. They can test each layer for all kinds of physical and chemical characteristics.

When scientists drill for ice cores, using a meticulous process that keeps the trace elements pristine and frozen hard for future analysis, they find all kinds of valuable data: compressed air bubbles that sample the atmosphere of the time when the snow fell; chemicals, dust and signs they can interpret to tell them about temperatures, winds, precipitation and much more. Some of what they are learning is startling—particularly when it comes to abrupt climate change in the planet's past.

The North Greenland Ice-core Project, or North GRIP, began in the mid-1990s as the successor to a series of such projects dating back to the 1960s. It uses a drill developed for a similar project in Antarctica. Because the ice is so thick and heavy, at the bottom of the glacier it can be pressured into a molasses-like liquid that is neither ice nor water—but it is slippery. As we have seen, the ice sheet itself is always moving at different speeds, so that it is not one river of ice but many different streams converging, shearing apart and breaking off. The Greenland ice sheet is always releasing icebergs that will drift slowly southwards, and this contributes to the continued movement of the ice from the higher ground.

In order to tell as orderly a year-over-year story as possible, ice cores need to be as cleanly layered as they can be. This gets complicated if you are sampling deep down into a moving river of ice. This deforming flow has thwarted previous efforts to obtain ice cores that could reveal two hundred thousand years of earthly events. Ideally, the ice-core samples go right down to the bedrock. For this reason, the research camps in Greenland are at the high point of the ice sheet, where it sits over the peak of a buried mountain ridge. The ice near the bottom of the glacier has been forged into huge crystals, sometimes the size of a baseball. The air compressed in this ice can seek to expand very quickly; in fact, samples not properly handled can explode at the surface, before anyone gets a chance to look at them.

Since Greenland is Danish territory, the University of Copenhagen is involved in overseeing the project with a large number of American partners.[2] The researchers are seeking to understand many issues, such as the relationship between climate and greenhouse effect in an unpolluted atmosphere (although that may be partially illusory for the period since the industrial revolution). How could the North Atlantic climate get 7°C warmer in fifty years at the end of the last glaciation? Could it happen again? How long did the warm period previous to ours last, and how will our own warm period end? Are natural climate changes predictable or random? Can we make predictions about climate change influenced by human activities, or anthropogenic changes?

There are also projects underway to monitor the ice flow and the weather, as well as to deepen understanding about the geology and ocean currents of the region. The central East Greenland coast was the place where Europe and North America broke apart 60 million years ago, and the earth's crust and upper mantle here are typical of areas where diamonds have been found in other parts of the world, so there is great interest in the potential for diamond mining. Italy has also been testing ice-penetrating radar here.

Whereas in Greenland, the ice-core drilling is going down to the bedrock, in Antarctica, which is much higher, the most exciting projects are going through the ice sheet at the Russian base over Lake Vostok and to the bedrock at Dome C, a French-Italian station. Data from these ice cores are allowing the study of seven hundred thousand years of climate and planetary change. The data confirm that today's carbon dioxide levels are higher than they have been in all that time. To date, the researchers have not pierced the ice dome over Lake Vostok because there is no international consensus about how to do so without contaminating a uniquely pristine environment. Researchers have high hopes for their study of Lake Vostok, which they believe is similar in makeup to the ice-covered moon of Jupiter, Europa.

The ice just above the lake contains microbial organisms that the researchers believe are from the lake itself. In other words, the ice just above the lake is probably refrozen lake water as opposed to glacier ice from precipitation, and the lake under-neath it is likely the habitat of unique creatures that thrive in the deep cold waters. Because of its complexity, this sensitive habi-tat will require the negotiation of a special international proto-col for cooperation. It may seem surprising that there would be a liquid lake under 4 kilometres of ice sheet, but the pressure of the ice sheet lowers the freezing point. Together with the heat generated by the earth below the bedrock, it combines to main-tain a liquid body of water. There may be life in any or all of Antarctica's seventy subglacial lakes, including Lake Vostok (which is comparable in size and depth to Lake Ontario) or in a lake under the South Pole; or possibly in the sediments at the bottom of these lakes. If the lakes are isolated from each other, it is even possible that they contain microorganisms entirely unique to each lake. All of this information is considered important to space exploration, as it simulates conditions on other planets or satellites such as Europa, Ganymede and Titan.

In preparation for this work, the United States Antarctic Program, which coordinates almost all U.S. research in Antarctica under the management of the National Science Foundation (NSF), has begun non-invasive research to gain the best possible understanding of Lake Vostok's physical characteristics. Researchers from the University of Texas at Austin have done work in aero-geophysical surveying, radar sounding, laser altimetry, magnetics and gravity, and the analysis is done at the Lamont Doherty Earth Observatory at Columbia University (LDEO).[3]

In the summer of 2004, researchers from LDEO and Rensselaer Polytechnic Institute in New York State announced they had successfully mapped the Vostok lakebed with non-invasive technologies such as laser altimeters, ice-penetrating radar and gravity measurements collected by aircraft.[4] They estimate that the lake contains roughly 5,419 cubic kilometres of water. They were surprised to find that a huge ridge in the lake has probably created two different environments to study. The top of the ridge is only 198 metres below the bottom of the ice sheet, while the water ranges from 396 metres deep in the northern basin to 792 metres deep in the southern one. They think the water takes between 55,000 and 110,000 years to cycle through the lake, and that the two basins may be completely different chemically and biologically. The next step will be to develop a device that could take samples of the lake and its bed without contaminating it. That is probably a long way off at the time of writing.

An Implacable Record

Ice cores from the Greenland ice sheet currently shed light on "only" about 115,000 years of the planetary story, although they are consistent with the Vostok data in many respects. Some of the more interesting findings are also very sobering: for example, it took less than two years for radioactivity from the 1986 explosion at the Chernobyl nuclear power station in Russia to show up in ice cores at the South Pole. Cores from both Antarctica and Greenland allow researchers to pinpoint very precisely when atomic-bomb testing began in the mid-1950s with a spike in radioactivity when various countries stepped up their atmospheric testing just before signing the 1963 Test Ban Treaty; the treaty committed signatories to restricting their nuclear explosion tests to underground. As more and more countries signed the treaty after 1965, the Antarctic ice cores show that radioactive fallout dropped sharply.[5]

We can track the impact of human activities since the Industrial Revolution through the growth patterns of carbon dioxide, methane, nitrous oxides from coal- and oil-burning power plants, cars, factory emissions, heating and cooling, sulphates and nitrates. Carbon dioxide, methane and nitrous oxides have gone up in sync with population growth. Sulphates started rising around the turn of the twentieth century, in part because of the rise of coal-fired power plants, and in part because of volcanic activity in the Caribbean. Every time there is major volcanic activity, the ice cores show spikes in sulphate content. Nitrates only began to rise quickly when the number of people who owned cars grew phenomenally in the 1950s, and when oil-fired power plants began to appear. Again, the appearance of the U.S. *Clean Air Act* in 1972 is the starting point of a levelling off in sulphates and nitrates in the ice cores.[6]

The ice cores also suggest why the Viking settlements in Greenland might have disappeared near the end of the fourteenth century. Data from cores in both Antarctica and Greenland show that in periods where the seas are stormier because of greater spreads in temperature between the tropics and the poles, the wave action throws more sea salt up into the atmosphere. When it comes down on the polar ice caps, the sodium levels in the cores shoot up. The higher sodium levels correspond exactly to the advent of the Little Ice Age, which lasted from about 1400 to well into the nineteenth century, when the unfortunate Europeans were dying in record numbers on the Arctic ice. The Vikings were probably killed off by unusually cold and longer winters beginning in the late 1300s.[7]

As scientists rewind the tape of history by examining these ice cores, they also generate computer models to predict the future. By testing these models against the historical data, they can gain some confidence that they are beginning to understand the incredibly complex systems that make up our planet's climate and evolution. But even if the models can be made to work fairly well against the known past, this does not mean that they will work to predict an unknown future. Faulty assumptions or faulty data, especially if they occur early on in the calculations, can be profoundly misleading. Besides, much of the change we now know or suspect is coming is likely to be completely disruptive and non-linear in nature. Whether or not humans are responsible for this, it projects a frightening scenario.

As humans, with very brief lives in geological terms, we cannot help feeling alarmed that increased levels of carbon dioxide and other greenhouse gases could be triggering radical change in such things as our available water supply, the climate where we live, or increased radiation from the sun (and therefore increased risk of skin cancer) as the gases cause the depletion of the ozone layer. The earth does not live in human time, and it has apparently gone through other radical changes. But the evidence is accumulating that the accelerated rate of change we are now witnessing is unprecedented in the last half million years. One thing is certain: in the frozen heart of the world's ice lies the key to understanding many of these vital elements of our life on earth. No wonder the ice guys are excited.

■ ■ ■

LIVES ON ICE

INESCAPABLE BEAUTY

Ice cores are only one of the tools scientists are using to understand the evolution of the planet. The findings from ice-core research must be analyzed in conjunction with those from many other areas. Peter Mackinnon, an Ottawa consultant who works frequently in China, originally wanted to be an astronomer or an astrophysicist. During his undergraduate studies in the late 1960s, he was chosen to work in solar geophysics and magnetism with a group of people who were inventing tools to be used to decode the magnetic signatures on the ocean floor.

This was at a time when the phenomenon that had previously been known as continental drift was coming to be known as plate tectonics. "Magnetic signatures" was not an expression that meant a great deal to me when he and I first talked, but he made it sound simple: "When magma comes out of the earth, it has minerals in it. Some of those minerals are magnetic . . . iron has certain properties that make it polar in nature, so we have a magnetic field that exists around the earth, the magnetic north and south poles, as we call them. When you have magnetic material in a liquid, it has the freedom to orient itself to the direction of the poles. But of course, it does not stay magma: it solidifies; it freezes and becomes rock above the salt and the ocean floor. Therefore, if you take a sample of the ocean floor, carefully taking today's orientation, then measure the magnetic field of where the dipoles are pointing, you'll find that they are probably pointing somewhere different than where north is today."

Analyzing of the patterns of these differences allows scientists to map these changes over time. The solidified magma closest to the spreading is the youngest, and that farthest away is the oldest. These time series, spilling in both directions, support the notion that from time to time the magnetic field flips, with the North Pole becoming the South Pole and the South Pole becoming the North Pole (solar system research shows this happens on other planets as well). When that happens, it reorients the magnetic particles in the liquid elements of magma. When you look at the ocean floor, you see patterns that are very striking. For hundreds and thousands of kilometres, these bands record the historic oscillation of the changing magnetic fields. This has proven to be one of the most important ways of determining the history of plate tectonics. At first, this doesn't sound as if it is related to ice, but in fact, it led Mackinnon to work with W.S.B. (Stan) Patterson, one of the world's leading authorities in the dynamics of ice sheets, and the author of the definitive *Physics of Glaciers*.

As a computer programmer for the geophysics team, Mackinnon was an expert in building models. Patterson asked him to look at how ice flows and deforms, or changes its shape, owing to gravity. In working on the model to demonstrate this, Mackinnon came across the work of a French physicist named Labourie, whose paper on the simplicity, in relative terms, of the movement of ice sheets or continental plates, he found "really elegant."[8] Labourie's work suddenly clarified for Mackinnon that ice is a rock made of a single kind of molecule that deforms under flow and pressure. The implication was that in order to understand how the planet was formed and might evolve, you have to take into account a combination of factors that would include sculpting by ice sheets, as well as plate tectonics, weather conditions and so on. This insight was challenging and intriguing for someone with Mackinnon's background.

Mackinnon signed on with Stan Patterson to do both the computer modelling and the fieldwork for his research. For ten years, he went on ice expeditions to the Arctic: "Basically, you knew when you were going, but you never knew when you were coming back. You had a mission, and you were going out to try and accomplish the mission." Mackinnon said he used to think about how easy he and his colleagues had it compared to the Franklin expedition. Still, this was before the days of GPS. They were too near the magnetic pole to use compasses, so they navigated by the sun. Once or twice a day, they would radio their weather and safety conditions. They were self-reliant, to say the least: "You'd sleep in a tent, so every morning, when you'd wake up you would have to break the ice off the inside of the tent. Your pot of water from melted snow that you had made for tea the night before would be frozen next to you. I mean, is that rough? It's just different; it's not really, really rough. The rough parts were when we were traversing under difficult environmental conditions. . . . I was known among my colleagues as the human crevasse detector. I would fall into crevasses as an easy way to find them. I actually had more skill, I guess, at reading the texture of the surface. This is rather complicated because it's a million shades of white and blue. So more often than not, I would say: there is probably a crevasse there and we would have to find our way around. But other times, I would find it the hard way!"

What kinds of people are attracted to such a life? Again, the idea of beauty resurfaces, in the dual form of experience and creation. Mackinnon says he was excited by the lure of gathering original knowledge, and the higher purpose of trying to understand the environment. For many of his colleagues, office routines were deadly, and the idea of exploring virgin wilderness was irresistible. Mackinnon was also a serious amateur photographer. His work from these exotic places began to get professional exposure: coffee table books, magazines such as *Life* and postage stamps. With his usual cheeriness and excessive modesty, he says: "That was good because it paid for all the equipment." The Canadian government's official collection contains 150 of his photographs, and they appear in a number of books as well.

To the Moon . . .

Jamie Rossiter, another Canadian, came to glaciology via lunar experiments. As a young graduate student, he went to work for Dr. David Strangway, who had come from MIT. Strangway had contracts with NASA to study moon rocks and to design an experiment to go to the moon using electrical waves to study the upper layers of the moon. By 1970, he was Chief of NASA's Geophysics Branch, responsible for the geophysical aspects of the Apollo Missions.

The technology involved in Canadian experiments was radio-wave detection. It behaves in ways that may seem counterintuitive for the average person. Radio waves do not transmit through conductive materials such as rocks, but do go through resistant materials such as air—and ice. This had been discovered tragically during World War II, when a few pilots crashed over Greenland. Their radar altimeters were telling them that they were within a safe distance of the ground, but in fact, the signals were going straight through the massive ice sheet and hitting bedrock far below. Needless to say, this was very dangerous.

By the time Rossiter was a graduate student, it was well known that moon rocks were different from most earth rocks in that they were extraordinarily resistant electrically, and that radio waves would go through them. Figuring out how to use radio waves to analyze the structure of the moon was a challenge, but the WWII history gave the NASA scientists the idea that glaciers could double for moon rocks in their experiments.

Rossiter missed a first trip to Switzerland in 1959, but after two months with the team he was sent off on a reconnaissance mission to Alberta to investigate the potential of the Athabasca Glacier, which offered the rare advantage of having a conveniently accessible toe right at a public roadside. He flew to Calgary, rented a car and drove up alone to the point just north of Lake Louise where the Icefields Parkway was gated and closed for the winter. He got out of the car, walked around the barrier and up to the toe of the glacier, quite pleased with himself for having located a great spot to bring the teams from MIT and NASA to finish the work. When he returned to the site with the team members, he discovered to his horror that he had been blithely wandering around an area where the surface ice was riddled with "mill holes"—places where the boulders absorb heat from the sun, and bore their way down into the glacier. These shafts, about a metre wide, went down several metres; they get covered with a cornice of snow, which may or may not support the weight of a human.

"As I think back on this, it sends shivers up my spine. Had I gone down one of those, I would still be there!" says Rossiter. "And of course, I was by myself and no one knew exactly where I was." As it happened, Rossiter's team discovered that while radio-echo sounding worked really well on truly cold glaciers, on temperate glaciers like Athabasca, there was an anomaly:

whenever the radio signal hit a puddle, it couldn't see through it. This is what made the technology, and its use on ice surfaces, relevant to the moon mission. As Rossiter says, "When you are designing multimillion-dollar experiments to go on a very limited payload . . . there are very political 'small p' politics—scientific politics, decisions about what experiments go and what don't. And the reason ours was chosen was that it was probably the only experiment that had a chance of discovering whether there was any moisture in the moon . . . so it did have that kind of impact on understanding the makeup, composition and history of the moon."

Rossiter followed Strangway to Houston, Texas, for a year, travelled for a while, and then did his doctorate at the University of Toronto, where he used the backup unit for the space experiment to study permafrost and ice sheets in the Arctic. In 1972, the experiment he had worked on with Strangway did go to the moon on the Apollo 17 Mission. Oddly, the successful moon mission seemed to reduce the immediate demand for lunar scientists, but opportunities for ice scientists were expanding. I heard from several others I interviewed about their careers that this was partly driven by oil exploration in the Arctic and the North Atlantic. Rossiter took a job with the Centre for Cold Ocean Resources Engineering (C-CORE) at Memorial University of Newfoundland. His job involved developing techniques for measuring ice thickness and ice properties from aircraft, helicopters and ships. There, he fell in love with the people of Newfoundland, and with the ice.

For Rossiter, "as someone who has worked in the Arctic and worked with ice, there is another sense that I would have of ice which is more artistic or ethereal. And certainly the beauty of the ice and the beauty of the natural environment in which I was privileged to work for a number of years is a warm memory." One of his favourite anecdotes is arriving as a young scientist in Twillingate, a northeastern coastal town in Newfoundland, and asking a local where he might get access to the ice. The Newfoundlander took Rossiter and his colleagues around the bay to a place where there was easy access down to the ocean, and "of course the bay was full of ice," says Rossiter. In his distinctive Newfoundland accent, the local said with a twinkle in his eye: "There you be, byes, hice to yer likin'!"

REDUCING ICE RISK

One recurring theme among these "ice guys"—to this day, women are rare on the ice—is a deep understanding of the awesome force of nature that is not common among urban people. Some, such as Ian Jordaan and Richard McKenna, both of Memorial University of Newfoundland, spend much of their time developing ways to help people operate with maximum safety and efficiency under icy conditions. This applies to oil and gas exploration, military applications, or construction projects, such as the 13-kilometre Confederation Bridge, the fixed link between Prince Edward Island and New Brunswick, which is the longest bridge over ice-covered waters in the world. The project was similar in scale to the Chunnel between England and France, but the ice factor added to its complexity. Jordaan, a civil engineer whose doctorate focused on concrete and steels, dated his involvement with ice to working on behalf of a Norwegian company to certify oilrigs for insurance purposes.

His work involved equipping project engineers to make decisions under uncertainty. How much pressure should a structure be able to resist? What is the probability of materials being exposed to forces beyond their resistance? What is the marginal cost of adding strength and weight to a point that might not be breached for two hundred years? When is the cost justified, and when is it not?

It is not always best to confront the ice head on. That is why icebreakers have spoon-shaped hulls that slide up over the ice and weigh it down until it breaks, rather than trying to slice through it. For the Confederation Bridge, Jordaan and his team therefore recommended cone-shaped foundation pillars. Their work showed that this optimal shape would cause the ice to climb up and crash back, breaking it up and preventing it from attacking the integrity of the structure. The destructive potential of the ice means it has to be taken very seriously, and an entire group of specialized professionals does exactly that. Jordaan's team, of which Paul Barrette was a member, made beautiful ice slides and illuminated them to discover and codify crystal structure—all for practical purposes, of course. Richard McKenna of C-CORE said: "Ice is such an incredible material. It always asks questions of you. Even if you are trying to get a quick answer or solve a quick problem, it is never quite as easy as you expect. So people always go into that little more detail, and I think it attracts inquisitive people, pretty down-to-earth people. That's what makes up the fraternity."

C-CORE has been around for more than a quarter of a century, dealing with ice issues for the resource industries, but also for the terrestrial application of space technology, including work for NASA. Oil and gas operations off the east coast of Newfoundland and Labrador face a 30 percent premium in costs because of ice, so C-CORE's work matters a great deal to them. The ice risk is far greater in some years than others.

Icebergs are counted as they cross the 48th parallel, 48° North, which is about the latitude of Paris. In some years, more than two thousand icebergs cross the line. Occasionally, onshore northeast winds will blow the bergs into the Strait of Belle Isle, and then into the Gulf of St. Lawrence. Sea-ice coverage is also a big issue for oil platforms off the east coast of Newfoundland and Labrador. In the High Arctic Beaufort Sea, drilling platforms have actually been built out of ice, using the same technology as snowmaking in the ski hills, but that is not feasible off Newfoundland.

The work done at Memorial's C-CORE was key in deciding how to build the fixed link bridge between Prince Edward Island and New Brunswick. The challenge, as always, was to come up with a design that made sense environmentally, economically and in terms of safety. Too much emphasis on safety results in designs that are too massive and costly to be built. Not enough attention to safety results in catastrophe. Elegant solutions are prized under these circumstances. The length of the Confederation Bridge across ice-choked waters resulted in high-end quality and safety decisions, well above industry standards. The bridge was designed with twice the lifespan (one hundred years instead of fifty) and a safety index, based on many factors, that is well above the industry norms.

The bridge design and building code applications of the project were world-leading: integrated into the design were hundreds of thousands of sensors to monitor five main areas: dynamics, which includes winds and earthquakes; short- and long-term deformation, which involves steel and concrete behaviour; thermal stresses; ice stresses, a major factor in the Atlantic; and corrosions. As well as collecting these data, the project was designed to look at load combination—the interaction of the different stresses, and seismic phenomena. The data would be gathered, managed and analyzed for twenty years, making it one of the world's great sources of knowledge and support for ice experts.

Scientists and engineers are often reluctant to admit that anything they do is less than logical. I asked McKenna if he was ever irrationally seduced by the beauty of ice. He said: "I think it's in the shape and form of it. I like to see those shapes and they fascinate me in terms of the visuals and the very subtle variations in colour and tone and texture. Those things go through my mind when I lie awake at night. Those are the things that I see and feel. . . .You can look at ice crystals in a little microscope and then you can pull yourself back to a satellite, eight hundred kilometres out and you have almost the same sense of things . . . you are looking at very large floes and here you are looking at crystals that are a couple of millimetres across and yet there are similar patterns and forms in those, and a lot of similarities in all the different scales . . . and they are all within day-to-day existence."

■ ■ ■

Richard McKenna's notion of the beauty and majesty of ice at every scale resonated strongly for me. I have met only one person who has actually experienced it in this way, however: Dr. Roberta Bondar, scientist, physician, astronaut and photographer. She has seen and photographed ice from space, and from close up. She has also thought about it, with a scientist's grasp of its significance, an environmentalist's passion about its future, and an artist's eye for its beauty.

As a crewmember of the space shuttle *Discovery* in 1992, Dr. Bondar was the first Canadian woman in space. She holds the NASA Space Medal and is an Officer of the Order of Canada and a Laureate of the Canadian Medical Hall of Fame. She studied professional nature photography at the Brooks Institute of Photography in California. Those who have worked with her call her a Renaissance woman, and speak with awe of the range of her abilities. Her friend and colleague Christine Yankou told me of the time Dr. Bondar took a fall into wet mud while working with her large-format Hasselblad camera in the wild.[9] The camera was badly affected, but not so Roberta Bondar's spirits: she hiked back to her vehicle with the Hasselblad, took it apart completely, cleaned it thoroughly and reassembled it so that she could finish her photo shoot—which she did. Later, she drove it into town and took it into the repair shop, explaining that there was one tiny screw that she had been unable to find. It seems the Hasselblad specialist technicians dined out on that one for a long time!

Dr. Bondar's extraordinary intellectual breadth and depth have led her to think about and discuss the subject of ice in many ways beyond the idea of beauty. Her contributions in the fields of science and medicine are great. But in addition, she has chosen to spend a great deal of time documenting, photographing and writing about icy landscapes in ways that suggest that the idea of true beauty may well be her highest priority and her most widely known legacy.

As the first neurologist in space, specializing in neurophthalmology—how we see and record the world around us—Roberta Bondar was able to link her various disciplines through her photography. From 302 kilometres above the earth, she took pictures that transformed the ice into abstract paintings of startling beauty. And just as Richard McKenna says, what is remarkable is the clear kinship of the images she has recorded from the earth, in the heart of remote places, with the companion pictures taken from space.

Her image of an ice scene in Ellesmere Island, Nunavut, in brilliant May sunshine is a *trompe l'oeil* tease.[10] This is the time of year when the darkness disappears for the summer, and night and day become one on Ellesmere. There is no way of appreciating the size of scale of the ice formations we are seeing in this picture. Is it a close-up of small chunks of melting ice at the water's edge, reflected so perfectly in the still cold sea? Or are we looking at gigantic glacier fingers extending into the sastrugi? The crystalline blue and white shapes, the reflection of the silver light—none of it conveys to the brain the information that would be needed to understand the individual proportion of the elements of this landscape.

In the very next photo in the book, *Canada: Landscape of Dreams,* there is only the memory of ice: the scars left by its passage thousands of years ago. The striking image of a Georgian Bay sunset is accompanied by a quote from Margaret Atwood:

"The lake, vast and dimensionless, doubles everything, the stars, the boulders, itself, even the darkness that you can walk so long in it becomes light." Here is a small, tight stand of heartbreakingly beautiful white pines, waving their long, paint-brush branches. Their size and place in the photo situates us in the human scale of the landscape. The sparseness of the trees shows how they struggle for existence, even thousands of years after the grinding and polishing of the pink-and-grey granite by the passage of the long-ago ice. Here, beauty is what the ice has left behind.

CHAPTER ELEVEN

"The ultimate function of the vessel is not specified at this stage,
apart from the fact that it must be unsinkable . . ."
—Deputy First Sea Lord of the Admiralty, 1943

ICE AS HISTORICAL CATALYST

In 406, on the last cold day of December, the Rhine River turned to ice. This freeze-up opened a passage for some fifteen thousand hungry Germanic tribesmen with their wives and children. These Suebis, Vandals and Alans poured into Roman Gaul, where only Frankish mercenaries were on guard; the professional Roman legions had been called home to Italy, which was also threatened by incursions at the time. Rome's failure to defend the edges of its empire was like the blossoming of algae. Within a year, Britain saw three different emperors proclaimed. The third of these, Constantine III, crossed into Gaul to get a piece of the action there, exposing his domestic front to raids from the Picts, Scots and Saxons. The Britons rebelled, expelled the Romans and established their own government. By AD 410, the Roman Emperor Honorious had given up on Britain and directed the British cities to take care of their own defence; Rome itself had been breached and sacked.

The invading Saxons overwhelmed the Britons over the next decades, as they buried coin, plate and jewellery in an attempt to ensure that their more advanced Roman civilization could re-emerge at some future time. In his masterful *How the Irish Saved Civilization*, Thomas Cahill identified the opening of this ice road across the Rhine as the tipping point in the fall of the Roman Empire, and the beginning of the Dark Ages:

> *On the last, cold day of December in the dying year we count as 406, the river Rhine froze solid, providing the natural bridge that hundreds of thousands of hungry men, women, and children had been waiting for. They were the barbari—to the Romans an undistinguished, matted mass of Others, not terrifying, just trou-blemakers, annoyances, things one would rather not have to deal with—non-Romans. To themselves they were, presumably, some-thing more, but as the illiterate leave few records, we can only surmise their opinion of themselves.*

There is great irony in this one weather event leading to the fall of the mighty Roman Empire, with all its powers and abil-ities to master the forces of its time. We now know that Europe was in the middle of a mini ice age at the time. This had tripped the regions north and east of the Rhine into famine. The Germanic tribes knew they would starve unless they could reach a place with more clement weather to grow food and to raise animals for meat. No matter how much they feared the Roman soldiers, they feared starvation more. And with the help of that ice road, they pushed through and destroyed the myth of the invincibility of Rome once and for all.

A conversation with the brilliant historian Margaret Macmillan (author of *Paris 1919*) yielded another story where ice played a determining role in history. Some 756 years after the Barbarian hordes crossed the Rhine, the people of Russia faced a similar pincer movement of aggression. In the east, the Mongols were invading. In the west, Pope Innocent III's Baltic crusade had been raging since 1198 when Bishop Hermann von Bushoeven of Tartu (in Livonia) gathered enough resources to invade northern Russia. The Teutonic Knights had long had their eye on the "pagan" Russian menace, and leapt at the chance for action. Prince Alexander Nevskii of Novgorod raised an army to defend his people against the Germans.

There is some controversy over whether the decisive battle on the frozen Lake Peipus (some accounts say it was on Lake Chudsko) in 1242 actually happened the way Sergei Eisenstein dramatized it in his 1938 classic movie *Alexander Nevsky*. It is a spectacular scene, with the knights (portrayed as brutish blond behemoths) making a wedge-shaped breach in the heroic Russian regiments. In the movie, clever Alexander, having positioned his troops on the thickest ice near the shore, leads his troops to surround the Teutons and force them onto thin ice in the middle, which breaks up and drowns the big, heavily armed Germans and their horses. It is one of the great battle scenes of all time, and it is almost impossible to remember today what a groundbreaking and innovative piece of moviemaking it was.

The historical accounts are sketchy and contradictory, so I like to imagine that the Battle on the Ice actually did happen the way Eisenstein envisaged it. Of course, and as all film students know, every Hollywood battle scene from *The Charge of the Light Brigade* to *Braveheart* is indebted to Eisenstein's brilliant camerawork and editing. The music is quite possibly the best film score of all time. The battle is a perennial favourite of model and diorama-makers, as well as of gamers and makers of battle scenarios, both online and in person. Prokofiev's minutely synchronized composition, particularly the Battle of the Ice, is a seamless part of the whole, and will be familiar to many modern moviegoers as the inspiration for John Williams' theme from *Jaws*. The Prokofiev music was so remarkable that the composer later responded to requests to adapt it for orchestra, and it is frequently performed as the *Alexander Nevsky Cantata*.[1]

The Battle on the Ice is legendary as a seminal event in determining the fate of Russia and its culture. The film very nearly never saw the light of day, however. When Stalin approved its production in 1938, he wanted it so badly (to whip up patriotism for an expected war effort) that he ordered entire units of the Russian army to serve as extras. Ironically, the highly effective battle of the ice scenes were shot in July, during a heat wave, on a huge level field covered with sodium silicate to look like ice. Unfortunately, by the time the film was released, to great reviews, it was on the wrong side of Russian-German relations: Stalin had just signed the 1939 non-aggression pact with von Ribbentrop, and criticizing Germans was strictly verboten. This was reversed in short order when Hitler invaded Poland, revealing himself to be as perfidious as the celluloid Germans.

In real life, the routing of the Teutonic Knights actually did dissuade the Germans from invading Russia until Napoleon decided to try it again in 1812. He too found the cold, the snow and the ice too much to overcome, and had to retreat with horrendous losses, his army decimated and his empire crumbling.

■ ■ ■

I visited the stunning rooms of the Hermitage Museum in St. Petersburg on a hot summer holiday when it was closed to the public and I could take my time appreciating its beauty. The Hermitage survived the German siege of Leningrad (as St. Petersburg was known during most of the Soviet regime) virtually intact: only one of its thousand rooms took a direct hit. Ice was not the obvious thought to have in that time and place . . . and yet, it played a starring role in the siege of 1941 as well.

In fact, the ice road on Lake Ledoka is credited with saving many lives in a time of desperation, death and destruction. Hitler ordered an attack on Leningrad (now and previously St. Petersburg) on June 22, 1941. His directive said: "Wipe the city of Petersburg off the face of the Earth. The defeat of the Soviet Union leaves no room for the continued existence of that large urban area. Finland, too, sees no point in the continued existence of that city so close to its new border. . . . A tight siege should be imposed on the city and fire from all calibres of guns and incessant bombing raids should reduce the city to ashes . . ."

The city sent away as many women and children, as much plant machinery and art as it could before all hell broke loose. All the available workers either joined the home guard or helped to convert the remaining factories over to making military equipment. The city was bombarded mercilessly, and choked off from its sources of food, fuel and supplies. The power plants and waterworks stopped running. In the brutally cold winter of 1941–42, Leningrad residents froze in ruined houses and starved on miniscule bread rations. There were no fats, meat or sugar, and people began to die in the streets. They could not even bury their dead because the soil was frozen hard, and therefore many bodies remained in the streets.

The military council decided that Lake Ledoga was their only hope, and on September 12, 1941, they were able to get two barges with grain and flour to Cape Osinovets from the eastern side of the lake. For nine hundred days, this became known as the Road of Life, the only way to get anything in and out of the besieged city. When the lake froze over, they began to build a winter route across the ice, which was known as Military Motorway 101. They had to build it in severe frost and gale-force wind conditions. The visibility was often nil, and the ice would sometimes collapse under them.

The Germans would bomb the passing cars and rake them with artillery fire, even when they moved at night using flickering flashlights. Some of the heavily loaded vehicles got caught in holes in the ice. Nevertheless, the amounts of food that did make it through allowed them to increase bread rations so that by December 1941, workers were getting 12 ounces a day, and office workers, dependants and children could have 7 ounces—still a pathetically small amount of food.

The most famous personality on the ice Road of Life was truck driver Maxim Tverdokhleb, who brought the children of Leningrad tangerines from Georgia for New Year's Eve 1942. He had to drive in bright moonlight, making him an easy target for two dive-bombing Messerschmitts. He made it with a badly wounded arm, a shattered windscreen, a pierced radiator and forty-nine bullet holes in his truck, but the children of Leningrad got their tangerines from sunny Georgia.

The suffering in Leningrad during those nine hundred days is impossible to fathom, and we can only salute the spirit of its people. They kept on working; they took care of their sick; they planted vegetables in the parks and along the streets. Marshal Georgy Zhukov later wrote in his memoirs: "War history had never before seen such battlefield valour and home front heroism as was displayed by the unbending defenders of Leningrad."

The most telling story of the siege lives on today: the brilliant Russian composer Dmitri Shostakovich's *Symphony no. 7*, an anthem to the spirit of Leningrad. The composer had refused to leave the city with the other members of the Philharmonic Society early in the war. He dug trenches and fought fires while the Nazi incendiary bombs rained down on the city. And he wrote transcendent music in homage to his defiant people, to whom he broadcast this radio message on September 20, 1941: "An hour ago I finished writing the second part of my big new symphony. . . . Why am I telling you this? Because I want all the Leningraders who are listening to me to know that life goes on and we are all doing our duty . . ."

A call went out to recruit eighty musicians to play the symphony, since the Leningrad radio orchestra had dwindled below the necessary size to play Shostakovich's music. Musicians were given special passes; many of them were malnourished, their hands calloused and bloodied from combat duty. They rehearsed for 15 minutes—they and their emaciated conductor Karl Eliasberg all holding on to their energy for dear life. He later recalled the world premiere of *Symphony no. 7*: "The chandeliers were all aglow in the Philharmonic Hall jam packed by writers, artists and academics. Military men were also very much in presence, most of them right from the battlefront . . ."

This must surely have been one of the most moving sights of that time—or any time. Eliasberg, trembling, his tuxedo having grown much too large for his starving body, lifted his baton. The hall swelled with the magnificent chords of the most beautiful music Shostakovich had ever written. When it was over, no one could move for a moment. Then people leapt to their feet, crying fierce tears of joy and applauding as if their hearts would burst. The musicians hugged each other as if they had just won an earth-shaking battle and survived. A German soldier, hearing the radio broadcast of the concert, was stunned: "When I heard Shostakovich's seventh symphony being broadcast from the famine-stricken Leningrad I realized that we would never be able to take it. Realizing that, I surrendered . . ."

Three years later, in January 1944, the Red Army took back Leningrad, and the ice road was allowed to melt away, like the resolve of the German Army.[2]

■ ■ ■

THE HABBAKUK

While Leningrad was under siege, the British were contemplating a scenario that is one of the stranger ice tales I have encountered: the story of the *Habbakuk*, an aircraft carrier made of ice that was planned to patrol the North Atlantic near the end of World War II.[3] I first heard about the story from Canadian scientist Jamie Rossiter, a former glaciologist who now runs the e-learning programs at CANARIE, a Canadian government network.[4]

The story finds Winston Churchill in a steaming bath (one of his very favourite places—he even travelled with a folding canvas bathtub) at his country residence, Chequers, sometime late in 1942, at the height of World War II.[5] The Allies were becoming desperate for a break in their luck. All kinds of strange ideas were being floated to try and reverse the course of the war. Lord Louis Mountbatten, then the chief of combined operations for the British war effort, had found one he liked. Arriving at Chequers, he rushed upstairs and unceremoniously burst into the bathroom with a parcel in his hands. Few other men would have dared to do this, but Mountbatten was no shrinking violet. He had something important to demonstrate. He told Churchill that he had a block of new, top-secret strategic material that he wanted to put into the bath. This he did immediately, dropping the contents of his parcel—a chunk of ice—into the hot water between the prime minister's naked legs.

Both men watched closely as the ice floated, intact, without melting. This was no ordinary ice. In fact, it looked more like frozen porridge. It was a building material developed by an eccentric English inventor named Geoffrey Nathaniel Pyke and named *pykrete* in his honour. Pyke was brilliant, if an odd duck. He had appeared at Mountbatten's office looking like a hobo, and told the chief of combined operations, "You need me on your staff because I'm a man who thinks." He had been thinking for a long time: Lord Zuckerman described Pyke as "not a scientist, but a man of a vivid and uncontrollable imagination, and a totally uninhibited tongue."

As a teenager, Pyke had used a false passport to sneak into

Germany during World War I, and to convince the *Daily Chronicle* to buy his dispatches from Berlin. The Germans nearly shot him as a spy, and then interned him in a camp from which he made a daring escape with a companion. On his return to England, he was trumpeted as a public hero by the *Daily Chronicle*; he wrote a book and gave lectures on his experience. In the 1920s, dissatisfied with the educational options for his young son, he used a small fortune acquired in the futures market (he had cornered a quarter of the world's tin market) to found a short-lived alternative school that is credited with virtually inventing progressive elementary education in Great Britain.

Unfortunately, he was ruined financially in the market crash of 1929 and the school had to close. During the Spanish Civil War, he invented a way to save coal by fitting bicycle pedals to shunting engines, and he fitted sidecars to Harley-Davidson motorcycles to carry hot food to the front and bring casualties back. Some of his ideas were off the wall and never adopted, such as sending dogs with brandy barrels around their necks into the Romanian oilfields so that the guards would get drunk, making it easy for commandos to take over. Other ideas, such as different sledge designs to help with travel in occupied Norway, or to blow up Germans with torpedoes released backwards on ski slopes, actually received support at the experimental stage.

Pyke's strength was leaps of the imagination: Why ice? Why not ice? In theory, ice is not an ideal building material: it is brittle on impact, it deforms under pressure, and its behaviour is difficult to predict. But it also offers advantages, which Pyke had reinforced significantly with the simple use of wood pulp. Adding 14 percent wood pulp into freezing slurry boosts the mechanical strength and crush resistance of the resulting ice to the properties of brickwork. The material can be moulded and planed like wood, and it melts very slowly. This super-ice takes the mechanical strength of ice from an unreliable fracture point of anywhere from 5 to 35 kilograms per square centimetre, to a fairly constant 70 kilograms per square centimetre. A 1-inch column of this stuff will support a car, and it melts very slowly in relation to pure ice. It is quite eco-friendly (not that eco-friendliness was a big concern in 1943, with Hitler occupying most of Europe).

The implications, Pyke thought, were phenomenal for the British war interest. He saw the possibility of the largest ships ever built, with the inherent capacity to repair them at sea. Existing aircraft carriers could only carry lightly armoured little planes with folding wings. The pykrete "berg-ships" could potentially hold full-sized airplanes with proper runways. With minimal energy, you could keep refrigeration equipment on board that allowed the ship to stay at sea for long periods. This equipment could be used to shoot supercooled water at any developing fractures or chips in the boat, but also to put the enemy out of commission: BLAM, your hatches are sealed! BLAM, your guns are blocked! BLAM, your guards are frozen solid! Mountbatten loved this kind of stuff. Pyke easily convinced the British commander to commission him and his associate, Martin Perutz, to produce and test large quantities of pykrete for future use.

On April 9, 1943, the Deputy First Sea Lord of the Admiralty issued a directive (which is still kept at the Fleet Air Arm Museum at Yeovilton in Somerset). It said: "The ultimate function of the vessel is not specified at this stage, apart from the fact that it must be unsinkable . . ."

Pyke and Perutz set up shop on Patricia Lake, near Jasper, Alberta. The prototype, just over 18 metres long and 9 metres wide, 6 metres high, weighed 1,000 tons, and sported a tin roof. The pykrete blocks were mounted on a wooden frame built with 3 x 6 studs and 3 x 8 floor joints. It only took a 1-horsepower motor to keep it frozen. The structure was insulated and cooled. Simultaneous experiments in front of the Chateau Lake Louise near Banff determined that the ship would need a hull at least 11 metres thick to deliver on the requirement that it be virtually invulnerable to bombs or torpedoes. The eventual *Habbakuk* would be designed as either a "relay floating air base" for long-range aircraft, an aircraft carrier for shorter-range anti-submarine patrols, an advance fighter base, or a cargo carrier. Potentially, it could be an aircraft carrier for the perennially useful Spitfires, which were too large to fit on the standard aircraft carriers of the time. Churchill was inclined towards large floating platforms to support the landings planned for the reoccupation of Europe. The British were also very concerned with their losses from German U-boats in the "mid-Atlantic air gap." Merchant shipping was highly vulnerable because of the limited range of patrolling aircraft and had suffered heavy losses.

Pyke thought great numbers of berg-ships could be built cheaply. They would be constructed of 12-metre blocks of ice; would be between 600 and 1,200 metres long, between 92 and 183 metres wide, up to 40 metres deep, with walls 9 to 12 metres thick. When it was built, the pykrete ship would dwarf the world's biggest existing oceanliner, the *Queen Mary*, whose tonnage was just 4 percent of the *Habbakuk*'s planned weight.[6] This meant that if a torpedo hit, it would make a crater 1 metre deep and 6 metres across, and all they would have to do is blast it quickly with a mixture of sea water, wood pulp and cold air, circulating through the ship in galvanized iron pipes.

The sheer size of the potential boat made it an oddity. Some of the military brass thought it would not be very useful because it would be impossible for such a large craft to operate in stealth. Pyke had an answer for that too. In his first *Habbakuk* memo, he wrote: "Surprise can be obtained from permanence as well as suddenness."

With his usual flamboyance, Mountbatten set out to prove the value of the pykrete boat idea at a secret meeting of the Allied chiefs of staff at Quebec City's Chateau Frontenac in August 1943. (Since the cost of the first ship had mounted to an estimated $100 million, Mountbatten was determined to get the Americans to pick up the tab for it.) As tension mounted in the anteroom where senior staff waited, two shots rang out from behind the closed doors. "My God, the Americans are shooting the British!" yelled British Air Marshall Sir William Welch, summoning the guards. As they rushed to the rescue, they found Lord Mountbatten surveying the mayhem with his smoking pistol while several of the officers present were laughing.

Mountbatten had presented a demonstration using a block of pure ice and a block of pykrete. Pulling out his pistol, he had shot each block. The ice had shattered on impact, but the bullet aimed at the pykrete had ricocheted and clipped the trouser leg of Fleet Admiral Ernest King. The officers were duly impressed, and there was soon an agreement between Churchill and Roosevelt to build the massive ship.[7] The Pentagon, however, was not big on British eccentrics. (Pyke was tall, with a straggly beard and messy clothes. He often appeared without socks, and once, for a meeting with the prime minister of Canada, Mackenzie King, showed up with his fly wide open because the zipper was broken.) With Mountbatten's departure from combined operations in October 1943, Pyke was forced off the project and transferred to the Admiralty, where he was neutralized.

In the end, the team removed the on-board machinery, and left the rest of the *Habbakuk* on Patricia Lake. The pykrete held up remarkably well through the hot summer, but eventually it melted into the lake. The project had been overtaken by technological progress (the atomic bomb), the low price of steel that made traditional aircraft carriers more affordable, and American activities in the Pacific. Pyke kept trying to promote his ideas to influential people, but eventually, discouraged, he shaved off his beard, swallowed a bottle of sleeping pills, and signed off from a world that did not seem to appreciate his genius. It was the winter of 1948, and he was only fifty-four.

In the 1970s, scuba divers found the remnants of the wooden frame on the lakebed. The archaeology department of the University of Calgary studied them, and in 1988, the Underwater Archeological Society of Alberta marked the site with an underwater monument. The following year, the National Research Council of Canada and National Parks erected a plaque on the shore of Lake Patricia, commemorating this colourful episode in the history of World War II.

In an article he wrote for *The New Yorker* in 1985, Pyke's colleague Martin Perutz speculates that the *Habbakuk* might never have been successful anyway because of design flaws.[8] But to this day, glaciologists who understand the mechanical properties of ice wonder why no one has ever taken pykrete any further. The last demonstration I know of took place on July 22, 2000, when J. Gordon Holley froze ice and pykrete in 1-gallon milk jugs for one week, shot both with a .243 rifle at 325 feet, and posted the pictures on his website devoted to "science theatre."[9]

THE MAUNDER MINIMUM COMES TO CREMONA

Beautiful music has always uplifted the soul. But it turns out the world's most beautiful violins may have achieved their iconic status thanks to Europe's Little Ice Age (mid-1400s to mid-1800s). The world's most beloved violins, and the most expensive, are the finite number of instruments still in existence produced by Antonio Stradivari and his colleagues, the master violinmakers of Cremona, Italy. Working in the seventeenth century, these skilled craftsmen may well have used special varnishes or wood treatments that resulted in the rich, brilliant sound of the instruments they left behind. (The delightful Canadian film *The Red Violin* follows such an instrument through the centuries.) But two American scientists have another theory, which appeared in 2003 in an obscure scientific journal called *Dendrochronologia*.

Dr. Lloyd Burckle of Columbia University's Lamont-Doherty Observatory in Palisades, New York, who specializes in global climate change by studying the lives of tiny sea creatures, was thinking about the coldest point of the Little Ice Age, Maunder Minimum (a 70-year period between 1645 and 1715 during which there was a lack of solar activity) when he realized that Stradivari's birth date was a year before the period started. Comparing the dates, he found that Stradivari's golden period, when he produced the most valuable violins, was from 1700 to 1720.

Dr. Burckle got in touch with Dr. Henri Grissino-Mayer, a tree-ring-dating expert, or dendrochronologist, at the University of Tennessee's Laboratory of Tree-Ring Science. Dr. Grissino-Mayer had recently authenticated the world's most famous Stradivarius violin, widely known as the "Messiah," in England. He developed a five-hundred-year chronology, beginning in the year 1500, for sixteen high-elevation forests of larch, spruce and pine in areas from the west of France to southern Germany. What he discovered was that the period of the Maunder Minimum coincided with a unique period of slow growth that caused the trees to produce very narrow, dense rings.

The two scientists wrote: "We would suggest that the narrow tree rings that identify the Maunder Minimum in Europe played a role in the enhanced sound quality of instruments produced by the Cremona (Italy) violinmakers." The noted that "narrow tree rings would not only strengthen the violin but would increase the wood's density. . . the onset of the Maunder Minimum at a time when the skills of the Cremonese violinmakers reached their zenith perhaps made the difference in the violin's tone and brilliance."[10]

No two handmade violins are the same, of course, and many, though not all, experts consider that the Cremonese masters have never been surpassed. But still, it is a very intriguing idea that a Little Ice Age could influence the standard by which violins are judged for centuries to come, and that as a result we could personally hear the world's most beautiful music half a millennium later.

■ ■ ■

The Maunder Minimum may have provided Stradivari with the best possible wood for making violins, but it also froze the Rhine River again, as it had in 406. This time, it touched off a wave of immigration to the New World. From the year 1702, agents for William Penn, the Quaker founder of Philadelphia, had been recruiting in the Palatinate, in what is now Germany. His offer of religious freedom, a peaceful existence and cheap land must have been very tempting, given the difficult times and extreme cold climate they were suffering. But the winter of 1708 was the last straw. In early October, it got intensely cold. By November 1, people said firewood would not burn in open air! By January 1709, wine and spirits had frozen into solid blocks of ice, birds were falling dead in mid-air and saliva was bouncing off the ground like hail. The Seine, the Rhone and Rhine Rivers froze; even the sea along the coast froze enough to bear heavy carts. People began to die, livestock did not make it through the winter and when spring came late in 1709, the fruit trees and vines were all dead.

This followed hard on two years of miserable crop failures, and there were no better days in sight. The people of the Palatinate had been buffeted for thirty years by wars and religious persecution. Now, they faced starvation. It was the final blow. Over the next sixty years, there would be a mass exodus of Palatines, lured by promises of freedom in the "promised land" of Pennsylvania posted in German throughout the Palatinate. William Penn himself visited, selling Pennsylvania as a haven for the poor.

The British got into the act as well: Queen Anne, the newly crowned Queen of England, was a relative of the ruler of the Palatinate, and a great Protestant sympathizer. As the successor to the Catholic King James II, she orchestrated a number of measures that threw a lifeline to the unfortunate Palatines. In 1709, Britain passed a law that gave citizenship to any foreigner who pledged allegiance to the British Crown and professed the Protestant faith, all for the cost of one shilling. Speculators with patents in the colonies sent recruiters to the Palatinate with offers of forty acres of land, paid transportation and maintenance. There was an ulterior motive: the British hoped to shore up the Protestant population in the colonies to provide a human buffer against the French-Canadian Catholics just to the north (who would have included my ancestors).

The Elector Palatinate was not at all pleased to be losing his subjects, and he threatened death to all emigrants. The bravest Protestants left under cover of night, beginning in the spring of 1709. In short order, some fourteen thousand Palatines were camped under appalling conditions at Blackheath, Greenwich Heath and other sites near London. The British government was swamped by the unexpected success of the outreach initiative. Some of the Palatinates were sent to Ireland to shore up Protestant numbers there, but they did not get the free land they had been promised. The British packed off some three thousand Roman Catholics back to Germany, and a further thousand of the wretched emigrants went to Jamaica, the West Indies and South Carolina.

Of the original fourteen thousand emigrants, about three thousand went to New York from Britain, while others sailed from Rotterdam. At the time, such a journey was ghastly. The ships were full of vermin and disease. People had to carry their own food and water, which quickly spoiled. Families often had to share a bunk for the whole crossing of three to five months. The elderly, the sick and the little ones often died of dysentery, typhoid or small pox—either during the crossing, or shortly after getting off the stinking ship. When these people landed in New York City in 1710, they numbered about a third of the city's existing population of less than five thousand, and could not be absorbed immediately. They were therefore housed on Nutten Island, now known as Governor's Island.

The Palatines were quickly recruited to harvest tar and pitch from the pine forests of New York for England's massive fleet of merchant ships and her navy. Many were resettled to Livingston Manor and sections of New York along the Hudson River, the land they had been promised under their emigration contracts. The Palatines were known as hardworking, solid citizens. Their contracts said they had to repay Queen Anne for their passage from Britain after seven years but they quickly found they were caught between political changes back in England and unscrupulous businessmen in New York. Saying they felt they were being treated as indentured servants, they rebelled against their living conditions and determined to go elsewhere. One hundred and thirty families, close to starvation, decided to move to Schoharie. With the help of friendly natives, the first fifty families managed to begin living off the land in the fall of 1712; the second group arrived in March 1713, by way of Schenectady, walking 40 miles in deep snow and ice to get there. The roads in the area were not cleared until 1770.

By the following year, 1714, when the Palatines were beginning to feel that their little community would survive, the ownership of their land was challenged. They were in no mood to be trifled with, and they ran their tormentors (who may actually have had a stronger legal claim) out of town in a particularly undignified manner. Between 1720 and 1723, the majority was relocated to other areas, including Pennsylvania, but they were being used as human shields against the French and the natives. The Palatines learned English and coped with harsh weather and wild animals that destroyed their crops and livestock, proving themselves to be self-sufficient and loyal citizens. They had to have the patience of Job, because at the time it could take up to thirty years to get legal rights to your land. Still, by 1745, there were approximately forty-five thousand Germans in Pennsylvania, and in 1766, Benjamin Franklin complained that they made up a full third of the population.

The Palatines were thrilled to live in religious freedom and peace, something that was difficult to find anywhere else at the time. In the early years they suffered through swarms of locusts in 1732, severe earthquakes in 1737, two years of poor crops (1750–51) and three years of drought (1752–54). In 1763, they lost many small animals because a freak hailstorm dropped balls of ice the size of turkey eggs. In the very hard winter of 1780, 20 inches of ice formed on the ponds, and sheep and cattle had frozen ears. The ice had been the catalyst to persuade them to build a new life far from home. In their new home, they still had to deal with it, but they had their freedom. And so they persisted: their legacy is the prosperous, quiet enclave that would come to be known, misleadingly, as Pennsylvania Dutch country.

CHAPTER TWELVE

"Raw nature must be preserved, so that we never forget
the grandeur it can inspire."
–Douglas Coupland, *Souvenir of Canada*

ICE UP CLOSE FOR THE MASSES

Dozens of ships now ply the Alaskan waterways out of
Vancouver and Seattle, many of them carrying two to three
thousand passengers in accommodations ranging from standard to highly luxurious. These tourists are intent on seeing
the majesty of Alaska's glaciers. From the deck of a cruise ship,
lucky visitors can witness spectacular ice displays, such as this
one recounted by *Globe and Mail* travel writer Wallace
Immen: "After thousands of years locked solidly in a glacier,
ice lets out a mighty scream of relief as it breaks free. At first
there are vibrations like distant anonymous thunder. Then
comes a deep rumble and finally, the mighty snap of separa-
tion as a cliff of glimmering aquamarine ice tumbles into an
effervescent sea . . ."

Who wouldn't want to see such a sight?

In recent years, with the heightened sensitivity that arose
out of the tragic Exxon Valdez oil spill in 1989, the Alaskan
authorities have been expressing concern about bilge water
from all of these vessels sullying the state's pristine coastline,

leading companies such as Crystal Cruises to maintain a strict "nothing overboadrd" policy. Few places on earth are as spectacular as coastal Alaska. Immen describes "vistas of mammoth mountains, veil-like waterfalls and tongues of glistening snow" that are "embellished by the shocking pink of fireweed, verdant meadows and the regular appearance of otters, whales, eagles and brown bears." This is one of the rare environments to experience that combination of spectacular ice juxtaposed with vibrant, colourful life. Alaskans, understandably, are determined to keep it pristine.

The Alaskan border shares glaciers with Canada, the most glaciated territory in the world. Canada has 100,000 glaciers, some of them easily accessible to tourists—but not St. Elias, in the southwest corner of Yukon. It is the largest single icefield outside the polar caps, and the largest mass of granite anywhere in the world, but most of its visitors are scientists attracted by its unique wildlife and the learning it offers about global climate and human activities. It is probably the third most important place for ice-core research, after Greenland and Antarctica, and confirms that what is sent into the atmosphere anywhere on the planet, from Krakatoa to Chernobyl, ends up preserved in the ice.

THE COLUMBIA ICEFIELD

In the Canadian Rockies every year, however, a million visitors—many from Japan where mountain environments are considered sacred—show up to inspect the Columbia Icefield over the course of a few short months. At 325 square kilometres, it is the largest subpolar body of ice in North America. My husband

and I love to rent a convertible in June, when we have a tradition of visiting the Rockies. This allows us to get a full frontal feel for the majesty of the mountains and their mantles of ice—as well as the jewel-like lakes, their colours a reflection of various kinds of "glacial flour"—mineral and rock dust—scoured out and dumped into them by the melting glaciers.

There is nothing like the feeling of roaring up the Icefields Parkway with the top down (it is not always warm in early June, so well wrapped with the heater blasting if necessary) and looking up: Castle Mountain, that really looks like the fortress protecting the treasures to come just up the road; the Crowfoot Glacier, its steely aqua talons curled around the rocks; and the glistening, broad Athabasca, with its payload of tourists from all over the world. We do this even if there is driving rain: at highway speeds, there is a protective air bubble around the passenger cabin of the car, and not a drop falls on us. (We have gotten used to the stares from the Winnebagos in the passing lane.)

The icefields feed many glaciers and ultimately three oceans—the Atlantic, the Pacific and the Arctic, because they stand right at the watershed for the entire North American continent. But the Athabasca, one of the world's most accessible glaciers, is the one that receives the bulk of visitors. It was first measured in 1970, although it was photographed long before that by the members of a remarkable Philadelphia family.[1]

The Vauxes, one of Philadelphia's most prominent Quaker families, began studying the mountain glaciers in 1887, shortly after the opening of the Canadian Pacific Railway. George Vaux Jr. (1863–1927), William S. Vaux Jr. (1872–1908) and Mary M. Vaux (1880–1940) as well as George Jr.'s son George

(1908–1996) visited the Canadian Rockies (or Canadian Alps, as they called them) every single year up until 1940. Mary did all the technical work and most of the printing of the photographs, while her brothers shot most of them. She eventually married Dr. Charles Walcott, the famous geologist and invertebrate paleontologist; she was an active member of the Alpine Club of Canada, and a talented botanical painter. William's work concentrated specifically on the movement and physical features of glaciers.

The Vaux siblings were no amateurs: all three belonged to the Photographic Society of Philadelphia, and competed in its juried competitions. They exhibited their work there and gave lectures about it; Canadian Pacific liked it so much that the family benefited from free railway passes west from Montreal in exchange for use of their photos in publicity brochures. The Vaux photographs, taken from 1899 to 1936, have been published in a beautiful book, and many of the originals are now part of the permanent collection of the Whyte Museum of the Rockies in Banff, Alberta.[2]

If the Vaux family began as avid tourists, they ended up leaving a major artistic and scientific legacy. They continued coming to the Rockies for decades, leaving a unique collection of photographs, diaries and observations that is helping researchers today identify changes in the glaciers over the last century and more.[3] The collection includes mountains, valleys, waterfalls, glaciers, ice formations, campgrounds and the remarkable hotels and bridges of the Canadian Pacific Railway—often with people included to give a sense of scale. As they learned more about the ice, the Vauxes began measuring the glaciers (though not the Athabasca). Their detailed and expert observations and measurements are among the best tools that modern glaciologists have to help them understand what is happening to the Rocky Mountain glaciers. This is all the more remarkable because the genteel Vauxes, Philadelphia aristocracy, had to get to some of these wild places on foot and with mules, the women in long dresses and large hats because there were no roads at the time. Recent exhibits of their photographs have included the bulky cameras they used and their original equipment, such as ice axes and barometers, which make their adventures seem very real.

The Athabasca retreated about 1.5 kilometres between 1870 and 1970, but since 1970, it has been retreating at a speed that many glaciologists find alarming: another 0.6 kilometres, indicating the speed of melting in the last third of the twentieth century was much greater than in the whole century before. The glacier appears to have undergone a spectacular thinning as well since a 1906 photo, perhaps as much as 100 to 120 metres at its frontal edge by 1999.[4] No one knows what role human activities are playing in this accelerated melting, although extensive research into the issue is ongoing.

For visitors to the Columbia Icefield, specially designed buses weighing 30,000 kilograms carry visitors up onto the Athabasca, which is up to 350 metres of solid ice down to the bedrock. Despite their jumbo size (the wheels alone are taller than I am) these "Snocoaches" look like little ants once they are up on the glacier. Tourists can get off the bus and step onto the glacier, but there are signs duly warning them about the danger of crevasses, deep fissures caused by freeze–thaw cycles, and movement in all bodies of ice. Visitors who intend to go up onto the glacier should bring sensible footwear with good traction, fleece jackets and mittens, even in high summer. The water that drains from the Columbia Icefield is among the purest, freshest water in the world. In celebration of this, tourists on the Athabasca glacier often dip a cup into a melt pool to sample the cold, clear liquid.

Ice Hotels

If the glaciers are among the true natural wonders of the world, people are also interested in man-made wonders. The world's few ice hotels are attracting increasing numbers of tourists, too. There is one in Canada, headed up by Quebec City resident Jacques Desbois, who has made a career out of taming the ice and bringing eager tourists to its beauty.

It all started innocently enough, in the winter of 1995. Desbois, like many Canadians, says he feels far more alive— "more efficient"—in cold weather. Since adolescence, he had made it a habit to build and sleep in igloos every winter, using traditional Inuit methodology (this is not something most Canadians, 80 percent urban-dwellers in the south of the country, would think to do, or even have any idea how to do). Each year he tried to improve his igloo-building technique. In the winter of 1995, when his two sons were three and five years old, he built an igloo in the backyard. The Desbois boys were in charge of deciding *when* they would sleep in the igloo. They picked a night when it was –35°C, and nothing would change their minds. Their father (along with their uncle) agreed to the plan.

Desbois had noticed that a local television station regularly carried what is known as a "kicker" item just before the weather forecast. It was always a lighthearted story, often weather-related. Amused by the boys' enthusiasm, he decided he would suggest their igloo adventure as that day's story. The days after Christmas are often slow news days and the station was grateful for the lead, sending a camera crew immediately to shoot the two generations of brothers preparing to sleep in their igloo. The next day, the phone started ringing off the hook. Other TV stations, radio stations and newspapers all started getting into the act. At week's end, Desbois was exhausted.

By the time a call-in show got involved, with callers attacking or defending his decision to let the little boys sleep in the igloo in such cold weather, Desbois began to hear something interesting in the callers' passion for the subject. In his mind, the wheels began to turn. Inuit, after all, have slept in igloos forever, in far colder weather . . .

The next winter, he started a business, providing an igloo-sleeping experience along with winter sports, such as snowshoe expeditions, dog-sledding and cross-country skiing. People responded and he did well, but Desbois wanted to take it further. Then a friend showed him a ten-line item in an issue of *Reader's Digest*, about an ice hotel in Sweden. He decided immediately that he too would build an ice hotel—in Quebec. Over the next year, he corresponded with the Swedish company by email, by "snail mail" and by telephone. By the time he made his first visit to Jukkasjärvi in Sweden's northern Lapland, accompanied by an engineer, they knew he was serious.

The Swedish hotel had first come to life in 1989 as a large igloo, built right on the ice of the Torne River. It was meant to house an art exhibit. After a few visitors who had spent the night in the igloo waxed enthusiastic about the quality of sleep they had experienced, the promoters decided to expand the concept. By 2004, the new Ice Hotel had sixty rooms and suites, a chapel, a pillar room, an ice bar sponsored by Absolut Vodka that *Newsweek* called "stunning," and a movie theatre.

When Jacques Desbois stepped into the lobby of the Swedish ice hotel in the winter of 1997, he suddenly understood ice as a medium. While snow is a structure of ice crystals and he had long been building igloos, the kind of snow he was used to working with had nothing to do with the crystal palace before him. Ideal igloo snow blocks, the kind the Inuit prefer to carve out of the arctic desert, have the texture, weight and insulating capacity of Styrofoam. This ice, harvested from the River Torne, was completely different: it was pure and dazzling, and illuminated with fibre optic light for maximum effect. Everything in the ice hotel—the pillars, chandeliers, furniture and sculptures—streamed with clear, light-bending radiance.

Now he understood why they called it an *ice* hotel, even though it contained many times more snow than actual ice. But what ice! "I really felt I had entered the belly of the winter," says Desbois. "The interplay of textures between the ice and the snow was absolutely startling; the association of the ice with the light, the luminosity . . . it revealed the suitability of the ice as a medium to express natural colours, according to the sunsets, to the position, the orientation, the source water of the natural ice from that Nordic Swedish river. I wanted to touch it; I wanted to see what artists could do with the medium. It was bewitching."

Desbois had always been in love with winter; now he was

seduced by the ice. He was determined to arrive at an agreement with the Swedes to create an ice hotel of his own. But for that to happen, he would need to master the methodology they had developed to construct the ice hotel, and a network of promotional partners to make it work. Over the next three years, he, his two partners and their consulting engineer would do just that.

The first year, they built an ice hotel just beneath the Montmorency Falls, close to the heart of Quebec City. This was a deliberate strategy to make it easy to get to, and to allow Quebec City residents to become familiar with it as a tourist attraction for day visitors. Desbois recruited a range of artists to design various sculptures, bas-reliefs and anthropological displays in his hotel. He drew on the talents of traditional woodcarvers from Saint-Jean-Port-Joli, a village famous for its bas-reliefs. His team developed tools for this work, adapting chisels, chainsaws and files for specific types of snow and ice. It was hard, physical work, starting from blocks of ice weighing almost 160 kilograms.

Slowly, the project took shape. The crystal-clear blocks used for this first Canadian ice hotel came from a big-city factory. They were made of Montreal's filtered tap water, and they had one idiosyncrasy that made them different from the Swedish ones: each retained the tiny mark of the tube used to remove air from the water. This tube ensured that the ice had maximum clarity. White ice is the result of air bubbles, often introduced by freeze–thaw cycles. These beautiful clear ice blocks, used on the ends of the hotel's tunnels, would have to be protected from the sun so they could stay that way. So they built large snow roof overhangs to keep their ice "windows" out of direct sunlight.

The second year, Desbois and his partners formed a partnership with SEPAQ, a for-profit Crown Corporation with an extensive tourism and recreation mandate, and agreed on a permanent site. The ice hotel would be located at the Duchesnay Ecotourism Station, 18 miles from the city, where a long-standing school of forestry and its residential facilities were being transformed into a four-star resort for business meetings and family vacations. A hotel and conference facility, spread over several buildings was already there, along with a whole range of available activities: hiking, snow-shoeing, dog-sledding, cross-country skiing, ice fishing, igloo construction, snowmobiling and winter field sports. The idea was that people would book package vacations; one night could be spent sleeping in the ice hotel, but with access to all the creature comforts the rest of the time. The Ice Hotel Canada would also have an Absolut bar, with ice tables in snow-cave alcoves, glistening ice pillars, sculptures and a huge ice-carved replica of the sponsor's famous bottle into which guests could enter, peer out through a large window, and have their pictures taken.

Whereas the Swedes had made classical round columns, the Quebecers carved the pillars, chiselling them like diamonds to reflect as much light as possible. In the bar, people could drink out of ice shooter glasses whose thick rims would slowly adapt to the shape of their mouths. Shots of liquor would be poured through a large bottle, held by a supersized human hand, all made of ice and resting on an ice bar. It was all very kitsch, and people took a childlike delight in it. Because of the thick walls, the temperature throughout the 3,000-square-metre ice hotel remains constant at −5°C. Since this is well below freezing, nonalcoholic beverages and drink mixes are stored in a standard refrigerator, to keep them warm enougn to stay liquid.

I was determined to experience all of this for myself. On the early March day that my daughter Sarah and I showed up at the Ice Hotel Canada, we were excited and a little apprehensive. We had seen the website; we knew it would be beautiful. But we also worried about such mundane issues as access to washrooms during the night. Sarah and I checked in at one of the old forestry school buildings, a relatively primitive facility in comparison to the rest of the operation. We had to check our bags until 9:30 p.m., when we would gain access to our room. We were told it was not a good idea to bring anything of value into the ice hotel: the rooms did not have doors, just curtains suspended on a rod anchored in the ice.

We decided to take the tour of the ice hotel right away. We were duly impressed. The large pillared lobby, known as the Grand Hall, included an ice lectern on which there was a guest book. We could read the enthusiastic scribbling of visitors from all over the world: California, Germany, England, Australia, New York, Philadelphia. We ducked into an intimate snow theatre, where a continuous video showed the construction of the hotel and promoted an Arctic adventure film. The theatre benches were covered with reindeer skins, as were all surfaces where people could be expected to sit for any length of time. A few thronelike ice chairs didn't have skins on them, and were clearly meant for show; but their sitting surfaces showed indications of occupation, a sign of the human incapacity to resist a throne. . . . The doorway to the bar was in the shape of the Absolut vodka bottle. The bar itself was the largest room in the hotel; it could accommodate functions with up to six hundred guests. Press events, business meetings and even weddings take place in the ice hotel each year; just off the bar was a chapel that served for the twenty-odd weddings a year. A large starburst had been sculpted over an impressive altar. The tunnels leading to the thirty-one guest rooms and "suites" were accessible from the bar and its adjacent courtyard. A Viking-sized barbecue and a large hot tub were the most prominent features of the courtyard. Our tour finished with two ice and snow art galleries.

We repaired to the dining room for an excellent dinner featuring venison, smoked salmon and other local specialties. The menu was sophisticated, but clearly intended to ensure enough calories to stay warm. Afterwards, we retrieved our bags temporarily, used the somewhat primitive shower facilities in the basement of the check-in building, and prepared to return to the ice hotel for the night. We found that sundown had caused a spectacular transformation: all the surfaces, whether the curved white snow walls or the ice columns, chandeliers and furniture, had taken on a brilliant radiance. This was magnified by the addition of artificial light, as fibre-optic lighting was cleverly deployed throughout the hotel to amplify the colour spectrums created by the ice itself: aquas, violets, pinks, blues, greens. It was truly magical, and new guests wandered around awestruck.

Sarah and I were summoned to the chapel and given our bedding bags. They contained $800 high-tech sleeping bags that seemed to weigh almost nothing. They were mummy-shaped, with no room to spare, with a hood to be brought up over our heads once we were ensconced. We were told that cotton, with its high moisture retention, was the worst thing to keep on our bodies if we did not want to get cold. While it seemed counterintuitive, we were told that nudity was best to retain body heat in the bags, designed to withstand temperatures as low as −35°C. For hygienic reasons, we were given a fresh little pillow that fit inside the hood, and a clean liner that felt like silk or micro-fibre, and prevented any bodily contact with the inside of the bag. Our instructors told us we should get into the bags fully dressed, and take our clothes—all our clothes—off inside, pushing to the bottom the items we wanted to be warm in the morning (as well as our bottles of water, which would freeze on the ice bedside table). Sarah and I looked at each other apprehensively as we received these instructions. I was a little squeamish, but the pillow and liner smelled lovely and freshly laundered, and I began to relax.

Our room was called the New York Suite. With "I ❤ New York" and the Stars and Stripes carved into the snow walls; an all-ice Statue of Liberty beamed internal light down on us. Under her diamond grin, we tried valiantly to undress inside the narrow bag liners. Very shortly, we were reduced to helpless giggles as we struggled to follow the instructions. We both regretted wearing long-sleeved pullover T-shirts that required major contortions to remove. Patrolling the halls for guests in trouble, a staff member heard the laughter and came to check up on us. "Would you like some help?" she asked discreetly from the other side of the curtain. "Yes, please," we gasped. She kindly came and helped us straighten out our bags, zipping us in. She turned off the lights that emanated eerily from under our bed. We were lying on an ice platform, topped with a thin queen-sized mattress covered with reindeer skins.

My nose began to feel cold in the first few minutes, but I covered it briefly with my hand and the sheet, and shortly I generated a bubble of warm air around the hood. Once my body accepted that it could not indulge in its usual nocturnal restlessness, I fell into a deep sleep, breathing the crystalline air with pure pleasure. It seemed only moments later that a staff member was waking us up with a choice of hot chocolate or coffee. I felt I had never had such as wonderful sleep—as if, somehow, the air there had more oxygen in it or something. I felt totally refreshed, and we tucked into a hearty breakfast with gusto.

The Quebec ice hotel has attracted fashion shoots, *Gourmet* magazine and a pop-rock video. This side of the business is a major revenue stream for the ice hotel, but it is also symptomatic of the growing place of ice imagery in popular culture. The experience was so real to me that I could not believe that Desbois and his crew would simply close the hotel on March 1 and watch it melt until the next year, when they would start building it all over again.

After the ice hotel in Quebec, others popped up in Finland and Alaska. The Aurora Ice Hotel at Chena Hot Springs Resort near Fairbanks[5] was much smaller, with just six rooms, but according to press accounts, its first visitor was just as thrilled with the experience as I had been in Quebec.

Artisans and sculptors from as far away as Turkey worked on its carving, shaping and sanding everything from towers and pillars to ice-crystal chandeliers lit by optic fibres. The Aurora was different from the other ice hotels in that its proprietors did not sign on for the ephemeral nature of the construction. They simply didn't like the idea of letting their entire hotel slip quietly into the closest body of water every spring. The Aurora Hotel was therefore built with 4,270 metres of 2.5-centimetre tubing pumping antifreeze chilled to 20-below zero at 1,500 litres a minute to keep the structure frigid—and rigid—all summer.

CARNAVAL

If you time a visit to the Ice Hotel Quebec-Canada in the first two weeks of February, you can also take in Canada's largest ice event: Quebec City's winter carnival, Le Carnaval de Québec. This event, which celebrated its fiftieth anniversary in 2004, attracts more than fifty-five thousand people to its annual parade in freezing weather. It is a hardy tradition that busloads of young people arrive from far and wide to pile into hotel rooms and party themselves into the ground. There are games, shows, maple syrup taffy pulls and crowd appearances by Bonhomme Carnaval, the event's big white mascot. He is a stylized snowman with a toque (a knitted hat with a tassel) on his head, and the traditional arrow-weave *"ceinture flêchée"* around his waist. Bonhomme is often accompanied by six Duchesses and a Queen of Carnaval—I remember how proud we were as kids when my cousin was chosen a *"duchesse,"* even though we lived far away from Quebec City and never made it there for the winter event.

In recent years, political correctness has made a dent in Bonhomme's harem, but he still treks out valiantly, the life of the party, overseeing his icy domain and the warm revelry that takes place throughout its duration. For all I know, teenagers are still carefully injecting vodka with a syringe into every orange in the bag they take on the bus to Quebec City. The wild side of Carnaval seems to have faded quite a bit, though, with the advent of more sophisticated and thoughtful events and the opening of a magnificent Museum of Civilization on the waterfront. You are more likely now to see families with small children enjoying the events, riding on horse-drawn sleighs through the streets and dipping into a trough of snow-cooled maple treats in the Old Town—a lovely relic of a simpler time. The Quebec City tradition includes an ice palace, which welcomes visitors. In 2003, the ice palace was made up of sixty-five hundred 34-kilogram blocks of ice.

St. Paul, Minnesota, also has a winter carnival. Its ice palace tradition, while not as reliable as Quebec City's, is more grandiose when it succeeds. But one difference between the two cities is that in Quebec City, they build an ice palace every year, because their weather permits it. The supply of ice is not a problem, nor is maintaining the palace once it is built. In St. Paul, the necessary conditions are rarely in place all at once. The 2004 palace was the first in twelve years, and the first since 1941 to permit visitors on the inside. There was a gap of thirty-four years between the 1941 palace and a modest 3,000-block one built in 1975. Two attempts in between suffered ignominious meltdowns and collapses. In the eyes of Jerry Ritter, an architect with the Twin Cities offices of the Leo A. Daly firm, which designed the 2004 ice palace, "If it happened every year, it wouldn't be as great."[6] When asked: "Why do we build ice palaces—these massively fragile, magically preposterous, strangely magnetic structures of frozen lake water?" Bob Olsen, who built the 1975 ice palace in St. Paul, said: "Because . . . we . . . can." Olsen claims to be one of two American "ice palace historians"—surely one of the more esoteric occupations around. Visiting an ice palace can be a traumatic experience— or at least F. Scott Fitzgerald thought so. He published a truly creepy story called "The Ice Palace" in a May 1920 issue of the *Saturday Evening Post.*

Ironically, the St. Paul tradition is said to have begun as the result of an insult sometime in the 1880s from a New York-based reporter, who called the place "another Siberia, unfit for human habitation in the winter." In 1886, the indignant citizens of St. Paul decided to show the world that Minnesota was a great, vigorous place and that ice and snow were assets, not liabilities. They looked north for inspiration: Montreal had a long tradition of ice-based festivities, dating back to the French colony. When the British took over after the Conquest in 1789, they continued the tradition and expanded on it. In 1883, Montreal built a magnificent ice palace, attracting fifteen thousand foreign tourists—an enormous influx at that time, when populations were much smaller, and travel much more onerous.

The burghers of St. Paul thought they could do even better—and they did. In 1886, they took advantage of a smallpox epidemic that had killed two thousand people in Canada, and caused the U.S. authorities to quarantine the province of Quebec, to spirit the ice-palace architects away and to build the first American ice palace. St. Paul's first ice palace was almost twice as big as Montreal's, and one hundred thousand people showed up to see the cornerstone laid. One of the reasons it was such a spectacular success was its groundbreaking use of electric lights. No one had ever seen so much artificial light in one place.

Moira F. Harris, in her book *Fire and Ice: The History of the St. Paul Winter Carnival*, wrote that the 1886 ice palace could easily have served as a city hall, courthouse, railroad station or post office had it been built in granite, but "electric lights, unusual at the time, created a rainbow effect on the ice blocks. When the ritual storming of the palace took place, rockets and other fireworks lit the sky, causing the ice to shine in spectacular colors, bringing magic to a winter night."

The road to success was not easy. Peg Meier of the *Star Tribune* told the story of the vicious rumours spread by "some evil-minded opponent of the ice palace scheme and an arch enemy to St. Paul's greatness." The first rumour was that St. Paul was too cold for ice, and that it would crack and crumble away if left outside. In a medieval-style castle 55 metres long, 49 metres wide, with a central tower 32 metres tall, that was a cause for some concern. But then the second rumour started: ice-bugs were worming away at each of the palace's twenty thousand ice blocks: "Everyone knows what a fearsome thing the ice-bug is, and how—small and almost microscopic in itself—it riddles the most solid blocks of ice with tiny holes until the whole thing becomes as substanceless and weak as so much tobacco ash," *Northwest Magazine* joked. Meier wrote that both rumours had been debunked, as well as the one that the palace been burned one day by spontaneous combustion.

Crowds poured into the elaborate ice palace, and the St. Paul's winter carnival was off to a great start: 150,000 people paid 25 cents each to get in, and the organizers were pleased to discover that they had made a profit from the very first year of its existence. In subsequent years, the ice castle was even bigger and fancier. In 1888, it stood nearly fourteen stories high, and six thousand people attended an Episcopalian wedding inside it. In 2004, one million visitors filed through, and security was a high priority, particularly on the day that the National Hockey League's All-Stars were in the building.

If the citizens and volunteers of modern St. Paul were proud of their ice-palace tradition, they were no longer alone in using it to attract tourism. Elaborate and massive as it was (a value of $8.4 million for a building that would only exist for seventeen days, including fifty-five thousand hours of donated time from the construction trades) the St. Paul palace was dwarfed by the huge Harbin Ice and Snow Festival grounds in northeastern China.[7] Fortunately for St. Paul, it didn't really have to compete: very few of its visitors would ever be able to go to China. But if they did, they would be amazed: it is kind of a Chinese Las Vegas in ice. Embedded coloured neon lights give lurid appeal to a whole city of ice: Egyptian pyramids, an Arc de Triomphe, and every kind of pillar, tower and windmill you can imagine, all carved out of huge blocks of ice. In fact, Harbin is known in China as "The City of Ice." In 2004, Air India even engaged Chinese artists to build a 15-metre-high ice replica of the Taj Mahal, hoping to woo Chinese tourists to India.[8] The structures glowed in shades of purple, pink, blue and green.[9]

Ice Lanterns

As part of its winter ice event, Harbin offers an Ice Lantern Festival. These ice lanterns (*bingdeng*) are descended from the fishermen's tradition of hollowing out blocks of ice for use as

hurricane lamps/lampshades. Manchurian ice lanterns had
been used to shield candles from the wind, with the added benefit of softly diffusing the light, for more than three hundred
years. Finland has a similar tradition, and its beauty is hard to
describe. Before I ever became aware of what Harbin was doing,
ice lanterns already had a sentimental value for me: my mother
had made them for my winter wedding. I loved the way they
had echoed my happiness the night I was married, as they
glowed with soft, warm light in the snowbanks along the path
leading to my sister's country house.

Harbin's Ice Lantern Festival is nothing like the simple, elegant presentation my mother developed, using only a child's
beach pail and her home freezer. It is a huge event, held from
January to March in a park named for a Chinese war hero. It
started off modestly enough in 1963, when Harbin residents
organized the first modern ice lantern show. Using moulds,
they created shapes, which they illuminated with candles. The
simple shapes quickly blossomed into fantastic pieces, from
the size of a mouse to the size of a city bus, filling the heart of
the city. The carvers use chainsaws to harvest huge blocks from
the frozen Songhua River and haul them to the park. They
weld them together with water to create sculptures of the U.S.
Capitol Building, Russian churches, ice pagodas, bridges,
landscapes and scenes from opera and theatre. Carvers come
from all over the world, including Great Britain, Malaysia and
the United States, to participate. At full tilt, the sound of
chainsaws and merry shouts fills the air as the sculptors work
frantically to finish their work by the deadline.

The Harbin ice lanterns have become world famous and

they go on tour from Europe to Vegas; there is a special relationship between the Chinese organizers and the people of Hortus Haren, in the Netherlands, who first welcomed guests from Harbin to their Mikado Hall in 1996. The following year, excited by the combination of ice with Oriental art, the town of Hortus Haren made an even bigger commitment, building a custom-designed cold hall from polyurethane panels and artificial cooling equipment to maintain the ice lanterns at exactly the right level of chill. *Image in Ice, the Frozen Art of China* was a huge hit, attracting crowds from all over Europe. In 1999, an eighteen-person team from Harbin created fifty illuminated animal carvings from Lapland lake ice. By this time, its fame had spread to North America, and Vegas had to have it: in the millennial year, Harbin's ice-lantern art became a star attraction at the Fremont Street Experience in Las Vegas. It had to happen.

Ice-Carving Contests

There must be something about wielding a chainsaw and a chisel on a material as clear and brittle as ice. People seem to be crazy about it. Ice-carving contests have grown to become an indispensable part of ice tourism. They are a challenge to mount: usually, people work with 136-kilogram blocks of ice that take at least three or four days to freeze. It's hard to work with, and often just when you think you have finally achieved success, a piece falls off, or the temperature changes, and it begins to melt. The carvings range from masterpieces of skill to monster pieces of kitsch.

Audiences all over the world seem to love ice sculptures, particularly in Japan. The Japanese military (or the closest thing to it) in Sapporo, northern Japan, has long used ice sculpture to soften its image. For fifty years now, members of the Japanese Self-Defence Force (SDF) have been hauling vast amounts of snow out of the mountains around the city, and pitching in to carve ice animals, figurines and palaces, in an effort to convince the public they are really good guys.

Only days before being sent to the front in Iraq, the largest deployment of Japanese troops since World War II, the SDF's men were busily carving ice in Sapporo. In 1954, at a time when there was still a lot of suspicion about militarization in Japan, this was pure spin-doctoring, trying to improve the organization's image. But in 2004, as the Snow Festival had grown to become the biggest event in Sapporo's yearly tourist calendar, the much-loved festival became the site of a show-down. Crowds showed up to protest the SDF's involvement in the War in Iraq: angered, the military threatened not to carve the ice. The threat worked. The protest stopped dead in its tracks, and the ice carvings appeared after all: a 50-foot Parthenon, for the Athens Olympic Games, and, for the base-ball-crazy Japanese, a huge bust of Hideki Matsui, who plays for the New York Yankees.

Japan was not the only place where politics has played a role in ice-carving contests. In Quebec City, carvers from fifty-six countries participated in the competition linked to Carnaval 2003. If you hadn't been paying attention, you might have thought the skilful Belgians were the ice carvers to beat. If experience were all that mattered, you would have been right. But everybody's attention was focused on some brand-new players who became the sentimental favourites the minute they appeared on the scene: the Kenyans—and they had a message to bring to the world.

Team leader Michael Kaloki, a twenty-eight-year-old free-lance television producer from Nairobi, had been to Quebec City's Carnaval when he was a student at Ryerson University in Toronto. That was where he first realized that ice was a material that could be sculpted. But how was the team going to become a great ice-carving machine in ice-poor Nairobi? Kaloki threw himself on the mercy of Mark Chira, the executive chef at the old Hemingway hangout, Nairobi's Hotel Stanley. Chef Chira was willing to help, but he had shocking news for the would-be carvers: he would fill his biggest stockpots with water and freeze it to give them a chance to try out carving rhinos and crocodiles, but they would have to work in his cold room, at a chilly −18°C. They threw on a few sweaters and coped with that.

They were in for a still bigger shock: in Quebec City, they would have to work outdoors, at temperatures hovering around −30°C. Their layered sweaters—all they could find in Nairobi—were just not going to cut it. Happily, the hospitable organizers loaned them real cold-weather gear, and they got on with carving their message to the world: an ice rhino with the name Kikiri, the Kiswahili word for "struggling." The rhino represented the struggle for his own species, but also for the disappearing ice on Mount Kilimanjaro and Mount Kenya, with its ensuing water shortage. The idea that tropical Africa has so much to lose with global warming and climate change is a new thought to most of us.

NOWHERE IS FAR ANYMORE

The farthest reaches of the planet—Ellesmere Island, Patagonia, Antarctica, the North Pole—are all becoming fashionable tourist destinations. For example, the January 4, 2004, edition of the *New York Times* devoted a full page to "Homage to Patagonia." It is somewhat incongruous to see tour buses against a pristine backdrop like Shadow Bay, the point of departure for ferries to remote glaciers. The falling Argentine peso has made this inaccessible place, Ushuaia, the world's southernmost city, a tourist attraction on a scale it has never seen before—to the point where it can be hard get into the most desirable hotels. The whole notion of being able to visit such remote places with all the modern conveniences, to suit your own schedule, is a startling and relatively new one. Ushuaia has always been nicknamed *"fin-del-mondo"* and thought of as the end-of-the-world place.

El Calafate is known for its spectacular glaciers, trekking or horseback riding on a sheep ranch; the magnificent Mount Fitzroy, at 3,350 metres of sheer granite and ice; Puerto Madryn for its whales and penguins; and the remote resort of Los Notros, overlooking the Perito Moreno Glacier, for splendid isolation in luxury (but not total isolation; for email junkies, there is an iMac in the bar). The Upsala Glacier calves into Lago Argentino in a lacy and unforgettable concoction of indigos and brilliant aquamarines.

Patagonia, Tasmania and New Zealand are the most frequent departure points for expeditions to Antarctica, a destination once reserved for hardy scientists and mad adventurers. In the pre-Christmas party season of 2003, I met at least six people at cocktail parties who told me they were setting sail for the southernmost continent, the new epitome of exotic tourism.

The coldest, windiest, driest, iciest and highest of all the world's land masses, Antarctica also has the longest nights, the longest days and the greatest concentration of wildlife. All these conditions are largely unchanged since humans first landed there. The surrounding frozen ocean varies from 3 million square kilometres in summer to 19 million square kilometres in winter. The continent is twice the size of Australia, and experienced a record low temperature of −89.2°C in 1983.

National Geographic Adventure magazine has ranked a Fathom Expeditions journey to Antarctica as one of the twenty-five greatest adventure trips in the world. Dave German, president and expedition leader, said their experiences emphasize wildlife, history and ice. He decided to form his own Antarctic travel company after leading the expedition that shot the IMAX film *Shackleton's Antarctic Adventure*. The film is remarkable in its replication of Ernest Shackleton's odyssey. Fathom offers travellers unique experiences that change their lives. More than ten thousand people land in the Antarctic each year, and more travel through its surrounding waters.

John Macfarlane, editor of *Toronto Life* magazine, made the trip with Butterfield and Robinson as one of one hundred passengers on the luxury cruise ship *Orion* in January 2004. He loved the experience of going out on side trips in the Zodiac over the six days they were moored in Antarctic waters, exploring the ice and the wildlife. He was exhilarated by the twenty-four hours of brilliant daylight, the range of crystalline blues, whites and silvers of the ice, and the abundance of wildlife. He saw hundreds of thousands of penguins, walked on a beach one day with at least two hundred elephant seals and saw one whale up close. At one point, he came face to face with a ferocious leopard seal—a somewhat frightening experience when he recalled that Shackleton had described an attack on one of his men by just such a seal.

Macfarlane enjoyed the combination of pure pleasure and learning, of experiencing the startling beauty of the place first-hand and hearing from the resident experts on the ship. Naturalists, ornithologists and geologists answered questions and discussed facts the neophyte passengers had never thought about. The reality of geological time was a revelation: Antarctica separating from Gondwanaland, the primeval continent of which it was a part at the equator. The displacement of tectonic plates happened over hundreds of millions of years, at 2 inches a year, exactly the rate of human fingernail growth. This explains why fossils of tropical fauna and flora are now lodged in the ice around the South Pole.

In two days' sailing each way, through the Drake Passage and six days' sailing around the Antarctic Peninsula, Macfarlane saw one vessel that looked like a working ship of some sort, one floating hotel and two sailing yachts. One of these, a 40-footer with two Frenchmen aboard, provided the enlightening spectacle of two legs of lamb hanging off the stern, relying on the salt water of the chilly southern ocean to cure the meat.

Macfarlane, an urbane, sophisticated journalist and publisher, is also an experienced wilderness canoeist and has travelled in the Arctic. What he remembers most is "the impression of vastness, desolation, and more ice than you've ever seen in your life—which is all the more interesting when you get your head around the idea that it has taken thousands of years for this ice to accumulate."

He says the trip made him a little more optimistic because "The world is behaving well in Antarctica. It's being managed for science and peace." Macfarlane found that the rules are taken very seriously. Everyone takes great care to prevent contamination of the pristine Antarctic: the Orion crew scrubbed each person's boots before and after visits to the mainland (they stayed on the boat at night). The dog teams that took Roald Amundsen to the pole would be forbidden on the continent today.

Still, an Antarctic or an Arctic expedition is not yet just a matter of routine. A careful reading of the cruise brochures shows that they always say they "hope to" visit each destination point. Exact routes and programs are always subject to weather and ice conditions; visits to scientific research stations always depend on final permission, which may be withheld. These Antarctica cruises remain a high-end, luxury affair, although there are more modest, down-to-earth experiences than the five-star *Orion*. Quark Expeditions, for example, uses former Russian icebreakers to offer expeditions that focus on learning, with extraordinary intellectual and logistical resources around both the north and south polar circuits. The expedition diaries for these cruises are freely available on the web, and offer a wealth of virtual experience.

POLAR BEAR MECCA

For many years, the town of Churchill, Manitoba, has been the gateway to the world's best polar bear–viewing opportunities.

Although there are other places around the North to see polar bears, especially in Alaska and Russia, nowhere do so many of these magnificent animals show up where people can get a good look a them. One reason for this is the particular way that Hudson Bay freezes up near Churchill—with an influx of fresh water that freezes earlier than the saltier waters of the bay in general. With the warming trend, the bears are waiting longer and longer for the ice to show up so they can hunt ringed seals more easily. Therefore, this earlier-forming ice offers a very attractive place to start their eating season, after a long summer of living off their fat.

There are a whole range of excursions available out of Churchill, from the more crowded tundra wagon convoys that carry forty or more people at a time, to smaller, more exclusive outings with twelve or fewer people. All depend on large vehicles with tires at least 1.5 metres wide, high above the ground with observation platforms to allow photography. In many instances, the tundra buggies even have windows that open. The bears are used to these vehicles, which can provide opportunities to photograph them from amazingly close up. In fact, the bears sometimes get too close, and the town of Churchill maintains a polar bear "jail" where they put troublesome bears that get too aggressive, or too close to the town. Unlike with humans, there is no due process and the bears get out of jail free; they are airlifted further into the wilderness before they do themselves or anyone else any harm.

Organizations like Earthwatch are encouraging wilderness tourists or ecotourists to participate in the intriguing study of polar-bear play fights, and to help them record observations:

noting how long each bout lasts, who plays with whom, and how intensely the bears play. The males are likely to confront each other "for real" to win females in the spring; but in the fall they grapple with each other on their hind legs, taking big swipes without hurting each other. Scientists want to know why: are they playing, establishing a social hierarchy, or just keeping in shape? As the bears spend more time without the ice they need to hunt, they must fast longer and they are exposed more to humans. No matter what is really going on, people love to watch the riveting action among these huge carnivores.

The Churchill excursions also bring people into contact with red and Arctic foxes, gyrfalcons, Arctic hares, snowy owls, willow ptarmigans and ravens, as well as the beautiful, stark, permafrost-rich tundra itself. Churchill is also part of a growing branch of ice tourism that centres on the idea of light—and particularly the famous aurora borealis and aurora australis, the northern and southern polar lights. The aurora borealis seems to appeal particularly to a Japanese clientele, among whom it takes on an aura of the sacred. Carson Schiffkorn owns the Inn on the River on the Teslin River east of Whitehorse, Yukon, near Johnson's Crossing. He is always amazed to see how much something that is taken for granted by Northerners can mean to someone who has never experienced it. The dancing curtain of coloured lights, mostly blue and green in the Far North (with the occasional appearance of rare red lights), results from charged particles from the sun, which follow the earth's descending magnetic field and crash into the upper atmosphere. The effect is dazzling, particularly in an ice-rich environment that can reflect the colours, and it is unique to the polar far ends of the earth. These kinds of ecotourism trips are not cheap—for example, a polar-bear excursion with Earthwatch out of Churchill, which would include the aurora, costs US$3,495 for six days.

Perhaps Fridtjof Nansen, the great Norwegian explorer, expressed it best: "In the flaming aurora borealis the spirit of space hovers over the frozen waters. The soul bows down before the majesty of night and death."

■ ■ ■

Despite the vast wilderness areas in North America, hikers are rarely more than about 32 kilometres from a road. By contrast, the new territory of Nunavut in Canada's Arctic has no roads outside its towns—none at all. Ellesmere Island is 4,000 kilometres from the nearest highway and 3,200 kilometres from the nearest tree. It can cost up to $20,000 to get a charter flight to go there. For a more modest ice adventure, you can call biologist Paul Wood in Newfoundland, and he will take you on a Wild Ice adventure including two days and one night for just $565 for two. It includes a bed and breakfast, a boat tour, a four-wheel-drive forest safari and a menu of chowder and home-smoked salmon with bottled iceberg water. You get to see icebergs up close in the water and caribou up close in the woods. Or you can simply go on your own to one of any number of beautiful national parks across North America. It's all there for the taking.

CHAPTER THIRTEEN

"Your biggest enemy is impatience.
You can't rush making a good sheet of ice."
—Dan Craig, Facilities Operations Manager, National Hockey League

SPORTS ON ICE

Imagine a prehistoric person, skating on a crystalline frozen lake in what is now Switzerland, around the year 3000 BC. He is wearing the fashionable sports accoutrement of the time: furs to protect him from the cold, and skates made from the leg bones of large animals, with holes bored in each end, tied on with leather straps. He is having a wonderful time . . . but probably, the skates are not tight enough—or the lake is not frozen enough. However it happens, those skates have come down to us in history as the oldest pair ever found . . . at the bottom of that Swiss lake.

Skating takes advantage of the physics of ice in a very clever way. The ice surface exposed to the air always carries a film of water that is ultrasmooth and silky. The physics of this water–ice film are endlessly fascinating to scientists because of how entirely different the film is from either water or ice itself, and because of the role it plays in everything from the design of airplane wings to the generation of lightning bolts. For our purposes here, suffice it to say that this silky film allows a skater to glide smoothly over what might otherwise not be such a smooth surface.

When I was a little girl, I dreamt of driving the Zamboni machine that repaired the ice between periods at hockey games, or halfway through figure skating sessions. This machine, I knew, dragged a wet cloth squeegee with hot water behind it, and filled in all the cuts and slashes that developed as skaters assaulted the ice, making it completely smooth and shiny again.

When I researched the origins of the Zamboni machine, I was shocked to discover that it was not a Canadian invention. Instead, Frank Zamboni was the Italian-American owner of the Iceland Skating Rink in Paramount, California, of all places! He patented his first successful ice machine in 1949, and it made its National Hockey League debut at the old Montreal Forum, one of the great pre-expansion hockey shrines in 1955, almost fifty years ago. Now American hockey fans are probably just as rabid as Canadian fans. But they are a lot lonelier. In Canada, hockey is almost a religion: about one in six Canadians play, and millions more watch the game on television. John Kerry is one of only about half a million Americans who play hockey; in contrast to Canadians, that makes about one in every six hundred! So hockey is 100 times more popular in Canada than in the United States.

When it comes to figure skating, however, the fan bases are much more comparable as a percentage of the population— perhaps because of the sexy female stars that keep coming out of the discipline, and the occasional scandal, such as the Tonya Harding story.

The National Hockey League's head ice guy, Dan Craig (all right, he's actually Manager, Facility Operations for the NHL, but I'll always think of him as the Ice Guy) taught me a lot about the kind of ice that professional sports demands. The enemy of quality ice—this surely comes as no surprise—is impatience. An ice sheet meant for hockey or figure skating (and they are not the same things) needs to be laid down patiently, controlling every little element to optimize athletic performance. And increasingly, to meet the demands of marketers and advertisers, it must also provide optimal brilliance and exposure for sponsor logos. This sometimes requires a delicate balancing act.

In the spring of 2004, Dan Craig's nightmare became a reality: Tampa Bay and San Jose both made the playoffs, which meant Dan and his team had to run back and forth between two hot-climate towns trying to keep the ice from going haywire on them. From the moment you open the doors to a professional arena, you are giving up control of the climate in the building. The warmer it is outside, and the longer the doors stay open, the tougher it is.

Dan is a hockey guy "from the school of life"; he learned his craft from high school on, as a part-time ice technician at the rink beside his school in Jasper, Alberta. He wound up running the recreation department in another small Alberta town, Bonneville, and learned a lot about water chemistry from managing the town pool. When he was offered the chance to take a course, he opted for a rink management course, and found his true love. At the time, the Edmonton Oilers were the best team in hockey. Their farm team told them about the wonderful ice in Bonneville, and they recruited Dan and his team to run the Coliseum. The rest is ice history (celebrated most recently with NHL's Heritage Classic game in November 2003 with outdoor ice produced by hometown boy Dan Craig and his team).

Dan's team kept on doing things just the way they had in northern Alberta. One day the "big guys" said they had to use de-ionized water from then on; Dan said he didn't think so . . . his team was number one for ice quality in the NHL, and they weren't going to jeopardize that. Dan says there are really just three things to remember about making a successful ice sheet for hockey: density, glide and clarity. "Don't ever mix them up," he says, "they go in that order. When you use pure water that is de-ionized or reverse osmosis, you reverse that formula, and you put clarity first." Bad idea, apparently, especially with the heavier, faster hockey players we have today, and the more sophisticated skates they wear. Pure water was great for brilliance, but it simply doesn't hold up to the density requirements for this new generation of players and equipment.

Hockey players want hard, fast ice—that's where glide comes in. This means keeping the ice at somewhere between 7.7 and −5.5°C—anything higher and the players feel as though they are struggling through sand. Figure skaters, on the other hand, care less about speed and more about grip as they push off to do their airborne manoeuvres.

"If your foot is stuck in the ice for one one-thousandth of a second, you have a problem. It's only the top thirty-seconds of an inch, but it feels like a magnet and you can't twist your foot out of it," says Dan. You have to strike exactly the right air balance between temperature and humidity to achieve the right ice texture. That's why Dan starts work at 5 a.m., and checks the data religiously on his laptop from all the NHL arenas where games are taking place that day. "If you lose your building in the first two or three hours of the day, it's a real battle. You have to keep the engineers on top of building control." He adds, "What makes good drinking water does not necessarily make good ice."

Great hockey ice depends on nucleating agents—minerals in the water that cause it to crystallize in a certain way. Teams get used to the particular feel and chemistry of their home ice, and the idea of "home-ice advantage" goes well beyond the fans cheering you on. In the past, developing a skill for skating on ice that was different from anywhere else really was a strategic advantage—and teams like the Boston Bruins in their old arena used it. Often, Dan is interviewed in the pre-game show for hockey junkies. They know how important his work is to the outcome for their beloved team, and he just keeps on trying to kill any home-ice advantage by making consistent, high-quality ice everywhere in the NHL.

Ice-quality reports are filed for every period of every game and critiqued before and after by each and every team that uses a given facility: outside air, inside air, humidity, ice-surface temperatures, ice-thickness reports, temperature of flood water, speed of resurfacing for two machines, when they changed the blades on the Zamboni, the ice surface at the edge of the boards (the Zamboni can't cut the last inch and a half)—it never ends, and Dan Craig and his people are constantly accountable. It's like the balance between church and state: tricycle racers, sumo wrestlers, baton twirlers—well, nothing against them, but they exist on sufferance. The ice is for the hockey players, and Dan Craig never, ever forgets that.

ICE FISHING

When it comes to ice fishing, that too tends to be a cross-border story: proportionally many more Canadians than Americans do it, but it is very big in all the states along the forty-ninth parallel, as well as in Alaska. Every place has its own definitions, though: in Wisconsin, it's an ice shanty; in Minnesota, it's an icehouse; and where I come from, it's a shack. Minnesota's Fishing Hall of Fame has a large section devoted to ice fishing, part of an industry that sells $2.4 billion worth of hunting and fishing equipment in the U.S. every year. There are an awful lot of ice-fishing fans, but they don't get much media coverage in the big cities. For example, the Jaycees in Brainerd, Minnesota, get 12,000 anglers from all over to their Ice Fishing Extravaganza. It employs 350 volunteers (Jaycees, the Girl Scouts, Boy Scouts and Woodland Good Samaritan Home) doing everything from hole drilling (100 volunteers take four hours to drill 24,000 holes in the ice at Hole-in-the-Day Bay) to running kiddie Olympics for 350 kids with a hot-air balloon overhead. The Brainerd Snodeos Snowmobile Club kicks off the process by making grid patterns with their sleds, and the augers follow. Thirty tents and booths offer beef sticks, fur hats, mini doughnuts, pizza, burgers and brats.

Meanwhile, in central Indiana, there is a bunch of guys who have started missing the Super Bowl for their Summit Lake ice-fishing extravaganza. They hang out at www.indianainfo.net and www.iceshanty.com normally, but on Super Bowl weekend, they have started getting together for a "braggin' rights" tournament. These guys are tough: they compete with a bunch of geese for the lake's 850 acres of ice. The geese interfere constantly with ice formation by landing on the water before the ice can solidify. In patches where there is open water, the Indiana fishermen take their chances with summer tackle—to the alarm of the authorities who end up rescuing casualties of thin ice on the edges of the "goose hole."

Lake of the Woods, on the Minnesota–Ontario border, is one of the first lakes to freeze up reliably in the winter; it is famous for its walleye, sauger and perch. Once the season starts, the motels fill up for 100 kilometres around the lake. Some two thousand ice-fishing shacks go up on Lake Mille Lacs the minute it freezes over, and it is very popular with the Twin Cities crowd (from Minneapolis–St. Paul). Occasionally, shallow lakes like Round Lake near South Shore, North Dakota (2 metres at its deepest) can suffer a complete kill if they freeze right through. The state's Game, Fish and Parks Department knows how much economic activity ice fishing brings in: it keeps restocking Round Lake, as well as Punished Woman Lake in the northeast.

Ice fishing is a world unto itself. If you saw the 1993 movie *Grumpy Old Men,* the kind of shack you saw then—a few boards over a hole in the ice—has probably met one of two fates in recent years: either it has been subjected to what I would call the deep-woods equivalent of a Martha Stewart treatment, or it has given way to a kind of guerrilla portability, driven by an ice-fishing icon named Dave Genz.

To be sure, there are still guys like Dale Bowman, a

Michigan reporter and angler who has his own website (www.dalebowman.com). He says he and his buddy Mike Arndt still like to keep it simple: they skip church on winter Sundays and drag a tent, two buckets of gear and a minnow bucket out onto a subdivision pond in the nexus of Woodridge/Naperville/Bolingbrook. They don't have a fancy shack, but Mike does have a few tricks up his sleeve. He sets up a gimmick, baited with golden minnows for the more active fish. This wind-driven "tip-up" jigs the bait for him, and makes his set-ups look like oilrigs in Texas. He uses regular tip-ups for less active fish, with just a "plain shiner" or a "roach." The catch ranges from bluegill to monster yellow perch and crappie. Mike has been fishing with his buddies on this pond since he was eight years old, and there is nothing those boys like better than staring at that hole in the ice and talking to each other sideways for hours on end.[1]

For those on the Martha Stewart end of things, it used to be enough to put up a few boards over a hole, but not anymore. The shacks that are staying in place are morphing into little palaces on ice—and right when the ice is becoming a lot less reliable. It's not unusual anymore to see shacks with windows and curtains, couches, TVs, satellite dishes and kitchenettes. Some families spend their whole weekends out on the ice, jigging their lines into an ice trench between the comfy seats. This trend seems to be bigger in Canada than in the United States and was the subject of hilarious but affectionate satirical coverage on the web-based CBC Radio 3 and on Rick Mercer's show on CBC Television in 2003.

Dave Genz, the ice-fishing legend, has worked his passion

into a whole business. He lives in Haven Township on the Mississippi River and is credited with modernizing ice fishing. While this has earned him a coveted berth in Minnesota's Fishing Hall of Fame and the attention of autograph hounds across ice-fishing country, you'll have to judge for yourselves whether or not this is a good thing.

At Joe's Sporting Goods in St. Paul they do a thriving business in newfangled ice-fishing paraphernalia. The hottest stuff used to come from Sweden, but now the Canadians and the Americans have caught up and surpassed the Swedes. Holographic lures imitate the flashy movement of fish scales under water. People used to use a simple wooden jiggle stick with a bobber and a length of line, or cut off the end of an ordinary fishing rod. Now there are customized ice-fishing rods, with sensitive tips and strong handles to fight the fish. The Buzz Stix rod even has a little battery-operated motor that will jig for you. The boys like to talk about which glow jigs work best where—green ones and red ones have been working well on Lake of the Woods and Red Lake, but not around Lake Walker.

Some people, hyped on high-speed Internet at home, are no longer willing to sit around and wait to see if there are any fish under the ice who might bite: these are the Dave Genz fans. They have adopted his ideas about portability and technology to locate the fish. They use underwater video cameras and GPS locaters, although they can't troll the way they would in the summer. Along with the guides who serve them, they now use a portable shack called the Fish Trap, invented by Dave Genz and mass produced (Dave's wife, Patsy, used to sew them up on her home machine). They set it up wherever the locaters tell them the fish are. They use snowmobiles to get there faster. And the anglers use their cell phones to tell their friends. Some worry that the ice can no longer protect enough fish to make this sustainable. It's not the way Grandpa used to do it, but it's a lot more efficient.

One thing that has also become more efficient, however, is the ability of the ice to trick people—in part because it is melting earlier and more often as the climate warms. All winter long in 2003, my Google ice alerts popped up and let me know: people were being rescued off the ice from Lake Erie, Lake St. Clair, in Ohio, Minnesota, Wisconsin, Pennsylvania and upstate New York. Every year, dozens of people misjudge the ice, or get cocky because they've had one too many, and end up crashing through it. If people don't stick to the marked ice roads, trucks can go down into the lake very easily—and they do. Needless to say, this can be deadly, especially after a few drinks. In the best-case scenario, if this happens to you and if you do not drown, you may have half an hour. But if the weather is very cold and you are very wet, you are in deep trouble. As we have seen in previous chapters, the behaviour of ice is not always predictable. Rescuing yourself or someone else who has fallen through ice can be a life-threatening proposition.

To add insult to injury, everybody takes a dim view of ice incidents: they'll rescue you, all right. But you can forget about getting your pickup truck, ATV or snowmobile back if it sinks into a lake. The insurance company won't honour your policy, the cops will charge you an arm and a leg—if they deign to bring your vehicle up from the shallows or the deep, and you'll probably get fined for polluting the water with oil and gas. And yet, people risk their lives and property on the ice all the time.

■ George Sailer tells Sara Ivry about being rescued from an ice floe in Lake Erie in the *New York Times Magazine*, February 15, 2004

"Rescues happen just about every year there's ice. The Coast Guard doesn't encourage you to go out; they say it's never safe. People don't pay a whole lot of attention to them. There have been ice fishermen since time began. We didn't know what to expect when we climbed into the copter, but there was no reaming us out or anything. When you have to depend on somebody to pull your tail out of the fire, you feel kind of sheepish about it. I don't know if the Coast Guard saved our lives, but they sure made it more convenient than standing out there.

"I can't get real enthused about going out again. I think about it, about the good times we've had on the ice. But you start to wonder if it's worth it. I miss it. There's something about competing with nature—that's what you're doing, really, when you hunt or fish. It's something that gets in your blood. As I said, I've lived along the lake, fished on it all my life. Still, I haven't been out this year."

Firefighters undergo specialized training regularly to make sure they know exactly what to do when the need arises. Here are a few tips on how to be safe on the ice:

1. Never count on the ice being of equal thickness everywhere. If you fall through, kick your feet until your body is horizontal.

2. Once you are out, roll away before standing up.
3. Use tools that will help you save others: a tree branch, milk jug or one of the buoys along the dock, for example.
4. Call for help.

Massachusetts firefighter Joseph W. Dupras Sr., concerned that four to five thousand people drown every year, many as a result of falling through the ice, decided to do something about it. His patented Personal Retriever—a kind of big soft Frisbee on a rope —is now carried on rescue vehicles in Middleboro, Randolph, East Bridgewater, West Bridgewater and Pembroke. It only takes a few seconds for a person weighed down by winter clothing or sports equipment to sink, and often rescuers are themselves trapped by unstable ice. The Personal Retriever is likely to save rescuers as well as victims.

ICE CLIMBING, HIKING AND HELI-SKIING

Among the more exotic ice activities, extreme ice climbers, hikers and heli-skiers fall under my definition of adrenaline junkies. Something drives them to need sensations that are simply not available in everyday life. I think it must be the need to experience exquisite and rare beauty, along with the actual physical sensation of pumping adrenaline, the body's response to stress and the need for action.

Take Guy Lacelle, one of the world's leading ice climbers— a quiet, unassuming athlete who inspires admiration among all his peers. He has established and repeated most of the extreme climbs in the Canadian Rockies, as well as elsewhere in the world. He climbs almost exclusively solo, spending fifty to sixty days on the ice each winter. If there is no ice available, he will climb rock faces; he has given up his former job and now plants trees in the summer, so as not to affect his availability for the right ice. Like many people who love that lifestyle, Lacelle spends a lot of time in Banff and Canmore, Alberta.

On the highway between the two towns, a pretty little ribbon of a waterfall is clearly visible, splashing down the cliff face, 150 metres high. A watchful passenger will see it clearly. The driver, needing to keep eyes on the road, will not have time. When this little waterfall freezes, it becomes a solid, freestanding column no bigger around than your arms can reach in many places. This is when it earns its reputation as the Terminator. It is one of the world's most difficult and challenging ice climbs.

The Terminator attracts daredevil climbers from all over the world. The dangerous and thrilling practice of climbing frozen waterfalls has become a global contest, with both amateur and professional athletes exchanging the secret locations of crystal pillars as they race to be first or fastest to conquer them. Equipped with crampons, gaiters, helmet, runners, ice screws, rope, belay devices, harness, ice axe and the right clothing, an ice climber has to have a very good sense of how the ice will sliver, shatter or break away. The techniques look a lot like rock climbing, except that this rock is far more treacherous. With climbers whose adrenaline pumps particularly around frozen waterfalls, the appetite for danger is even higher: I have seen a climber put his arms around a slim little column of crystalline fresh ice which will probably melt later in the day, and sink his axe into it and head on up. The thrill of scrambling up something so fragile and transparent must be extraordinary, but many climbers cannot even articulate the feeling. I know I was terrified just watching.

The equipment available today is so much better than what has ever been available before, that many people have come to think that ice climbing is easy. They are in for a rude shock if they ever tackle some of the truly challenging climbs on their own. The great German ice climber Reinhold Messner collaborated in the making of the *Shackleton* film for PBS. He and two of his colleagues undertook to replicate Shackleton and his men's climb of the daunting mountains in South Georgia—but surely not their exhaustion after a terrifying sea voyage in a lifeboat from Elephant Island, months of acute cold, food shortages, inadequate clothing and nothing more than boat screws in their leather soles, and an awl. Messner and his colleagues were filmed making the climb; they are among the world's very best ice climbers, and they could not believe the effort required. They gained a profound respect for their predecessors—and a new appreciation of their high-end equipment.

In a completely different genre, my vote for most fun-loving ice athletes goes to *Chicks with Sticks*, a Colorado-based organization that helps women learn to climb with other women. Here is a testimonial from Leigh McGuigan, a *Chicks with Sticks* participant who probably speaks for all ice climbers: "It's easy to understand how climbing serves as a metaphor for challenges that require courage, strength and commitment, and many of us know the feeling of lasting confidence that comes from persevering one step at a time through a formidable physical challenge."

PRACTICAL CONSIDERATIONS FOR ICE ADVENTURES

If you insist on visiting places that are under the metal disk on your globe, such as Ellesmere Island or Antarctica, then you need professional advice to stay safe and warm. There is no shortage of high-tech gear and expert guidance available, although all of it is expensive. But even armchair travellers can enjoy learning about what they might need if they ever did decide to venture into ice country.

If, like me, you are an urban person who has to watch food intake, then working hard in the cold offers the great luxury of allowing you to consume a lot of calories. Kobalenko (*The Horizontal Everest*), who has probably logged more miles hauling a sledge on Ellesmere Island than anyone else on earth, found that when he first tried extreme cold weather expeditions, he needed about 7,000 calories a day, both to keep up his energy for hard spring sledding and to stay warm. In his colourful style, he wrote: "My jaw ached from chewing, I got hemorrhoids from all the activity of a supercharged metabolism, and I ran out of things I wanted to eat. Even a whole strawberry shortcake every day palls after a while." While the hardship involved in eating a strawberry shortcake a day tugs at the heartstrings, it really makes you wonder how the early explorers survived on their meagre rations and with such inadequate equipment. The addiction to extreme ice sports and activities is such that people tend to overlook the serious inconveniences and dangers they present.

There is no doubt that ice tourism is growing in popularity, and in many cases it really does provide safe access to exotic adventure. But as so often happens where ice is concerned, the exotic can quickly turn to the tragic. Few events embody this so keenly as the 1998 death of twenty-three-year-old Michel Trudeau, youngest son of Canada's former prime minister. Trudeau, an experienced mountaineer and guide, was swept off a trail above a deep mountain lake by a sudden avalanche. His body, weighed down by the heavy equipment packs he was carrying, remains in the frigid emerald depths of Lake Kokonee despite valiant attempts by expert cold-water divers to recover it. Every year at least fourteen people die in avalanches in Canada's stunningly beautiful, and addictive, backcountry.

Avalanches happen when different weights of ice and snow crystals build up in unstable layers. They can be triggered by something as innocent as a handclap. If you are ever travelling in an avalanche zone and you hear cannons going off, that is probably the sound of safety officials triggering deliberate avalanches to prevent unpredictable ones that might kill people. This is a whole branch of wilderness management, backed by specialized science. At the ice conference in St. John's, I met Pramod Kumar Satyawali, a full-time researcher at the Snow and Avalanche Study Establishment in Chandigrah, India. He assured me that his discipline is taken very seriously in his country, and that there are many research projects left to be undertaken before we will have a clear idea of what to do about avalanches. The old cannon trick is primitive, and hope springs eternal that more sophisticated avalanche methods will be developed.

CHAPTER FOURTEEN

"A hundred Irishmen, with Yankee overseers, came from Cambridge every day to get out the ice. They divided it into cakes and these, being sledded to the shore, were rapidly hauled off. Thus it appears that the sweltering inhabitants of Charleston and New Orleans, of Madras and Bombay and Calcutta, drink at my well."

—Henry David Thoreau at Walden Pond, Winter, 1846–47

BUSINESS AND PLEASURE

For many years, I spent a week every summer at a remote cottage, the only one on a little jewel of a lake in the granite of the Canadian Shield. I spent my days reading and relaxing—there was no electricity—and occasionally getting into the canoe to check out the beavers. Several times a day, the loons would swoop in and serenade us with their haunting cry. When we played classical music on a solar-battery-powered CD player, the loons would move closer, swaying to the music.

At night, I slept in a solid log structure that had been on the lake at least since the 1920s. Before it housed guests, it was a storage place for huge blocks of ice carved from the surface of the lake in the dead of winter, and packed with sawdust or hay to keep it cool all summer. The icehouse now has windows and occasionally a bossy squirrel who thinks he owns it. I marvel at the work that must have been involved in hauling heavy cakes of ice from the surface of this rock-walled lake to the icehouse, and then out a mile to the nearest road when it was needed. Only the fact that it was such a precious commodity at the time can have justified so much effort.

The men would have come through the forest with horses and carts, bringing their tools, chains and pulleys to bring out the ice. They would have tried to keep the surface clear of insulating snow that might soften the ice, and waited until it was anywhere from 20 to 60 centimetres thick. Then they would have scored it with a ploughlike tool, and sawed it carefully into checkerboard squares. There were different ways of extracting the ice, but perhaps they lifted it out in rafts of several still-linked squares, or individually. This lake is relatively sheltered from the wind by its high granite shore, but the work would still have been dangerous and physically demanding. The men would have had to spend time away from their families to get it done, but it was very important work, part of the annual cycle of the harvesting of nature's bounty to survive.

In my family, this era of the ice business evokes a story of great sadness that ends in hope. The story begins on February 10, 1934, long before I was born.[1] My great-uncle Emile Couture, forty-eight years of age, was a small farmer from St-Henri de Lévis, northwest of the Maine border. In those days, without a car, the 20-kilometre distance between the farm and the city was too far to commute, so he and a group of men would board at a rooming house in Quebec City while they worked on contract to an ice harvesting company. This had become a regular winter occupation for the farmers in the region: about six weeks a year, they would harness a pair of horses to a wagon, pack their work clothes and head up to work on the St. Lawrence River. In effect, the natural ice harvest was part of their lives as farmers, and certainly an important boost to their meagre incomes. When this story took place, the natural ice business was already dying, a farming business being replaced by a manufacturing business offering a safer, more reliable supply, and a guaranteed return on investment.

This February 10 was a day that great-uncle Emile's children would never forget. Their mother, Clara, a tiny woman barely 1.5 metres tall, was expecting the family's nineteenth child at the age of forty-four. Three elder sons were studying for the priesthood in Quebec City. The day dawned bitterly cold as the men set out to do their dangerous work on the river ice. They used huge crosscut saws, chains and plows, large tools that are dangerous if the ice shifts suddenly.

That morning, Emile's friends saw his pair of horses come to a sudden stop and his cart jerk behind them. They rushed to him, knowing immediately that there was something wrong. They found him spread-eagled on his wagon, stricken by a heart attack. They rushed him to a hospital, to no avail. He had made his last trip to the ice. Well into the night, the riderless horses came home, without Emile. My brave little Aunt Clara lost her nineteenth child shortly after birth, but her eighteen others all had good educations and did well. Not one of them every worked on the ice, and by the time they were adults, no one was even buying it in that form any more.

THE ICE OF KINGS
The ice trade in Canada at one time was significant, working in

symbiosis with the forest industry, which supplied the sawdust to insulate the ice cakes, and the seasonal labour. But Queen Victoria and her colonial representatives in Madras, Calcutta and Bombay all got their ice from Massachusetts.

Victoria was not the first monarch to demand ice for her table—it was a sought-after luxury in Mesopotamia four thousand years ago, where they built ice stores. The Greeks used snow to chill their wines, and Nero's slaves carried ice down from the Apennine Mountains. Nero liked to serve sorbets made with nectar, fruit pulp and honey at his decadent dinners.

The Chinese were cutting and storing ice in 1000 BC, and their emperors enjoyed desserts made from snow and ice, flavoured with fruits, wine and honey. Around 500 BC, the Egyptians and Indians would make ice on cold nights by putting out water in earthenware pots and keeping the pots wet. Sometimes they used saltpetre to hasten the process. Legend says the Chinese taught the Arab traders to combine syrup and snow into a kind of sorbet, and that they in turn taught the Venetians and Romans how to do it. Alexander the Great (fourth century BC) is said to have liked iced beverages. The earliest ice cream is probably the buffalo, cow and goat milk concoctions made with ground rice and fermented in Tang China between 907 and 618 BC. The stuff was thickened with flour and flavoured with camphor, a substance most of us today would associate with a strong medicinal smell. King Tang of Shang had ninety-four icemen on his staff, so it was definitely something to be taken seriously.

In the sixteenth century, Catherine de Medici of Florence married Henry II and became Queen of France, bringing her cookbooks and her Italian chefs, who made *sorbetto*. Charles I of England is said to have bought a recipe for "frozen milk" from a French chef. When eggs and cream became available, they were added so that the dessert became known as "cream ices." Around the same time, someone invented custard and began adding it to the cream ices. This remained an upper-class dessert until it could be produced more easily and in a stabler form that did not need as much expensive ice to store it frozen.

In the seventeenth century, wealthy British households began to build semisubterranean brick vaults to house ice. The servants would collect ice in the winter and put it into these vaults, packing the ice in salt and wrapping it in flannel strips. It would be stored underground to keep it frozen until summer.

At least three hundred years ago, the Turks were making *salep dondurma*, orchid ice cream, out of milk, sugar and orchid tubers (the tubers are called "fox testicles" in Turkish). They would bring ice and snow down from the Taurus Mountains to mix with salt and water to superchill the mixture and freeze it as they beat it with metal rods. As with all ice cream, this beating process prevents the crystals from clumping as they form, and gives the ice cream the smooth, creamy texture people love so much. To this day, the orchid ice cream is said to have aphrodisiac and other health benefits. Because of the high mucilage content of the tubers, its texture is so consistent and elastic that children make skipping ropes out of it, and people often eat it with a knife and fork.

THE BOSTON ICE KING

Frederic Tudor, the protagonist of Gavin Wightman's delightful book *The Frozen Water Trade*, was a nineteenth-century Boston entrepreneur, ultimately very successful in the natural ice business after a lifetime of fighting to convince investors, workers and customers it was a real business. At first, he was ridiculed: who would want to buy something that was freely available in winter and that would not keep?

With his associates, Tudor fostered important innovations that made the business more viable. He started out exporting to the Caribbean with his brother William, but soon discovered that the U.S. South was a more profitable market. In building two large icehouses in Havana and Charleston, South Carolina, he learned a great deal about the physics of heating and cooling. In the early days of Tudor's business, his men broke chunks of ice off lakes and rivers with pickaxes and sawed them into more manageable chunks once they had landed them.

This was both difficult and inefficient, so one of his suppliers, Nathaniel Wyeth, invented an ice plough. Drawn by horses with spiked shoes, this plough would cut regular grooves in the ice, making it possible to harvest large numbers of regular ice cakes. These rectangular cakes could be stacked in warehouses with sawdust or straw insulation, and they melted more slowly than the irregular chunks. The blocks had to be kept sufficiently apart that they would not refreeze together.

Wyeth also invented pulley mechanisms to get the ice out and into storage. By the 1880s, the Midwestern ice companies were harvesting vast amounts of ice just to supply the beer companies and Chicago's meat packers. Swift & Co. pioneered assembly-line abattoirs with refrigerated railcars, enabling them to outmanoeuvre East Coast meat companies. The revolution in refrigerated transport changed global trade.

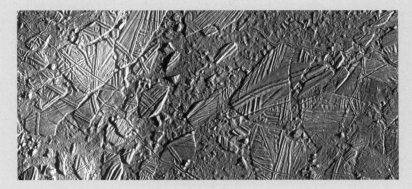

This colour-enhanced image from NASA's Galileo space mission shows a patch of the surface of Europa, one of the moons of Jupiter, that measures about 70 by 30 kilometres. The white and blue areas were blanketed by a fine dust or ice particles when a large crater called Pwyll was created some 1,000 kilometres to the south. Big blocks of ice that blew up intact at the same time probably made the small craters visible in the photo. Dr. Robert Pappalardo says Europa operates much like a lava lamp, sending warmer ice from deep below up to the surface in a constant movement.

The data to create this image arrived at the Jet Propulsion Laboratory in Pasadena, California, over five months between September 1996 and February 1997. To view images and data received from Galileo on the World Wide Web, go to http://galileo.jpl.nasa.gov. Background information and educational context for the images can be found at www.jpl.nasa.gov/galileo/sepo.

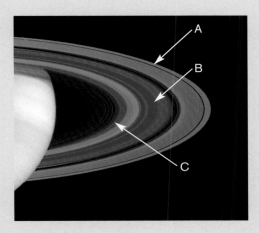

Saturn's fascinating rings are largely made of ice and dust; they are surprisingly thin. This is the most detailed look to date at the temperature of Saturn's rings, which are colour-coded in this false-colour image from the Cassini spacecraft. The data show that the opaque region of the rings, such as the outer A ring (on the far right) and the middle B ring, are cooler, where-as the more transparent sections, such as the Cassini Division (in red just inside the A ring) or the inner C ring (shown in yellow and red), are relatively warmer. For more information about the Cassini-Huygens mission, visit http://saturn.jpl.nasa.gov and the instrument team's homepage, http://cirs.gsfc.nasa.gov/. (NASA/JPL/GSFC/Ames)

This may be the most famous Viking ship in history. The Gokstad ship, excavated in Norway in 1880, has clean, fast lines that made it ideal for war and for slipping through the ice. It is in the Viking Ship Museum in Oslo. Before the Gokstad find, no one really knew what these ships looked like. To this day, admirers and imitators build them and sail them. There is an interesting compendium of this kind of activity at www.digitalnorseman.com/vships/shpintro.html. *(Ian Morrison)*

Gjøa, a sturdy little ship, was the first to navigate the Northwest Passage between 1903 and 1906. Had it been larger, it would not have survived the icy shoals. Its seven-man crew was commanded by the great Roald Amundsen, who was also first to reach the South Pole. Many believe he may also have been first to the North Pole. Since 1972, *Gjøa* has rested on the grounds of the Fram Museum in Oslo. *(Ian Morrison)*

This picture of the *Fram* coming out of the water permanently in 1932 hangs on a wall below deck. The museum subsequently built around the most important ship in the history of popular exploration allows access to all the original artefacts. The website is worth a visit too: www.fram.museum.no/en/. *(Ian Morrison)*

The *Fram*'s round hull was reinforced with stout wooden ribs that helped it survive a three-year drift in the pack ice of the Arctic Ocean while Sverdrup mapped it—making an inestimable contribution to polar knowledge, still in wide use a century later. Sverdrup never emerged from Nansen's shadow, and he committed suicide back in Oslo. *(Ian Morrison)*

The grand hall of the Ice Hotel Quebec-Canada is filled with light and crystalline reflections from its carved ice pillars. The use of fibre optics embedded in the ice maximizes the brilliance of the light and creates an overall effect that is quite stunning for the first-time viewer. *(Courtesy of Ice Hotel de glace Québec-Canada)*

Passengers of the *Crystal Harmony* are treated to a helicopter expedition over magnificent Alaskan glaciers. The ice has become a huge asset to the tourism industry wherever there is permanent ice, such as Alaska, Greenland and Antarctica. Conversely, places where the ice is visibly deteriorating, such as Mount Kilimanjaro and the European Alps, are seeing a noticeable drop in their tourism revenues. *(Courtesy of Crystal Cruises)*

In 1845, a rival enterprise on Lake Wenham near Boston opened successfully in London and Liverpool, advertising its wares as "Concentrated Wenham." In Cockney, this quickly became "concentrated venom," which led *Punch* to suggest it might be poisonous. Even though Tudor had founded the whole business and was by far the largest operator at the time and the Wenham company lasted just a short time abroad, the Wenham name circulated for many years in England and in India, as a kind of generic name for American ice. It never had such cachet at home, even though it remained available in the domestic market much longer.

Aside from its cooling pleasures in food and drink, and its helpful contribution to delaying food spoilage, the Anglo-Indian community believed firmly in the ice's medicinal benefits, that it cured illness when applied to the face or the body. In the burning hot Indian climate, the demand for the Massachusetts product was so great that panic could set in—or at the very least anger—if the ships were delayed. The July, 1850 edition of the *Bombay Telegraph and Courier* reported:

> *We are without ice! The supply is used up. The little chilly building between the Supreme Court and the Scotch Kirk is denuded of its treasures. Dirty water and sawdust is all it contains. . . . If there were any such thing as public spirit in Bombay we might hope for the adoption of measures to preserve us from the recurrence of the present evil. . . . There is now an interregnum: King Tudor has laid down his ice-sceptre. . . . There should therefore be an agitation throughout the city . . . against the abominably sudden and inexplicable cutting off of our supply of ice.*[2]

If ice was still a much-desired luxury in Bombay and in Europe, in America it had become an institution. *De Bow's Review* said everyone in America could have it if they wanted it:

> *In workshops, composing rooms, counting houses, workmen, printers, clerks have their daily supply of ice. Every office, nook or cranny, illuminated by a human face is also cooled by the presence of his crystal friend. . . . It is as good as oil to the wheel. It sets the whole human machinery in pleasant action, turns the wheels of commerce, and propels the energetic business engine. In every house almost there is a vein of ice, beginning with the blocks in the cellar and going through the refrigerators and filters on every story to the attic. We use it seven or eight months of the year—all the year in the south; and even in New York there are a number of families who ice their Croton [drinking water from Lake Croton, to the north of the city] throughout the winter. In this latter particular, and in the too free and careless use of it in the hottest days of summer, the abuse of the luxury consists. It is considered by physicians as a tonic; but an excess, as in the use of intoxicating liquors, will, in all probability produce diarrhea.*[3]

■ ■ ■

As people found more things to do with ice, such as preserving fresh food, the market demand for it began to explode. Whereas ice had at first been considered a great luxury, North American users began to popularize its use through decentralized storage, and then home delivery, first by horse-drawn wagons, and eventually by trucks. Individual wooden iceboxes, usually oak with a zinc-lined ice compartment, made it possible for middle-class households to have their own personal refrigeration devices. The iceboxes had a drainage pan that had to be emptied about three times a day as the ice cake in the upper box melted.

As refrigeration spread, so did a number of other benefits: less food spoilage and food poisoning, the ability to choose a preferred temperature for eating certain foods, and for the first time ever, increased diversity of food sources. Fresh food is generally healthier than pickled, salted, canned or dried foods. The health benefits were enormous, not to mention the pleasure derived from liberation from the monotony of a diet based solely on local meat and produce that could be pickled, dried or otherwise stored for the winter.

In 1876, Charles Tellier carried a meat shipment from Buenos Aires to Rouen in Normandy. The boat, called *Le Frigorifique* ("the refrigerator"), was a precursor of a huge meat trade to Europe. Around the same time, fishing boats added refrigerators, enabling major increases in ocean transportation of food. The volume of transportation by sea increased from 1 million tons in 1788 to 5 million in 1861, and reached 12 million by 1913.

The difficult and labour-intensive nature of the natural ice business prompted inventors to seek other solutions, and by the middle of the nineteenth century, there were steam-powered machines able to make ice. This solved the supply problem for the American South and the Indian market, both of which were largely using artificial ice by the 1880s. The growth of ice manufacturing was stimulated by a warm winter in 1889–90, which reduced the amount of natural ice available, and by a shutdown of the New England ice trade with the South during the Civil War.

Beer companies such as Milwaukee's Pabst and Montreal's Molson required plenty of ice to keep their lager near freezing temperatures. German-style lager beers were only a winter product until enough ice was available to support its low-temperature production process year-round.

The use of large cakes of ice under railway cars allowed the first refrigerated cars for transporting California lettuce and fruits over the winter. With fans blowing over the ice and into the cars, this was also the first form of air conditioning aboard trains, and it was used on some North American lines into the early 1970s. Ice pans were also placed under funeral caskets to keep the corpse from deteriorating during visitations to people's houses, as was then the custom. One account tells of a ninety-year-old who would get up in the night to turn off leaky faucets—not because of a sense of economy, as her grandchildren always thought, but because of the chilling memory of the dripping sound in the pan beneath her own grandfather's casket in the night when she was a child.

Spadina House—Ice and Style

I recently joined the board of Toronto's Historical Houses—museums intended to showcase life in our city's history. One of the sights that have most impressed me is the icebox at Spadina House, a gracious manor once occupied by a prominent Toronto family. As befits a large family whose members loved to entertain, their icebox was huge! Whereas I had always thought of iceboxes as the early and tiny cousins of the modern refrigerator, the Spadina House version is closer to today's hotel meat locker. It is also beautifully finished: the dairy and egg part of it is like a modern fridge built into the side of a wooden structure the size of a small room. It is lined with a smooth, heavy white ceramic material. The other part accessible from inside the house is a walk-in metal-lined compartment the size of a small room. It was for meat. The icebox component, where the ice was delivered and kept, is above these two compartments, and it is only accessible from outside the house. So a horse-drawn wagon would pull up outside, deliver the huge block of ice into the compartment, and leave again, without disturbing the occupants. Before the days of electricity, this was luxury indeed!

A LABOUR-INTENSIVE INDUSTRY

The natural ice business was backbreaking and labour-intensive, but it provided welcome income to workers. In the winter of 1879–80, U.S. Census Bureau figures show that thousands of workers were employed in the business, and between 8 and 10 million tons of ice were harvested.

In early December 1931, the Alberta Ice Company in Calgary received hundreds of applications when it announced it would be hiring about seventy men to harvest its 50,000 tons of ice from an artificial lake west of the city. The company used especially equipped trains to supply the ice to points all across Alberta and southern British Columbia. All over Canada, northeastern and Midwestern U.S., natural ice enterprises were able to supply large geographical areas. Those on the eastern seaboard, however, were trading globally from the beginning, supplying the Caribbean, the southern states, Britain and India. At its peak, it was a huge business: ice from New York's Hudson River and the lakes and streams of New England was sent around the world in insulated ships.

America's love affair with ice began in the nineteenth century, when it became what Wightman called "the first refrigerated society," and no other country is as addicted to ice in drinks. Tudor's entrepreneurial talents extended to marketing and training bartenders to use ice in cocktails. Americans remain under the influence of his enterprising nature, whether they realize it or not. The pervasive use of ice in drinks is particular to Americans. In many cultures, water would never be served full of ice cubes—something which happens as a matter of course in most North American restaurants.

Non-Americans are often mystified to see Americans drinking a carbonated soft drink full of clinking ice cubes before noon, or to be served sweetened iced tea when they expect a hot brew. The origins of iced tea date back to the beginning of the era of refrigeration, but most accounts agree that it was widely popularized and commercialized at the St. Louis World's Fair in 1904. A group of tea producers from India and Ceylon had a pavilion at the fair, but were not doing very well in the July heat. Their British coordinator, Richard Blechynden, who may have previously tried iced tea in the American South, decided to pack glasses with ice and serve the tea cold. The producers soon had line-ups at their counters, and the rest is history. The waffle cone was also pioneered at the St. Louis World Fair, and ice cream would become a strategic asset in World War II—the American military used it systematically as a morale booster.

The Scots believe that ice ruins their magnificent single malt scotches, and they do have a point about the chemical transformation that arises when ice is dropped into whisky. The cold reduces the flow of wonderful aromas to your nose, and dampens the distinctive taste of the whisky. Chill filtration, in which whisky is taken down below the freezing point, removes the cloudiness in the whisky, but also some of the flavour, which is why the practice is controversial.

The natural ice business continued in Canada and the eastern seaboard until the 1920s, but as the Hudson River and other bodies of water suffered from the careless disposal of sewage and manufacturing waste, people became more and more concerned about pollution. Already by 1907, Hudson River ice often contained the typhoid bacteria. The small motors needed to power electric refrigerators began to be more easily available in the 1920s. By 1937, there were 3 million such refrigerators in American homes. By the 1950s, the iceman's visits had entered history. Today, the refrigerator is North America's most used appliance, present in 99.5 percent of American homes.

THE EXPENSIVE STRUGGLE TO BE ICE-FREE

The management and removal of ice is a big business, especially in cities. Not that you would want the title, but Moscow, Helsinki and Montreal are always pulling the blanket over which one of them is the world's top snow-and-ice city. In the eighteen years that I lived in Montreal, I always heard that the city simply budgeted $1 million a snowstorm to clear the streets and sidewalks as efficiently as possible and get on with life. Cities with less ice and snow experience are often paralyzed under a light dusting of snow.

If you are from Timmins, say, or Winnipeg, it is really quite amusing to watch drivers in New York or Vancouver struggle with the occasional little snowfall. Sometimes, they just abandon their vehicles until the weather improves.

True winter lovers will say that the snow simply adds beauty and the character-building challenge of coping cheerfully with any inconvenience. But there actually are certain hard costs involved: for example, car thefts increase because people leave their cars running while they run an errand or simply to warm it up before they get in; farmers worry about calves being born wet and exposed to extreme cold in the fragile hours after birth.

The true and costly impacts of ice happen when it gets in the way of human activities. When ice weighs down high-voltage power lines and breaks them, the whole economy grinds to a halt. When a freak ice storm hits, transmission wires can snap and take out the power in entire cities and regions. The 2001 ice storm in Quebec sent residents into shelters for two weeks and marked forests with dead and crippled trees that remained visible for years afterwards. Even places as far south as Georgia and Alabama have had ice storms in recent years. When ice coats airplane wings and car windshields, it can cause fatal accidents. Or it can simply make city streets and sidewalks impossible to navigate, causing serious falls that can threaten an elderly person's independence for life.

Dr. Victor Petrenko of Dartmouth College in New Hampshire sees a huge business opportunity in this. He has discovered that the semiliquid film at the ice surface has an electrical conductivity that is not halfway between that of ice and water, but rather 10 billion times more conductive than either. This astounding discovery has enabled him to use ice as a proton semiconductor. He has designed a solar power cell that uses large surfaces of ice itself as the semiconductor to achieve very low-cost power generation. This uses up large ice surfaces, but it is so laughably cheap and clean that it might make an ideal way to power research stations in the Arctic and Antarctic.

He is in the process of patenting a whole series of inventions that use the electrical conductivity of the ice to de-ice everything from airplane wings to power lines, and to customize the traction of tires on icy roads. His inventions will facilitate the creation of high-performance, energy-efficient icemakers, and they will make ski waxes obsolete for those who choose to use his "electronic-wax kick-off mechanism." It uses low-voltage current to prevent ice from adhering to the skis, with adjustable friction. This does away with the time-honoured ritual of maintaining a range of ski waxes for every conceivable cross-country skiing condition, and maybe the traditionalists won't like it. But some people will . . . and that will be good business for Dr. Petrenko!

Ice Imagery

There are plenty of businesses that use ice imagery to further their commercial interests. The clarity, purity and coldness of ice play into popular imagery in an interesting way. Steuben

Glass has a whole series of beautiful crystal sculptures featuring Inuit life—a hunter waiting patiently over a seal's breathing hole, for example.

Products as diverse as mineral water, makeup, vodka and cars have used ice imagery in recent years, most very successfully—so successfully that several companies now show only silver cars. In New York, Chicago and Los Angeles, clarity, purity and cold play well: guerrilla marketing firms convince their clients that branded ice pops should be the latest cool free giveaway used in street-level promotions of products aimed at youth.

The nature and behaviour of ice itself have also played into its creative use. Beer companies such as Labatt's have used ice-crystal formation to concentrate the flavours in their beer. The contrast of sharp cold and heat are sometimes used in what is called contrast therapy, to get the blood pumping when there is sluggish circulation or an injury; but also to give pleasure or to titillate. Think of Baked Alaska, a dessert that involves covering shaped ice cream with meringue and baking it very quickly at high temperatures—it's the counterintuitive nature of it, hot and firm next to cold and creamy, that makes it so good. Or the "ice-cube scene" in the movie *9 and a Half Weeks*, in which Mickey Rourke runs an ice cube over Kim Basinger's body. It was very eighties, very daring for its time, but titillating because of the sharp contrast between body heat and the cold shock of ice on skin. In the theatre, you could hear people draw their breath in when the ice cube made contact.

THE YIN–YANG OF ICE

The action of ice on the human body is interesting and controversial: Western medicine believes firmly in its usefulness, whereas Chinese medicine mostly rejects it. The standard advice for a trauma or strain injury is RICE—Rest, Ice, Compression and Elevation. The ice shrinks the blood vessels and tissues at the site, restricting blood flow and preventing swelling. In Chinese medicine, this is considered unwise except for severe traumatic injuries, where it helps to slow down bleeding.

On the contrary, traditional Chinese doctors believe that increasing blood flow to an injured area, often with heat, is important to oxygenating and healing it. Some of the great beauties of the twentieth century believed in the use of ice to firm up breast and facial tissues, and they might in fact have had a point, if the advice was rigorously followed.

Plunging whole bodies into ice is a form of torture, but one willingly undergone by a forty-one-year-old Singapore monk, the Venerable Shi Ming Yi, who is also the chief executive officer of the Ren Ci Hospital. Every year, the venerable monk pulls an endurance stunt to raise money for his institution. The 2004 version of the stunt involved standing chest-deep in a plastic container filled with 1,000 kilograms of ice cubes. He planned to stay as long as he could in the ice to raise $5 million for the hospital, and to enter the *Guinness Book of World Records*. He was hooked up to a vital-signs monitor to keep track of his heart rate, oxygen levels and breathing pattern, while a thermal scanner and an ear thermometer kept track of his body temperature. Because extreme cold will make a person drowsy, doctors standing by also intended to speak to him throughout the stunt to ensure that he stayed lucid. The sides of the plastic container were designed to fall away instantly when he decided he had had enough.

In rehearsals for the stunt, the venerable monk found that he suffered very minor skin burns from the ice, but his thoughts conquered all: "The ice will be cold and painful," he said, "but I'll think of it as showers of love and compassion for the patients, and from the people who are making the calls to donate money." This may seem an odd paean to the pleasure that ice can give, but it certainly establishes how broad is the range of possibilities.

CHAPTER FIFTEEN

"We do not think clearly in megatons or picture generations much beyond our grandchildren. Nonetheless, the earth has become our garden; it behooves us to cultivate it with wisdom."
—Alison Jolly, Ethologist

LESSONS FROM AN ICE ADVENTURE

To many people, it seems, writing a book about ice is an odd idea. Indeed, why fixate on just one phase—albeit the most mysterious, most fascinating and little-understood phase—of the most common element on earth, water? How is it possible to describe, meaningfully, the manifestations of ice, from the universal to the microscopic, from the societal to the personal? Its beauty is unique and endlessly captivating. Its majestic and gargantuan progress has literally carved the planet, and blown away men and their supposedly invincible machines like matchstick toys.

When Nero sent slaves into the mountains to gather ice for early versions of fruit sorbets to be served at his decadent dinners, he was one of a long line of men and women to harness ice for pleasure and adventure. As we have seen, by the mid-nineteenth century, it was possible to harvest ice as a commercial crop, part of the bounty of nature improving the quality of life. Once the natural sources of ice close to cities had been fouled, ice factories sprang up to meet the demand for the precious, perishable crystal all around the world.

We have gone from a time when brave explorers conquered the unimaginable on hair-raising expeditions that took them away for years to today, when high-tech sportsmen reach the poles while promoting themselves on the web through their satellite videophones. Adrenaline junkies seek out the most fragile, dangerous ice forms to climb under impossible conditions. This long progression from force of nature to necessity of civilization and ever-more-extreme sports demonstrations may have fooled us into thinking we control our world, but the ice still holds surprises.

To those who know how to read it—on land or sea, in the sky or in space, the ice holds the key to unfathomable mysteries, revealing both past and future. It never lies. Whether it hangs in the sky or falls out of it in the form of giant hail missiles; whether it rumbles down the mountainside or melts quietly into the sea, its place in the earthly ecosystem is of great import to us, and its presence or absence is a harbinger of life in worlds beyond our own. Perhaps this is why we are so fascinated with all the miniature and controllable forms of ice in our lives, and why we attach its name to substances as diverse as seductive diamonds and deadly drugs.

Despite the might and majesty of our cryosphere—all of the earth's frozen water and soil—embodiments of the raw power of nature are melting away faster than we can measure the consequences of their loss. Some of the grandest spectacles our ancestors and we have known will be nowhere visible to our children and grandchildren, except on screens and in picture books. Vital questions we must seek to answer are what role human activity is playing in these developments and how we will adapt to our new circumstances.

Throughout recorded history, there has always been a fearful fascination with ice, an attraction to it as a frontier to be explored, often with the illusion of possible conquest. Many have died seeking to satisfy this intense curiosity and desire. What has been little understood until very recently was the role of the ice in the health of our planet and the living creatures that inhabit it.

Pure, clean water is so necessary to life that most of us understand the need to care for our water supply. For example, most people living in a developed society today would not dream of dumping raw sewage into their lakes and rivers. And yet it is only a short time ago—perhaps three or four generations—that our ancestors thought nothing of emptying the morning slop bucket into open channels in the streets, never connecting these actions with subsequent epidemics and shortened lifespans. We have moved beyond that now, in the immediate ways that we can see. What is it now that we do not see, and what does the ice have to teach us about it?

The cryosphere is everywhere around us, whether we realize it or not. It affects us whether we live in the tropics or at the poles, driving extreme weather and climate change before it. The more we know about it, the more we know about our future and ourselves. The ice cores reveal the closed aspects of the earthly system, how what happens in one place affects the whole. In that sense, the ice cores are putting us in our place. Inexorably, as they bring to the surface evidence of global patterns, chemistry and consequences, they will make it as unthinkable to dump noxious chemicals into the earth's air and water as it would be today to empty a chamber pot on a city street.

The study of ice is also giving us a different perspective on time, bringing us closer to the understanding of aboriginal peoples who have remained bound to the earth in a more direct way than most of us. If you imagine the earth's whole existence mapped on a twenty-four-hour clock, as if its 4.6 billion-year history had begun one day ago, the first single-celled fossils would not have appeared until eighteen hours, or 3.5 billion years ago. The first fish would have appeared two hours, or 400 million years ago. At one minute, or 2 million years ago, the last ice age began; the Industrial Revolution, when humans began seriously polluting the planet, started less than a second—just three one-thousandths of a second ago—on this imaginary twenty-four-hour clock. If you held your arms out to measure this span of time, and you filed the tip of one fingernail lightly, you would have removed the entire history of humans on earth.

So much for self-importance. I am not a scientist, and there are many competent professionals working on the ice issues explored in this book. They are generating studies, sounding alarms and trying to make themselves heard, which is not easy. Sometimes they are not good at explaining, and often, the rest of us are not good at listening. We are busy; we flee complexity. But there is hope.

There are wonderful teams of people working together

across borders, across ideologies, across personalities. Just as explorers worked for hundreds of years to map the Arctic and the Antarctic, today's scientists are rising above their differences and their interests to map deeper, more meaningful realities that have been hidden from us. This new generation of scientists, in my experience, is wonderfully open to guiding us into their treasure store of knowledge.

Every day, new information becomes available—often so much of it that we become fearful and we back away. Those who know most, and hope for a better world, will need resources and support in the future to make whatever difference they—and we—can. There are projects underway, particularly in the Russian Federation, financed by the U.S., Canada, Denmark, Norway, Sweden and others, to address some—but certainly not all—of the most urgent and egregious situations, particularly to help our circumpolar neighbours in Russia and Eastern Europe to recover from the industrial practices of the Communist era.

Around the Arctic rim, which should be the most pristine place on earth (after Antarctica) rusting hulks, from abandoned factories to nuclear submarine wrecks, are not even identified and monitored as they leach everything from radioactive wastes to long-banned pesticides into the fragile northern ecosystems. The ice is carefully preserving this evidence of human folly and arrogance. We have no idea, as yet, what will happen as a result—what havoc these circumstances will wreak on people and on the planet.

■ ■ ■

The effects of all this are far-reaching and complex. No one has yet figured out how to protect their own children and grandchildren from poisoned air and water. Everyone has a stake in changing the behaviours that got us here. The community of concerned citizens and scientists cuts across all nationalities and societies. But governments, communities and industries are not all equally aware, committed and responsible.

Reconciling ice time and human time, in the sense of taking responsibility for actions that may only bear fruit long after we are gone, is one of the most difficult things we have to do. And yet, we must. Dr. James Hansen of NASA's Goddard Institute for Space Studies, one of the fine scientific minds focusing on these issues, is committed to speaking out in ways that will actually influence decisions and behaviours to make a difference.

He believes there are ways to mitigate the global-warming time bomb, and that these actions will yield a cleaner, healthier atmosphere. He believes that we may even, eventually, be able to slow or stop the process of climate change that is underway. For example, he talks about cost-effective and practical technology that could rapidly reduce the soot emanations that are blackening so much of the world's ice and snow—destroying its capacity to reflect the sun's energy away from the earth. This one simple thing would help. He is among many who believe we could do so much more to be responsible custodians of this blue, green and white planet.

The unique beauty of ice is at the core of our humanity: you cannot abandon yourself to the experience of looking—truly looking—at a single snow crystal or an image of Antarctica from space, and not be moved by the heart-wrenching, fragile, awesome beauty of it. And once you have truly looked, you can never be the same again.

NOTES

CHAPTER ONE

1.   Water makes up 92 percent of blood plasma, 80 percent of muscle tissue, 60 percent of red blood cells and 50 percent of most other tissues, according to the *Columbia Encyclopedia*.
2.   This was announced in Japan on March 28, 2002.
3.   The authors, Peter Schwartz, CIA consultant and former head of planning at Royal Dutch/Shell Group, and Doug Randall of the California-based Global Business Network say climate change "should be elevated beyond a scientific debate to a US national security concern." The report was commissioned by Andrew Marshall, an influential Pentagon defence advisor over the past thirty years. It was leaked to *The Observer* in the U.K. and made public on February 22, 2004 under the headline "Now the Pentagon tells Bush: Climate Change will Destroy us."
4.   Canada, Denmark, Finland, Sweden, Iceland, Norway, Russia and the United States.
5.   Geophysicists Mark Simons at the California Institute of Technology (Caltech) and Bradford Hager at M.I.T. have shown that incomplete glacial rebound can account for a substantial portion of the Hudson Bay gravity anomaly.
6.   See www.ig.utexas.edu/research/projects/plates/750.htm?PHPSESSID= ac6723ea09fa7c0687109a625cd5323e.
7.   See www.museum.state.il.us/exhibits/ice_ages/images/laurentide.mpg.

CHAPTER TWO

1.   Pumice, which is forged in molten lava, with trapped air bubbles, also floats.
2.   Only five other substances, of the ones we know, share this trait of becoming less dense when frozen with H_2O: plutonium, geranium bismuth, silicone, antimony and gallium.
3.   This image brings to mind controversial Japanese research by Dr. Masaru Emoto, which concluded that the molecular structure of water actually is affected by music. You can learn more about Dr. Moto's observations and see some remarkable photographs at www.hado.net.

4. See *The Snowflake Man* by Duncan C. Blanchard (*Weatherwise*, 1970, 23(6), 260–69) for a delightful account of Bentley's life.
5. All of Bentley's work has been catalogued by the University of Wisconsin at www.ssec.wisc.edu/library/bentley.htm.
6. A short film on the site shows Bentley at work in 1917, and describes his methods. See http://snowflakebentley.com/vid.htm.
7. See http://nsidc.org/antarctica/megadunes/dunes.html.
8. See http://www3.nf.sympatico.ca/paul.alcock/.
9. The berg that hit the Titanic on April 14, 1912, and caused it to sink off the coast of Newfoundland was also considered medium-sized, probably between 60 and 120 metres long, and between 15 and 30 metres high.
10. The Drake Passage in the southern oceans is also sometimes called Iceberg Alley, because it sees hundreds of icebergs calving from the Antarctic ice shelf.
11. "Day of the Viking: At this foggy spot, the idea of Canada was forged," Will Ferguson, *Maclean's*, July 1, 2001.
12. Arctic adventurers who melt glacier ice to drink in a saucepan say it sizzles like bacon for the same reason.
13. See the Glossary at the end of this book.

CHAPTER THREE

1. More than 24.7 parts per thousand salt.
2. US National Parks Service figures.
3. See UNESCO's International Year of Fresh Water (2003) website at www.wateryear2003.org/.
4. Runoff is the source for all human diversions or withdrawals for irrigation, industry, municipal uses, navigation, dilution, hydropower, and maintenance of aquatic life including fisheries.
5. See www.unesco.org/water/wwap/facts_figures/basic_needs.shtml.
6. See the Glossary for more complete definitions.
7. Contrary to what many people think, the ground and the air just above it are often at quite different temperatures.
8. This term is often used in metallurgy, where it usually refers to an industrial process intended to strengthen an alloy.
9. A strict definition of permafrost is rock or soil remaining at or below 0°C for two years or more. It can contain more than 30 percent ice, or almost none. The National Snow and Ice Data Center in Boulder, Colorado, maintains a map of permafrost in the northern hemisphere on its permafrost page at http://nsidc.org/sotc/permafrost.html.
10. The research on the Somerset Island lake is published online in *Proceedings of the National Academy of Sciences*, 2004. The abstract can be found at www.pnas.org/cgi/content/abstract/0307570100v1.
11. Dr. Greg Dash is an Emeritus Professor of Physics and Adjunct Principal Physicist at the Applied Physics Laboratory at the University of Washington, and the co-instructor of Transition School Physics (since 1999). He earned his

Ph.D. in Physics at Columbia University in 1951. Professor Dash is a Fellow of the American Physical Society, and was awarded a Guggenheim Fellowship and the Physical Society's Davisson-Germer Prize for electron and atomic physics. He was a Visiting Distinguished Professor in Israel (1974–75) and France (1977, 1982, and 1986), directed the NATO Advanced Study Institute in Sicily (1979), and served on the Advisory Committees of the National Science Foundation and the National Magnet Laboratory. In addition to teaching at the Transition School, Professor Dash continues to conduct research in the physics of ice and in surface science. He is the author of numerous articles. He has authored and/or edited three books and published over 200 research articles and reviews in physics journals.

12. See http://lasp.colorado.edu/icymoons/.

CHAPTER FOUR

1. A joint Norwegian-Canadian research project at Churchill, Manitoba, led by Nils Øritsland, of the Norwegian Polar Institute in Oslo, and working with live-trapped bears from southern Hudson Bay greatly advanced the understanding of polar bear physiology, and in particular the bear's heat-exchange systems.

2. Fisheries and Oceans Canada maintains an interesting web page about the species at www.dfo-mpo.gc.ca/zone/underwater_sous-marin/ArcticCod/artcod-saida_e.htm.

3. R. Maxwell Savage, *The Ecology and Life History of the Common Frog* (London: Sir Isaac Pitman and Sons, 1961).

4. Kenneth B. Storey and Janet M. Storey, "Lifestyles of the Cold and Frozen," *The Sciences*, May 1999.

5. Ibid.

CHAPTER FIVE

1. The United States (Alaska), Canada, Denmark (Greenland), Iceland, Norway, Sweden, Finland and Russia all border on the Arctic Ocean. All except Iceland have indigenous peoples living within the Arctic region.

2. See ILO-Convention 169, "Convention Concerning Indigenous and Tribal Peoples in Independent Countries."

3. According to Jens Dahl, a Danish authority on the subject, "The Arctic Region is defined from a combination of geographical and political factors. This implies that indigenous peoples living in geographically non-Arctic regions in some instances should be included if they are inhabitants of an Arctic country. Thus, the Natives of southern Alaska and Eastern Siberia are included, while the Dene Indians might be excluded after the carving out of a Nunavut territory from the Canadian Northwest Territories. Finally, if an indigenous group considers itself as being part of the Arctic this should also be considered. Thus, in Russia I will include all the so-called "26 Small Peoples of the North and Far East," and other indigenous groups of the same

geographical area (Russian North and Far East), including the two major groups, Komi and Yakut, but, for example, not the Buryat living north of Mongolia, who have their own autonomous republic."
4. Vílhjalmur Stefánsson and Gisli Palsson (ed.), *Writing on Ice: The Ethnographic Notebooks of Vílhjalmur Stefánsson* (Lebanon, NH: University Press of New England, July 2001).

CHAPTER SIX

1. It is difficult to know whether or not Pytheas would have reached as far as Iceland, which has twenty-four hours of daylight in July and August, but short nights, like the ones he described in Thule, in June and September.
2. Strabo's *Geographical Sketches* were completed about AD 23. He spoke of work by Eratosthenes and Hipparchus, but none of their work survives. Strabo spoke only briefly about the problem of projecting a sphere onto a two-dimensional flat plane. He is clear about one thing: his intention is to aim his work at statesmen with an interest in people, natural resources and land, not mathematicians.
3. R. Chevallier, "The Greco-Roman Conception of the North from Pytheas to Tacitus," *Arctic* 37, no. 4 (Dec. 1984): 341–46.
4. It was not until Peter the Great pushed the Swedes out of Russia in the Great Northern War that their hold was broken. The war lasted twenty-nine years. Peter founded St. Petersburg in 1703 as part of the effort to keep the Swedes out, and to give him a Baltic gateway.
5. This site at the University of St. Andrews in Scotland carries an excellent summary of Ptolemys career at www.gap.dcs.st-and.ac.uk/~history/Mathematicians/Ptolemy.html.
6. There is much material from the original expedition diaries in Robert McGhee's splendid book *The Arctic Voyages of Martin Frobisher: An Elizabethan Adventure* (Montreal & Kingston: McGill-Queen's University Press, Canadian Museum of Civilization, 2001; British Museum Press, 2002). McGhee's own lively and well-researched account has been very useful here.
7. By the twentieth century, Arkhangelsk was an ice-free port because of global warming.
8. It was probably Baffin Island cobble, with flecks of sparkly mica in it.
9. McGhee, *The Arctic Voyages*, p. 74.

CHAPTER SEVEN

1. Charles Arnold, of the Prince of Wales Northern Heritage Centre in Yellowknife; Jim Tuck, Chief Archaeologist at the Colony of Avalon, Newfoundland; and Robert McGhee of the Canadian Museum of Civilization; Bill Fitzhugh and Réginald Auger of the Smithsonian Institution.
2. Lieutenant George W. DeLong, U.S.N., Commander, 1879 DeLong expedition; go to www.arcticwebsite.com/DelongImage.html.

3. Peter McFarlane and Wayne Haimila, *Ancient Land, Ancient Sky: Following Canada's Native Canoe Routes* (Toronto: Knopf, 1999), p. 37.
4. James Bay was named in his honour.
5. Commemorated in Foxe Basin.
6. Owen Beattie and John Geiger, *Frozen in Time* (Saskatoon: Western Producer Prairie Books, 1987).
7. Go to www.doughoughton.com/webpage/image/60/a60880.jpg for a picture of his tomb in St. Magnus Cathedral in Kirkwall.
8. The following reproduces the text of Dr. Rae's letter to the admiralty regarding the encounter with the fate of the Franklin expedition, and Charles Dickens' indignant response:

From Dr. John Rae's Report to the Hudson's Bay Company

April 1854. We were now joined by another one of the Natives who had been absent seal hunting yesterday, but being anxious to see us, visited our snow house early this morning, and then followed up our track. This man was very communicative, and on putting to him the usual questions as to having seen "white men" before, or any ships or boats—he replied in the negative; but said, that a party of "Kabloonas," had died of starvation, a long distance to the west of where we then were, and beyond a large River;—He stated that, he did not know the exact place; that he had never been there; and that he could not accompany us so far.

The substance of the information then and subsequently obtained from various sources, was the following effect: In the spring, four winters past (1850), whilst some Esquimaux families were killing Seals near the shore of a large Island named in Arrowsmith's Charts, King William's Land, about forty white men were seen traveling in company, were seen traveling southward over the ice and dragging a boat and sledges with them. None of the party could speak the Esquimaux language so well as to be understood, but by signs the Natives were led to believe that the Ship, or Ships, had been crushed by the ice, and that they were now going to where they expected to find deer to shoot. From the appearance of the Men (all of whom with the exception of one Officer, were hauling on the drag ropes of the sledge and were looking thin)—they were then supposed to be getting short of provisions, and they purchased a small Seal or piece of Seal from the natives. The Officer was described as being a tall, stout, middle-aged man; when their day's journey terminated, they pitched Tents to rest in.

At a later date the same season, but previous to the disruption of the ice, the bodies of some thirty persons and some Graves were discovered on the continent, and five dead bodies on an Island near it, about a long day's journey to the north-west of a large stream, which can be no other than Great Fish River (named by the Esquimaux *Ool-koo-i-hi-ca-lik*), as its description and that of the low shore in the neighborhood of Point Ogle and Montreal Island agree exactly with that of Sir George Back. Some of the bodies had been buried (probably those of the first victims of famine); some were in a tent or tents; others under the boat, which had been turned over to form a shelter, and several lay scattered about in different directions. Of those found on the Island one was supposed to have been an Officer, as he had a telescope strapped over his shoulders and his double-barrel gun lay beneath him.

From the mutilated state of many of the bodies and the contents of the kettles, it is evident that our wretched Countrymen had been driven to the last dread alternative—cannibalism—as a means of prolonging existence. A few of the unfortunate Men must have survived until the arrival of wildfowl, (say, until the end of May), as shots were heard, and fresh bones and feathers of geese were noticed near the sad event. There appears to have been an abundant stock of ammunition, as the powder was emptied in a heap on the ground out of the case or cases containing it; and a quantity of ball and shot was found below the high-water mark, having probably been left on the ice close to the beach. There must have been a number of watches, compasses, telescopes, guns (several double-barrelled), etc., all of which appear to have been broken up, as I saw pieces of these different articles with the Esquimaux, and, together with some silver spoons & forks, purchased as many as I could get. A list of the most important of these I inclose:

One silver table fork—crest, an animal's head with wings, spread above.
3 Silver table forks—crest, a bird with wings extended.
1 Silver tablespoon, crest, with initials F.M.R.C.
1 Silver tablespoon & 1 fork—crest, bird with laurel branch in mouth, motto spero meliora
1 Silver table-fork—initials H.D.G.S.
1 Silver tablespoon, 1 tea-spoon, and 1 dessert-fork—crest, a fish's head looking upwards with laurel branches on each side
1 Silver table fork, initials A.M.D.
1 Silver table fork, initials G.A.M.
1 Silver table fork, initials J.T.
1 Silver dessert spoon, initials J.S.P.
1 Round Silver plate, engraved 'Sir John Franklin K C H'
1 Star or Order, with motto 'nec aspera terrent, G.R. III, MDCCCV.'
2 Pieces Gold Watch Case
1 Case silver gilt pocket Chronometer & dial
1 small silver pencil Case
1 piece of an Optical Instrument
1 gold Cap Band
2 pieces (about 2 inches) gold Watch Chain
2 Sovereigns
1 Half crown
4 Shillings
2 leaves of the Students Manual

1 surgeons Knife
1 Scalpel
2 Knives
1 shoemaker's knife
1 pocket Compass Box
1 Ivory Handle of a Table Knife, marked "Hickey"
1 narrow tin case, marked "Fowler"
1 narrow tin case, no cover, marked W.M.

Charles Dickens, "The Lost Arctic Voyagers," December 2, 1854
We have stated our belief in the extreme improbability of this inference as to
the last resource, can be rested, first on close analogy, and secondly, on broad
general grounds, quite apart from the improbabilities and incoherencies of the
Esquimaux evidence: which is itself given, at the very best, at second-hand.
If it is to be inferred that the officer who lay upon his double-barrelled gun,
defended his life to the last against ravenous seamen, under the boat or elsewhere, and that he died in so doing, how came his body to be found? That
was not eaten, or even mutilated, according to the description. Neither were
the bodies, buried in the frozen earth, disturbed; and is it not likely that if
any bodies were resorted to as food, those the most removed from recent life
and companionship would have been the first? Was there any fuel in that desolate place for cooking "the contents of the kettles"? If none, would the little
flame of the spirit-lamp the travellers may have had with them, have sufficed
for such a purpose? If not, would the kettles have been defiled for that purpose at all? Some of the corpses, Dr. Rae adds, in a letter to the Times, "had
been sadly mutilated, and had been stripped by those that had the misery to
survive them, and who were found wrapped in two or three suits of clothes."
Had there been no bears thereabout, to mutilate the bodies; no wolves, no
foxes? Lastly, no man can, with any show of reason, undertake to affirm that
this sad remnant of Franklin's gallant band were not set upon and slain by the
Esquimaux themselves. It is impossible to form an estimate of the character of
any race of savages, from their deferential behaviour to the white man while
he is strong. The mistake has been made again and again; and the moment
the white man has appeared in the new aspect of being weaker than the savage, the savage has changed and sprung upon him. There are pious persons
who, in their practice, with a strange inconsistency, claim for every child born
to civilisation all innate depravity, and for every savage born to the woods and
wilds, all innate virtue. We believe every savage to be in his heart covetous,
treacherous, and cruel, and we have yet to learn what knowledge the white
man—lost, houseless, shipless, apparently forgotten by his race, plainly
famine-stricken, weak, frozen, helpless, and dying—has of the gentleness of
Esquimaux nature.
    It is in reverence for the brave and enterprising, in admiration for the
great spirits who can endure even unto the end, in love for their names, and

in tenderness for their memory, that we think of the specks, once ardent men, "scattered about in different directions" on the waste of ice and snow, and plead for their lightest ashes. Our last claim in their behalf and honour, against the vague babble of savages, is that the instances in which this "last resource" has been permitted to interpose between life and death, are few and exceptional, whereas the instances in which the sufferings of hunger have been borne until the pain was past, are very many. Also, and as the citadel of that position, that the better educated the man, the better disciplined the habits, the more reflective and religious the tone of thought, the more giganti-cally improbable the "last resource" becomes . . . In weighing the probabilities of the "last resource," the foremost question is—not the nature of the extrem-ity; but, the nature of the men. We submit that the memory of the lost Arctic voyagers is placed, by reason and experience, high above the taint of this so easily allowed connection; and that the noble conduct and example of such men, and of their own great leader himself, under similar endurances, belies it, and outweighs by the weight of the whole universe the chatter of a gross handful of uncivilised people, with a domesticity of blood and blubber.

Dr. John Rae, Rebuttal to Dickens, 23 December 1854
The objection offered that my information was received second-hand, I con-sider much in favour of its correctness. Had it been obtained from the natives who had seen the bodies of our dead countrymen, I should have doubted all they told me, however probable their tale might have appeared; because had they, as the usually, do, deposited any property under stones in the neigh-bourhood, they would have had a very excellent cause for misleading me.

I do not infer that the officer who lay upon his double-barrelled gun defended his life to the last against "ravenous seamen"; but that he was a brave, cool man, in full possession of his mental faculties to the last; that he lay down in this position as a precaution, and, alas! was never able to rise again; and that he was among the last, if not the very last, of the survivors. The question is asked, was there any fuel in that desolate place for cooking the contents of the kettles? I have already mentioned in a letter to the Times how fuel might have been obtained. I shall repeat my opinion with addi-tions:—When the Esquimaux were talking with me on the subject of the dis-covery of the men, boats, tents, & C., several of them remarked that it was curious that no sledges were found at the place. I replied that the boat was likely fitted with sledge-runners that screwed on to it. The natives answered, that the sledges were noticed with the party of whites when alive, and that their tracks on the ice and snow were seen near the place where the bodies were found. My answer then was, That they must have burnt them for fuel; and I have no doubt but that the kegs or cases containing the ball and shot must have shared the same fate.

Quoting again from the article on the lost Arctic voyagers. "Lastly, no man can with any show of reason undertake to affirm that this sad remnant of Franklin's gallant band were not set upon and slain by the Esquimaux themselves?"

This is a question which like many other is much more easily asked than answered; yet I will give my reasons for not thinking, even for a moment, that some thirty or forty of the bravest class of one of the bravest nations in the world, even when reduced to the most wretched condition, and having firearms and ammunition in their hands, could be overcome by a party of savages equal in number to themselves. I say equal in number, because the Esquimaux to the eastward of the Coppermine, seldom, if ever, collect together in greater force than thirty men, owing to the difficulty of obtaining the means of subsistence. When Sir John Ross wintered three years in Prince Regent's Inlet, the very tribe of Esquimaux who saw Sir John Franklin's party were constantly or almost constantly in the neighbourhood. In the several springs he passed there, parties of his men were travelling in various directions; yet no violence was offered to them, although there was an immense advantage to be gained by the savages in obtaining possession of the vessels and their contents.

What appears to me the most conclusive reason for believing the Esquimaux report, is this: the natives of Repulse Bay, although they visit and communicate for mutual advantage with those further west, both dislike and fear their neighbours, and not without cause; as they have behaved treacherously to them on one or two occasions. So far do they carry this dislike, that they endeavoured, by every means in their power, to stimulate me to shoot several visitors to Repulse Bay, from Pelly Bay, and from near Sir John Ross's wintering-station in Prince Regent's Inlet.

Now, is it likely that, had they possessed such a powerful argument to excite—as they expected to do—my anger and revenge as the murder of my countrymen, would they have not made use of it by acquainting me with the whole circumstances, if they had any such to report?

Again, what possible motive could the Esquimaux have for inventing such an awful tale as that which appeared in my report to the secretary of the Admiralty? Alas! these poor people know all too well what starvation is, in its utmost extremes, to be mistaken on such a point. Although these uneducated savages—who seem to be looked upon by those who know them not, as little better than brutes—resort to the "last resource" only when driven to it by the most dire necessity. They will starve for days before they will even sacrifice their dogs to satisfy the cravings of their appetites.

One or two facts are worth a hundred theories on any subject. On meeting some old acquaintances among the natives at Repulse Bay, last spring, I enquired about other that I had seen there in 1846 and '47. The reply was, that many of them had died of starvation since I left. Among these was one man whom I well knew—Shi-ma-keck—and for whom I enquired by name. I learnt that this man, rather than endure the terrible spectacle of his children pining away in his presence, went out and strangled himself. Another, equally well known to me, being unable, I suppose, to support the pangs of hunger, stripped off his clothes, and exposed himself to cold, until he was frozen to death.

Rich, E.E., Johnson, A.M: Rae's Arctic Correspondence 1844–55
London: The Hudson's Bay Record Society, 1953. Maps (some folding and partly coloured). Extra illustrated with colour photocopy of a "Map of the Arctic Exploration from which resulted the first information of Sir John Franklin's missing Party; by John Rae. 1854. Rae was the first to adopt the Eskimo way of life during his explorations, and ate, travelled and lived like the Eskimos: this may be partly responsible for his successful expeditions in the Arctic. Excellent historical introduction, accompanied by Rae's letters written from the Arctic." This copy is No 1122 of a Limited Edition which is issued only to subscribers to The Hudson's Bay Record Society. John Rae's correspondence with Hudson's Bay Company on Arctic Exploration 1844-55. (Ref. #ACC-C100). . Limited Edition. Hard Cover. Fine. 7" x 10" Tall. Canadian History. ARCTIC EXPLORATION JOHN RAE HUDSON BAY CANADIAN HISTORY. Catalogs: Canadian History. (Inventory #004687) www.biblio.com/glossary.php?action=search&dcx=10016252

CHAPTER EIGHT

1. Sir Robert Borden had a surprisingly good understanding of the north and its people. Governor-General Adrienne Clarkson evoked this in her Stefánsson Memorial lecture: "In 1921, our Prime Minister, Sir Robert Borden, wrote an introduction to the book [Stefánsson's *The Friendly Arctic*]. In it, he said that, for anyone who read Stefánsson's *My Life with the Eskimo*: "Many preconceived ideas of these great northern territories must disappear forever."

He added: "There seems to be much truth in Stefánsson's observation that the cold of the Arctic deprives no one of either health or comfort if he understands conditions, realizes necessary precautions and, making good use of his common sense, governs himself accordingly."

Borden also spoke about the deprivation experienced in Europe at the end of the Great War, when heating fuel was scarce, even in London, England. The cold was such that he had to seek firewood from the Canadian Corps stationed nearby. He compared this to Stefánsson and his party who, at that very same time, were "sitting in their shirt sleeves hundreds of miles within the Arctic Circle comfortably housed in an edifice which was constructed of snow blocks in less than three hours."

As a Canadian, I find it wonderful to think that the prime minister of the time understood, through Stefánsson's writing, more than we might think about life in the higher reaches of the Arctic. As Borden explained, the Eskimo's "social organization, their conception of life, their ideas respecting the phenomena of nature and their practical adaptability to a difficult environment were probably similar to those which prevailed among our ancestors. They spoke several dialects of a remarkably complex language and in everyday life they used a vocabulary far exceeding that which we ordinarily employed. Through the accumulated experience of successive generations they had acquired habits of life admirably suited to their surrounding. For them the age of magic still existed and without difficulty they accounted for the most miraculous or impossible events. Kindness, hospitality and many social virtues adorned their lives. But contact with the white races has been seldom beneficial to any such type. When a primeval civilization comes into contact with ours, the new wine is too strong for the old bottle."

2. The *Mary Sachs* was a 30-ton, 60-foot schooner with twin propellers, built at Benicia, California, near San Francisco in 1898. She once served as a mail boat for the U.S. Postal Service.

3. From an interview with trader D.R. Stein, *The Daily Province*, Vancouver, November 3, 1919.

4. The following publications resulted from this expedition:

CANADIAN ARCTIC EXPEDITION 1913–18 REPORTS
XII. REPORT OF THE CANADIAN ARCTIC EXPEDITION 1913–18, VOL. XII:
THE COPPER ESKIMOS;
Part A: THE LIFE OF THE COPPER ESKIMOS by Diamond Jenness (1922), 277 pages, 9 plates, 69 figures, 2 maps. (OUT OF PRINT)
Part B: PHYSICAL CHARACTERISTICS OF THE COPPER ESKIMOS by Diamond Jenness (1923), 89 pages, 12 illustrations, tables. ISBN 0-660-02413-6. (OUT OF PRINT)
Part C: OSTEOLOGY OF THE WESTERN AND CENTRAL ESKIMOS by J. Cameron (1923), 79 pages, 8 illustrations, tables. ISBN 0-660-02414-4. (OUT OF PRINT)
Part D: THE DENTITION OF THE WESTERN AND CENTRAL ESKIMOS by S.G. Ritchie (1923), 7 pages. (OUT OF PRINT)
XIII. REPORT OF THE CANADIAN ARCTIC EXPEDITION 1913–18, VOL. XIII: ESKIMO FOLKLORE;
Part A: MYTHS AND TRADITIONS FROM NORTHERN ALASKA, THE MACKENZIE DELTA AND CORONATION GULF by Diamond Jenness (1924), 90 pages. ISBN 0-660-02415-2. (OUT OF PRINT)
Part B: ESKIMO STRING FIGURES by Diamond Jenness (1924), 192 pages, 229 figures. $5.00. ISBN 0-660-02416-0.
XIV. REPORT OF THE CANADIAN ARCTIC EXPEDITION 1913–18, VOL. XIV: ESKIMO SONGS;
SONGS OF THE COPPER ESKIMOS by Helen H. Roberts and Diamond Jenness (1925), 506 pages, 145 sheets of music. $9.95. ISBN 0-660-02418-7.
XV. REPORT OF THE CANADIAN ARCTIC EXPEDITION 1913-18, VOL. XV;

Part A: **COMPARATIVE VOCABULARY OF THE WESTERN ESKIMO DIALECTS** by Diamond Jenness (1928), 134 pages. $3.95.
ISBN 0-660-02417-9.
Part B: **GRAMMATICAL NOTES ON SOME WESTERN ESKIMO DIALECTS** by Diamond Jenness (1944), 34 pages. (OUT OF PRINT)
XVI. REPORT OF THE CANADIAN ARCTIC EXPEDITION 1913-18, VOL. XVI;
MATERIAL CULTURE OF THE COPPER ESKIMOS by Diamond Jenness (1946), 148 pages, 189 figures. (OUT OF PRINT)
5. Jerry Kobalenko, *The Horizontal Everest* (Toronto: Penguin, 2002), p. 53.

CHAPTER NINE
1. It is reproduced in Derek Hayes' *Historical Atlas of the Arctic* (Seattle: University of Washington Press and Vancouver: Douglas & McIntyre, 2003).
2. For more on IGY, go to http://ipy.gsfc.nasa.gov/egu.shtml.

CHAPTER TEN
1. Arctic Monitoring and Assessment Program, AMAP Assessment 2002: Persistent Organic Pollutants in the Arctic.
2. The Greenland Ice Sheet Project Two (GISP2) is being carried out by scientists from: the U.S. Army Cold Regions Research and Engineering Laboratory in Hanover, NH, Carnegie Mellon University the Desert Research Institute in Reno, Nevada, The Massachusetts Institute of Technology, Ohio State University, Pennsylvania State University, the New York State Department of Health, the State University of New York at Albany, the State University of New York at Buffalo, Lamont-Doherty Geological Observatory of Columbia University, University of Arizona, University of Colorado, University of Miami, University of New Hampshire, University of Rhode Island, University of Washington, the U. S. Geological Survey in Tacoma, Washington, and the University of Wisconsin. GISP2 is funded by the United States National Science Foundation Division of Polar Programs as a part of the Arctic System Science Initiative (ARCSS). The University of New Hampshire coordinates GISP2 scientific activities. The Polar Ice Coring Office (PICO) at the University of Alaska in Fairbanks provides logistical and drilling support. Permission to work in Greenland is generously provided by The Commission for Scientific Research in Greenland and the governments of Denmark and Greenland. The 109th TAG Air National Guard, Schenectady, NY, and the U. S. Air Force Military Airlift Command from McGuire Air Force Base in New Jersey provide air transport. The U.S. Air Force Space Command provides support at Sondrestrom Air Base in Greenland.
3. NSF's Office of Polar Programs has established a committee to study the possible scientific exploration of sub-glacial Antarctic lakes. Read the committee's charge at www.nsf.gov/od/opp/antarct/subglclk.htm. The international Scientific Committee on Antarctic Research maintains a site on the exploration of sub-glacial lakes at http://salegos-scar.montana.edu/.

4. Michael Studinger, of the Lamont-Doherty Earth Observatory (LDEO) at Columbia University, Robin Bell, of LDEO, and Anahita Tikku, formerly of the University of Tokyo and now at Rensselaer Polytechnic Institute.

5. J. Dibb, P.A. Mayewski, C.F. Buck and S.M. Drummey, "Beta Radiation from Snow," *Nature* (1990), 344, 6270, 25.

6. Data from D.M. Etheridge, G.E. Pearman and P.J. Fraser, "Changes in Tropospheric Methane between 1841 and 1978 from a High Accumulation Rate Antarctic Ice Core," *Tellus, Ser. B.* 44 (1992): 282–94; C.K. Keeling, J.A. Adams, C.A. Ekdahl, and P.R. Guenther, "Atmospheric Carbon Dioxide Variations at the South Pole," *Tellus*, 28 (1976): 552–64; T. Machida, T. Makazawa, Y. Fujii, S. Aoke, and O. Watanabe, "Increase in Atmospheric Nitrous Oxide Concentrations during the Last 250 Years," *Geophys. Res Lett.* 22 (1995): 2921–24; C. McEvedy and R. Jones, *Atlas of World Population History* (Penguin, 1978); P.A. Mayewski, W.B. Lyons, M.J. Spencer, M.S. Twickler, C.F. Buck and S. Whitlow, "An Ice Core Record of Atmospheric Response to Anthropogenic Sulphate and Nitrate, *Nature* (1990), 346 (6284): 554–56.

7. K.J. Kreutz, P.A. Mayewski, L.D. Meeker, M.S. Twickler, S.E. Whitlow and I.I. Pittawala, "Bipolar Changes in Atmospheric Circulation during the Little Ice Age," *Science* (1997).

8. See the *Journal of Geophysical Research.*

9. NASA's camera of choice: Dr. Bondar found that in space, she could hold two of the big cameras bound together, floating with very little effort. On earth, it was much tougher.

10. Roberta Bondar, *Canada: Landscape of Dreams* (Vancouver/Toronto: Douglas & McIntyre, 2002), p. 24.

CHAPTER ELEVEN

1. You can hear it on the Telarc CD-80143: Los Angeles Philharmonic Orchestra, André Previn; Christine Cairns, Mezzo-soprano; Los Angeles Master Choral, John Currie, Director.

2. I have drawn extensively for this account on *The Leningrad Siege* by Lyubov Tsarevskaya from the Voice of Russia, 2003.

3. An admiralty clerk's mistake resulted in the *Habbakuk* being named with the wrong spelling—but it was indeed a wondrous concept.

4. CANARIE's mission is to accelerate Canada's advanced Internet development and use by facilitating the widespread adoption of faster, more efficient networks, and by enabling the next generation of advanced products, applications and services to run on them.

5. This story appears in a delightful biography of inventor Geoffrey Pyke by David Lampe, *Pyke: The Unknown Genius* (London: Evans Brothers, 1959).

6. Pyke's memos can be found through the Public Record Office (www.pro.go.uk), Admiralty Files ADM 1/15672 and ADM 1/15677. There are also references in the *London Illustrated News*, March 2, 1946, pp. 234–37.

7. "War on Ice?" *Newsweek*, March 11, 1946, p. 51.

8. Martin Perutz, "Enemy Alien," *The New Yorker*, August 12, 1985, pp. 35–54.

9. For more on pykrete go to www.geocities.com/Broadway/1928/pykrete.htm.

10. Ontario's Lailey Vineyard, under the principle that the tightness of the wood grain in cold-climate trees might have something special to offer, is experimenting with aging its wines in Canadian oak.

CHAPTER TWELVE

1. For a photographic comparison of the Columbia Icefield between 1906 and 1998, visit www.whyte.org/time/rockies/glaciers/index.html.

2. *Exploring the Canadian Alps: The Vaux Family Rocky Mountain Photographs, 1899–1936* (Library Company of Philadelphia, 1996); another good book on the Vaux family that includes many of the ice photographs is *Legacy in Ice, The Vaux Family and the Canadian Alps* by Edward Cavell (Banff: Altitude Publishing and the Library Company of Philadelphia).

3. Now with the Whyte Museum of the Rockies in Banff, Alberta.

4. Luckmann et al., *Géographie physique et Quaternaire*, 53(3), 1999.

5. Home of the World Ice Art Championships.

6. David Hawley, "Why Build an Ice Palace? Because It's Really Cool," *Pioneer Press*, January 14, 2004.

7. *Harbin* is Manchurian for drying fishnets.

8. Air India said it would replicate the ice Taj Mahal in the northern Japanese city of Sapporo in February 2004 at another major ice sculpture festival. The popularity of such events appears to be spreading.

9. Have a look for yourself at www.chinaonyourmind.com/chinatravel/chinatravelnews/harbin_ice.html.

CHAPTER THIRTEEN

1. As neurolinguist Deborah Tannen has long established, men (unlike women) don't tend to need or want eye contact to have their most meaningful conversations.

CHAPTER FOURTEEN

1. My mother has provided me with this account from my late father's surviving family.

2. Quoted in Gavin Wightman's, *The Frozen Water Trade* (New York: Hyperion, 2003).

3. Ibid.

GLOSSARY

Ablation — All processes by which snow, ice, or water in any form are lost from a glacier; the loss of snow or ice by evaporation and melting.

Ablation area — The lower region of a glacier where snow ablation exceeds snowfall.

Accumulation area — The upper region of a glacier where snow accumulation exceeds melting.

Albedo — The fraction of incident radiation reflected by a surface. For example, in terms of visible light, white surfaces tend to be highly reflective, while darker surfaces tend to absorb more incoming radiation.

Amorphous water ice — At 120 Kelvin (−153°C) water/ice loses its distinct crystalline structure.

Arctic — The area lying above 66° 32' N (often rounded to 66.5° N). Along this line, the sun does not set on the day of the summer solstice, and does not rise on the day of the winter solstice.

Arctic air mass — Mass of very cold air in the Arctic regions, which invades lower latitudes at irregular intervals.

Arctic mist — A mist of ice crystals; a very light ice fog.

Arete — Sharp, narrow ridge formed as a result of glacial erosion from both sides.

Aurora — Luminous phenomena, in the form of arcs, bands, draperies, or curtains in the high atmosphere over high latitudes. Auroras are related to magnetic storms and the influx of charged particles from the sun. The phenomena are called **aurora borealis** in the northern hemisphere and **aurora australis** in the southern hemisphere. Also known as northern lights and southern lights.

Bay ice — Ice newly formed upon the surface of the sea. The expression is, however, applied also to ice a foot or two in thickness.

Berg — An iceberg.

Bergy bit — Large chunk of glacier ice (a very small iceberg) floating in the sea. Bergy bits are usually less than 15 feet high, and are generally spawned from disintegrating icebergs.

Bestet — The situation of a ship when closely surrounded by ice.

Bight — An indentation in a floe of ice, like a bay, by which name it is sometimes called.

Blink — A peculiar brightness in the atmosphere, often assuming an archlike form. The blink of land, as well as that over large quantities of ice, is usually of a yellowish cast.

Bore — The operation of "boring" through loose ice consists in entering it and forcing the ship through by separating the masses.

Brash ice — Accumulations of floating ice made up of fragments not more than 6 feet across; the wreckage of other forms of ice.

Cache — Literally a hiding place. The places of deposit of provision in Arctic travel are so called.

Calf — A mass of ice lying under a floe near its margin, and when disengaged from that position, rising with violence to the surface of the water. See Tongue.

Calving — A large mass of ice breaking off from a larger ice shelf, glacier or ice sheet into the water.

Catchment glacier — A glacier that receives nourishment from wind-blown snow.

Chattermarks — Striations or marks left on the surface of exposed bedrock caused by the advance and retreat of glacier ice.

Cirque — A glacially eroded basin shaped like half a bowl; a deep, steep-walled recess in a mountain, caused by glacial erosion.

Cirque glacier — A glacier that resides in basins or amphitheatres near ridge crests. Most cirque glaciers have a characteristic circular shape, with their width as wide or wider than their length.

Cirque lake — A small body of water occupying a cirque depression, dammed by a rock lip, small moraine, or both. See also Tarn.

Clathrates — Gas trapped in a crystallized ice cage structure under high-pressure. Sometimes known as "flammable ice."

Compressing flow — Flow that occurs when glacier motion is decelerating down-slope.

Constructive metamorphism — Snow metamorphism that adds molecules to sharpen the comers and edges of an ice crystal.

Contrails — Ice crystals that are suspended in jet aircraft exhaust.

Crevasses — Open fissures in glacier ice. Crevasses form where the speed of the ice is variable, such as in icefalls and at valley bends.

Crow's nest — A small circular house, like a cask, fixed at the masthead, in which the look-out man sits, either to guide the ship through the ice, or to give notice of whales.

Dene — The Athabascan-speaking peoples of northwest Canada and inland Alaska considered as a group.

Density — Density is the ratio of the mass of an object to its volume. Snow has a density averaging about 0.1, firn has a density of about 0.55, and glacier ice has a density of about 0.89. The density of unmineralized fresh water is 1.

Depth hoar — An ice crystal that develops within a layer of snow. Depth hoar is characterized by rapid recrystallization, usually caused by strong gradients in temperature, forming crystal shapes that resemble cups and scrolls. Typically found near the bottom of an annual accumulation of snow and most persistent on polar or subpolar glaciers where air temperatures are cold and annual snow accumulations are light.

Diamond dust — A type of precipitation composed of slowly falling, very small, unbranched crystals of ice which often seem to float in the air. It may fall from a high cloud or from a cloudless sky. It usually occurs under frosty weather conditions (under very low air temperatures). Also known as ice needles, frost in the air and frost mist.

Dock — In a floe, may be natural or artificial: the former being simply a small "bight," in which a ship is placed to secure her from the danger of external pressure; and the latter, a square space cut out with saws for a similar purpose.

Dorset — The most recent of the Paleo-Inuit cultures in the Canadian Arctic and Greenland, dating from 500 BC to AD 1400. Their sites are found in the coastal tundra regions of Newfoundland and Labrador.

Drain channel — Preferred path for meltwater to flow from the surface through a snow cover.

Drift — General term referring to any kind of glacially derived deposits.

Drifting stations (drifting ice stations) — Research stations on the floes of the Arctic Ocean.

Drumlin — A hilly remnant from the ice ages.

Emissivity — The amount of electromagnetic energy (primarily at wavelengths longer than 1.0 micrometre) that an object emits. For example, the earth emits long-wave radiation, much of which is in the infrared part of the electromagnetic spectrum. The earth also emits radiation in the even longer microwave wavelength regions. The emissivity of an object varies as the fourth power of its absolute temperature.

Equilibrium line — The boundary between the accumulation area and the ablation area.

Equilibrium zone — Zone of a glacier in which the amount of precipitation that falls is equal to the amount that melts the following summer.

Erratic — A boulder swept from its place of origin by glacier advance or retreat and deposited elsewhere as the glacier melted. After glacial melt, the boulder might be stranded in a field or forest where no other rocks of its type or size exist.

Esker — A sinuous ridge of sedimentary material (typically gravel or sand) deposited by streams that cut channels under or through the glacier ice.

Eustasy — Global position and changes in position of sea level.

Extending flow — When glacier motion is accelerating down-slope.

Fast ice — Sea ice which forms and remains fast along the coast, where it is attached to the shore, to an ice wall, to an ice front, between shoals or grounded icebergs. Fast ice may move up and down with changes in sea level. It may form in situ from sea water or by freezing of pack ice of any age to the shore, and it may extend a few yards or several hundred miles from the coast. Fast ice may be more than one year old and may then be prefixed with the appropriate age category (old, second-year, or multi-year).

Field — A sheet of ice generally of great thickness, and extending beyond the visual field which can be seen from a ship's masthead.

Fiord (sometimes spelled fjord) — An abrupt opening in the coastline admitting the sea, usually of glacial origin.

Firn — Firn is old snow that has been recrystallized into a denser substance. Snowflakes are compressed under the weight of the overlying snowpack. Individual crystals near the melting point have slick liquid edges allowing them to glide along other crystal planes and to readjust the space between them. Where the crystals touch they bond together, squeezing the air between them to the surface or into bubbles. During summer we might see the crystal metamorphosis occur more rapidly because of water percolation between the crystals. By summer's end the result is firn—a compacted snow with the appearance of wet sugar, but with a hardness that makes it resistant to all but the most dedicated snow shovelers! Firn has a density greater than 0.55.

Firnspiegel — A thin sheet of ice formed on the glacier surface by rapid refreezing of solar-heated snow or firn, usually at high elevations during spring.

Floe — The same as a field, except that its extent can be distinguished from the ship's masthead. A "bay-floe" is a floe of ice newly formed.

Floe piece — An expression generally applied to small pieces of floes, not more than a furlong square.

Fluted berg — An iceberg that is grooved into a curtainlike pattern; thought to be carved by small meltwater streams.

Fracture — Any break or rupture through very close pack ice, compact pack ice, consolidated pack ice, fast ice, or a single floe resulting from deformation processes. Fractures may contain brash ice and/or be covered with nilas and/or young ice. Length may vary from a few yards to many miles.

Frazil ice — Fine spicules or plates of ice, suspended in water. Frazil ice formation represents the first stage of sea ice growth. The frazil crystals are usually suspended in the top few inches of the surface layer of the ocean and give the water an oily appearance. In the open ocean the crystals may form, or be stirred to a depth of several yards by wave-induced turbulence.

Frost point — The highest temperature at which atmospheric moisture will sublimate in the form of hoarfrost on a cooled surface. It is analogous to the dew point.

Geyser — A fountain that develops when water from a conduit is forced up to the surface of a glacier; also called a negative mill.

Glacial advance — Glacial advance is the net movement of glacier terminus down-valley. Advance occurs when the rate of glacier flow down-valley is greater than its rate of ablation. Advances show a convex-shaped terminus.

Glacial drift — Glacial drift is the loose and unsorted rock debris distributed by glaciers and glacial melt waters. Rocks may be dropped in place by the melting ice; they may be rolled to the ice margins, or they may be deposited by melt water streams. Collectively, these deposits are called glacial drift. Till refers to the debris deposited directly by the glacier. Rock debris rolls off the glacier edges and builds piles of loose unconsolidated rocks called glacier moraine. Lateral moraines form along the side of a glacier and curl into a terminal moraine.

Glacial flour — Glacial flour is the fine-grained sediment carried by glacial rivers that results from the abrasion of rock at the glacier bed. Its presence turns lake water aqua blue or brown, depending on its parent rock type.

Glacial polish — Glacial polish is the levelling and smoothing of rock by fine-grained debris at the glacier bed. Coarser rocks may gouge scratches called striations.

Glacial retreat — Glacial retreat is the net movement of the glacier terminus up-valley. Retreat results when the glacier is ablating at a rate faster than its movement down-valley. Retreating termini are usually concave in shape.

Glacial till — An unsorted, unstratified mixture of fine and coarse rock debris deposited by a glacier. Also called till.

Glacier — A glacier is a body of ice showing evidence of movement as reported by the presence of ice flowline, crevasses, and recent geologic evidence. Glaciers exist where, over a period of years, snow remains after summer's end.

Glacieret — A very small glacier.

Glacier outburst flood — A sudden release of meltwater from a glacier or glacier-dammed lake sometimes resulting in a catastrophic flood, formed by melting of a channel or by subglacial volcanic activity.

Glacio(...) — Used as a prefix with another term to indicate relationship to glaciers

Grease ice — A later stage of freezing than frazil ice when the crystals have coagulated to form a soupy layer on the surface. Grease ice reflects little light, giving the surface a matte appearance. Grease ice behaves in a viscous fluidlike manner, and does not form distinct ice floes.

Great Ice Age — The Pleistocene Epoch.

Grey ice — Young ice 10–15 cm thick. Less elastic than nilas and breaks on swells. Usually rafts under pressure.

Grey-white ice — Young ice 15–30 cm thick. Under pressure more likely to ridge than to raft.

Growler — An iceberg less than 7 feet across that floats with less than 3 feet showing above water; smaller than a bergy bit.

Hail — Frozen raindrops. Also known as sleet.

Hanging glacier — A glacier that terminates at or near the top of a cliff.

Headwall — A steep cliff, usually the uppermost part of a cirque.

Hydrothermal alteration — Hydrothermal alteration is the alteration of rocks or minerals due to the reactions of geothermally heated water with minerals. The process weathers and weakens the rocks such that they may become unstable.

Hummock — A mass of ice rising to a considerable height above the general level of a floe, and forming a part of it. Hummocks are originally raised by the pressure of floes against each other.

Ice — The solid crystalline form of water. Ice is a mineral: hydrogen oxide.

Ice anchor — A hook or grapnel adapted to take hold upon ice.

Ice apron — A mass of ice adhering to a mountainside.

Ice belt — A continued margin of ice, which in high northern latitudes, adheres to the coast above the ordinary level of the sea.

Iceberg — A large floating mass of ice detached from a glacier.

Ice blink — White glare on the underside of low clouds indicating presence of ice, which may be beyond the range of vision.

Ice cap — A dome-shaped mass of glacier ice that spreads out in all directions. An ice cap is usually larger than an icefield but less than 12 million acres.

Icefalls — Icefalls are somewhat analogous to waterfalls in rivers. The flow of the ice down a steep gradient often results in crevasses and seracs.

Icefield — A mass of glacier ice, similar to an ice cap. An icefield is usually smaller than an ice cap, somewhat controlled by terrain, and often does not have a dome like shape.

Ice sheet — A dome-shaped mass of glacier ice that covers surrounding terrain and is greater than 12 million acres (e.g., Greenland and Antarctic ice sheets).

Ice shelf — Portion of an ice sheet that spreads out over water.

Ice stream — 1. A current of ice in an ice sheet or ice cap that flows faster than the surrounding ice. 2. Sometimes referring to the confluent sections of a branched-valley glacier. 3. Obsolete synonym of valley glaciers.

Ice wedge — Wedge ice comprises a series of ice veins (ice occupying cracks in permafrost) that are formed at the same location over time.

Ice worm — An oligochaete (hermaphroditic) worm that lives on temperate glaciers or perennial snow. There are several species that range in colour from yellowish brown to reddish brown or black. They are usually less than .04 inches in diameter and average about 0.1 inches long. Some feed off red algae.

Inuit — Native peoples of the Canadian Arctic and Greenland. The plural of the Inuit word inuk: "human being."

Innu — Formerly referred to as the Naskapi or Montagnais Indians, the Innu reside in Nitassinan (Eastern Quebec and Labrador). The Innu population is about 16,000 today, concentrated mostly in 13 villages.

Jökulhlaup — Icelandic term for glacial outburst floods. Jökulhlaups are sudden outbursts of water released by a glacier. The water may be released from glacier cavities, subglacial lakes, and from glacier-dammed lakes in side valleys.

Katabatic wind — Wind that flows from a glacier. A katabatic wind is caused by air that cools over the ice surface becoming heavier than surrounding air, then draining down-valley. Also called glacier wind.

Kinematic waves — Refers to a wave of ice moving down-glacier propagated by its increased thickness. The wave of ice may move at 2 to 6 times the velocity of surrounding thinner ice.

L'Anse aux Meadows — The only known Viking site in North America, L'Anse aux Meadows is located near the northern tip of Newfoundland. Found in 1960 by Helge Ingstad, it proves that Vikings reached North America around 1000 CE, five hundred years before Columbus.

Land ice — Ice attached to the land, either in floes or in heavy grounded masses lying near shore.

Lane of water — A narrow channel among the masses of ice, through which a boat or a ship pass.

Latent heat of fusion — The amount of heat required to cause a change of phase from solid to liquid, or the heat released when the phase change is from liquid to solid. In the case of melting snow, the phase change from ice to water requires a significant amount of heat—160 times that required to raise the temperature of the same amount of ice by just 1°C. Until the required amount of heat is supplied to completely melt all of the ice being considered, no further increase in temperature will occur.

Lateral moraine — A ridge-shaped moraine deposited at the side of a glacier and composed of material eroded from the valley walls by the moving glacier.

Lead — Any fracture or passageway through sea ice, which is navigable by surface vessels. A more general description of a lead is an area of open water or new ice between ice floes, although the term is generally applied to linear features. If the open area is very large, it may be called a polynya. A lead between the shore and the pack ice is called a coastal lead or shore lead, and a lead between the fast ice and the pack ice is called a flaw lead.

Magnetic Pole — Either of the two points (north and south) on the earth's surface at which magnetic meridians converge. The horizontal component of the magnetic field of the earth becomes zero at this point.

Mass balance — Mass balance describes the net gain or loss of snow and ice through a given year. It is usually expressed in terms of water gain or loss.

Medial moraines — Medial moraines form where two mountain glaciers bearing lateral moraines unite. They appear as dark streaks of rock along the glacier centre-line.

Meltwater conduit — A channel within, underneath, on top of, or near the side of a glacier that drains meltwater out of the glacier. A meltwater conduit is usually kept open by the frictional heating of flowing water that melts the ice walls of the conduit.

Microwave sensors — In terms of wavelength, microwaves range from 1 centimetre to 1 metre, and are much longer than the shorter visible (0.000381 – 0.0007874 millimetre) wavelengths. These longer wavelengths allow microwave energy to penetrate through atmospheric clouds. Because these sensors measure microwave energy, they do not rely on sunlight for illumination, which allows microwave sensors to acquire images regardless of time of day.

Microwave sensors are either passive or active sensors. Passive sensors detect and record naturally upwelling microwave energy emitted from objects. An active sensor generates its own beam of energy, generally via antennas, that sends a pulse of microwave energy in the direction of interest. The antenna then detects the returned energy patterns (backscatter) that indicate the presence of objects and their position relative to the sensor.

Radar (radio detection and ranging) was the original active microwave sensor that became widely operational with the onset of World War II.

Moraine — Rock debris deposited by a glacier. A mound, ridge or other distinct accumulation of glacial till.

Moraine shoal — Glacial moraine that has formed a shallow place in water.

Moulin — A nearly vertical channel in ice that is formed by flowing water; usually found after a relatively flat section of glacier in a region of transverse crevasses. Also called a glacier mill.

Mountain glacier — A glacier that is confined by surrounding mountain terrain.

Neoglaciation — Advances made by mountain glaciers since the great Pleistocene ice age.

Névé — 1. The accumulation zone of a glacier. 2. Firn.

Niche glacier — A glacier that resides in a small recess of the terrain. Also called a pocket glacier.

Nilas — A thin elastic crust of ice, easily bending on waves and swell and under pressure, thrusting in a pattern of interlocking "fingers" (finger rafting). Has a matt surface and is up to 10 centimetres thick. May be subdivided into dark nilas and light nilas. Dark nilas is less than 2 inches thick and very dark in colour. Light nilas is 5–10 centimetres thick and reflects proportionately more light than dark nilas, depending on its thickness.

Nipped — The situation of a ship when forcibly pressed by ice on both sides.

Ogives — Alternate bands of light and dark ice seen on a glacier surface.

Outburst flood — Any catastrophic flooding from a glacier. Outburst floods may originate from trapped water in cavities inside a glacier or at the margins of glaciers or from lakes that are dammed by flowing glaciers.

Pack ice — Term used in a wide sense to include any area of sea ice, other than fast ice, no matter what form it takes or how it is disposed. The pack can be described as very open (with an ice concentration of 1/10 to 3/10), open (4/10 to 6/10, with many leads and polynyas and the floes generally not in contact with one another), close (7/10 to 8/10, composed of floes mostly in contact), very close (9/10 to less than 10/10), and compact (10/10, with no water visible, called consolidated pack ice if the floes are frozen together).

Pancake ice — Newly formed ice, in numberless individual patches of "sludge," and giving the surface of the sea the appearance of handsome pavement. The individual ice cakes have upturned edges from banging together in the waves.

Patch of ice — The same as a pack, but of smaller dimensions.

Penitents — The extreme relief of ablation hollows found most often at high altitudes in the tropics. So named because the resulting spikes of snow resemble repentant souls.

Perennial snow — Snow that persists on the ground year after year.

Perfectly plastic solid — A solid that does not deform until it reaches a critical value of stress, after which it will yield infinitely. Some glaciologists say that ice is a perfectly plastic substance. (That is, brittle and capable of cracking like a solid, yet deformable and capable of flowing at other stresses.)

Permafrost — Permanently frozen subsoil, occurring throughout the Polar Regions and locally in perennially frigid areas.

Piedmont glacier — Large ice lobe spread out over surrounding terrain, associated with the terminus of a large mountain valley glacier.

Pingo — An Eskimo term for a perennial frost mound consisting of a core of massive ice with soil and vegetation cover. The size of a pingo can range from a few yards to tens of yards, in both diameter and height. Pingos can be found in continuous and discontinuous permafrost zones.

Pleistocene — The period of earth's history from roughly 2 million years ago to about ten thousand years ago, characterized by the advance and recession of continental ice sheets.

Polar day — In Polar Regions, the portion of the year when the sun is continuously in the sky. Its length changes from twenty hours at the Arctic/Antarctic Circle (latitude 66°33' N or S) to 186 days at the North/South Pole.

Polar glacier — Glacier whose temperatures are below freezing throughout, except possibly for a thin layer of melt near the surface during summer or near the bed. Polar glaciers are found only in Polar Regions of the globe or at high altitudes.

Polar night — In Polar Regions, the portion of the year when the sun does not rise above the horizon. Its length changes from twenty hours at the Arctic/Antarctic Circle (latitude 66°33' N or S) to 179 days at the North/South Pole.

Polynya — Any non-linear shaped opening enclosed in ice. Polynyas may contain brash ice and/or be covered with new ice, nilas or young ice; submariners refer to these as skylights. Sometimes the polynya is limited on one side by the coast and is called a shore polynya or by fast ice and is called a flaw polynya. If it recurs in the same position every year, it is called a recurring polynya. Polynyas range in size from relatively small to enormous

Pressure melting — Melting that occurs in ice at temperatures colder than normal melting temperature because of added pressure.

Push moraine — Moraine built out ahead of an advancing glacier.

Rafting — Pressure process whereby one piece of ice overrides another. Most common in new and young ice (cf. finger rafting). Finger rafting is a type of rafting whereby interlocking thrusts are formed, each floe thrusting "fingers" alternately over and under each other. Common in nilas and grey ice.

Randkluft — A fissure that separates a moving glacier from its headwall rock; like a bergschrund.

Red algae — An algae common on temperate glaciers and perennial snow. Its red colour sometimes prompts people to call it "watermelon snow," and it is said to taste like watermelon!

Regelation — Motion of an object through ice by melting and freezing that is caused by pressure differences. This process allows a glacier to slide past small obstacles on its bed.

Relict permafrost — Relict permafrost reflects past climatic conditions, usually colder temperatures, that differ from current conditions. This permafrost persists in places where it could not currently form.

Ridging — The pressure process by which sea ice is forced into ridges. A ridge is a line or wall of broken ice forced up by pressure. May be fresh or weathered. The submerged volume of broken ice under a ridge, forced downwards by pressure, is termed an ice keel.

Roche moutonnee — A roche moutonnee is a small asymmetrically shaped hill formed by glacial erosion. The upper sides are rounded and smoothed and the lower sides are rough and broken due to quarrying by the glacier.

Rock glacier — A glacier whose motion and behaviour is characterized by a large amount of embedded or overlying rock material. A rock glacier may be composed of: 1. Ice-cemented rock formed in talus that is subject to permafrost. 2. Ice-cemented rock debris formed from avalanching snow and rock. 3. Rock debris that has a core of ice; either a debris-covered glacier or a remnant end moraine.

Sailing ice — Ice of which the masses are so much separated as to allow a ship to sail among them.

Sea ice — Ice formed by ocean water. Generally only forms in the Arctic and Antarctic Oceans but patches of this ice can be carried a great distance by currents or winds.

Seracs — Seracs are the pinnacles of ice formed where the glacier surface is torn by sets of crevasses.

Sintering — The bonding together of ice crystals.

Shuga — An accumulation of spongy white lumps, a few inches across; they are formed from grease ice or slush and sometimes from anchor ice rising to the surface.

Sledge — A large sled usually pulled by dogs, used for transportation across snow and ice.

Sludge — Ice of the consistency of thick honey, offering little impediment to a ship while in this state, but greatly favouring the formation of a "bay-floe."

Slush — Snow that is saturated and mixed with water on land or ice surfaces, or as a viscous floating mass in water after heavy snowfall.

Snow — 1. An ice particle formed by sublimation of vapour in the atmosphere. 2. A collection of loosely bonded ice crystals deposited from the atmosphere.

Snow ice — Snow ice forms by refreezing flooded snow, creating an ice layer that bonds firmly to the top surface of a floe. Ice formed by this process and makes a significant contribution to the total mass of Antarctic sea ice. The snow cover of sea ice can become flooded by seawater via a number of mechanisms, in particular when the mass of snow becomes great enough to depress the ice/snow interface below sea level. The snow cover is porous and seawater can easily infiltrate from the sides of floes to form a slush layer at the ice/snow boundary. The snow may also become flooded by water rising up brine channels within the sea ice. With sufficiently cold temperatures, this slush layer freezes to form snow ice.

Splay crevasse — A crevasse pattern that forms where ice slowly spreads out sideways. Splay crevasses are commonly found near the glacier terminus.

Stream — A long and narrow, but generally continuous, collection of loose ice.

Striations — Striations are the scratches etched into the rock at the bed of a glacier. Their presence indicates grinding of sand and rock particles into the bed under considerable pressure. In some places, fine-grained debris polishes the bedrock to a lustrous surface finish called glacial polish.

Suncup — A suncup is a small depression on a snow or firn surface formed by melting and evaporation and resulting from direct exposure to the sun.

Surging glacier — A glacier that experiences a dramatic increase in flow rate, 10 to 100 times faster than its normal rate. Usually surge events last less than one year.

Tarn — A small mountain lake or pool, especially one that occupies an ice-gouged basin on the floor of a cirque.

Terminal moraine — A moraine formed at the down-valley end of a glacier. Piles of loose, unconsolidated rock at the glacier's down-valley end. The rocks may be pushed there by the forward motion of the glacier or dumped from the glacier's rounded surface.

Terminus — The down-valley end of a glacier. It is sometimes referred to as the glacier snout.

Thomson crystal — A large ice crystal found in deep, stagnant water-filled cavities of a glacier.

Tidewater glacier — A mountain glacier that terminates in the ocean.

Till — The unsorted rock debris deposited directly by the glacier without the extreme reworking by melt water. Also called glacial till.

Tongue — A mass of ice projecting under water from an iceberg or floe, and generally distinguishable at a considerable depth of smooth water. It differs from a "calf" in being fixed to, or a part of, the larger body.

Tracking — Towing along a margin of ice.

Trimlines — The sharp vegetative boundaries delimiting the upper margin of a former glaciation. The age differences of the ground surface are often visible because of different ages of the vegetation.

Water sky — A dark appearance in the sky, indicating "clear water" in that direction, and forming a striking contrast with the "blink" over land or ice.

Weathered ice — Glacier ice that has been exposed to sun or warm wind so that the boundaries between its ice crystals are partly disintegrated.

Young ice — Nearly the same as "bay-ice," but generally applied to ice more recently formed than the latter.

SELECTED BIBLIOGRAPHY

This bibliography refers only to books and print publications. Electronic publications are referenced in the endnotes.

Abley, Mark, ed., *Stories from the Ice Storm*, McClelland & Stewart, Toronto, 1999.

Admiralty Files ADM 1/15672 and ADM 1/15677, Public Record Office (www.pro.go.uk).

AMAP Assessment 2002: Persistent Organic Pollutants in the Arctic. Arctic Monitoring and Assessment Programme (AMAP), Oslo, Norway, 2004.

Atwood, Margaret, *Strange Things: The Malevolent North in Canadian Literature*, Clarendon Press, Oxford, 1995.

Barrett, Clarence, *Cape Breton Highlands National Park: A Park Lover's Companion*, Breton Books, 2002.

Bawlf, Samuel, *The Secret Voyage of Sir Francis Drake, 1577–1580*, Douglas & McIntyre, Vancouver/Toronto, 2003.

Beattie, Owen, and John Geiger, *Frozen in Time*, Western Producer Prairie Books, Saskatoon, 1987; newly reissued with a foreword by Margaret Atwood.

Blanchard, Duncan C., "The Snowflake Man," *Weatherwise* 23, no. 6 (1970): 260–69.

Bondar, Roberta, *Canada: Landscape of Dreams*, Douglas & McIntyre, Vancouver/Toronto, 2002.

Borghese, Elisabeth Mann, T*he Oceanic Circle: Governing the Seas as a Global Resource*, United Nations University Press, Tokyo, New York, Paris, 1998.

Breashears, David, *High Exposure: An Enduring Passion for Everest and Unforgiving Places*, foreword by Jon Krakauer, Simon & Schuster, New York, 1999.

Cavell, Edward, *Legacy in Ice: The Vaux Family and the Canadian Alps*, Altitude Publishing, Banff, Alberta, and the Library Company of Philadelphia, Philadelphia.

Chevallier, R., "The Greco-Roman Conception of the North from Pytheas to Tacitus," *Arctic* 37, no. 4 (Dec. 1984): 341–46.

Clark, Joan, *Latitudes of Melt*, Alfred A. Knopf, Toronto, 2000.

Columbia Encyclopedia, Columbia University Press, New York, 2001–04.

de Villiers, Marq, *Water*, Stoddart, Toronto, 1999.

Dibb, J., P.A. Mayewski, C.F. Buck, and S.M. Drummey, "Beta Radiation from Snow," *Nature* 344 (1990): 6270.

Dodd, John, and Gail Helgason, *Canadian Rockies Access Guide*, Lone Pine Publishing, Edmonton, Vancouver, Renton, WA, 1998.

Dyson, James L., *The World of Ice*, Alfred A. Knopf, New York, 1963.

Ehrlich, Gretel, *This Cold Heaven: Seven Seasons in Greenland*, Pantheon Books, New York, and Random House of Canada, Toronto, 2001.

Exploring the Canadian Alps: The Vaux Family Rocky Mountain Photographs, 1899–1936, Library Company of Philadelphia, Philadelphia, 1996.

Fagan, Brian, *The Little Ice Age: How Climate Made History 1300–1850*, Basic Books, New York, 2000.

Ferguson, Will, "Day of the Viking: At This Foggy Spot, the Idea of Canada was Forged," *Maclean's*, Toronto, July 1, 2001.

Fleming, Fergus, *Barrow's Boys: The Original Extreme Adventurers*, Granta Books, London and New York, 1998.

Fleming, Fergus, *Killing Dragons: The Conquest of the Alps*, Atlantic Monthly Press, New York, 2000.

Foster, Michael, and Carol Marino, *The Polar Shelf: The Saga of Canada's Arctic Scientists*, NC Press, Toronto, 1986.

Fowler, Brenda, *Iceman: Uncovering the Life and Times of a Prehistoric Man Found in an Alpine Glacier*, Random House, New York, 2000.

Grenfell, Sir Wilfred, *Adrift on an Ice Pan*, with an introduction by Ronald Rompkey, Creative Publishers, St. John's, 1992.

Hart, Matthew, *Diamond: A Journey to the Heart of an Obsession*, Penguin Group, 2001.

Hawley, David, "Why Build an Ice Palace? Because It's Really Cool," *Pioneer Press*, January 14, 2004.

Hayes, Derek, *Historical Atlas of the Arctic*, University of Washington Press, Seattle, and Douglas & McIntyre, Vancouver, 2003.

Hempleman-Adams, David, *Walking on Thin Ice: In Pursuit of the North Pole*, Orion Books, London, 1998.

Høeg, Peter, *Smilla's Sense of Snow*, trans. Tiina Nunnally, originally published in Danish under the title *Frøken Smillas fornemmelse for sne*, by Peter Høeg and Munksgaard/Rosinante, Copenhagen, 1992, translation copyright 1993 Farrar, Strauss & Giroux, reissued by Doubleday Canada, 2001.

Homer-Dixon, Thomas, *The Ingenuity Gap*, Knopf Canada, Toronto, 2000.

Horwood, Harold, *Bartlett: The Great Explorer*, Doubleday Canada, Toronto, 1977.

Hudson's Bay Record Society, London, 1953. Maps (some folding and partly coloured). Extra illustrated with colour photocopy of a "Map of the Arctic Exploration from which resulted the first information of Sir John Franklin's missing Party; by John Rae. 1854. Excellent historical introduction, accompanied by Rae's letters written from the Arctic." This copy is No. 1122 of a Limited Edition which is issued only to subscribers to the Hudson's Bay Record Society. John Rae's correspondence with Hudson's Bay Company on Arctic Exploration 1844–55. (Ref. #ACC-C100). Limited Edition. Hard Cover. Fine. 7" x 10" Tall. Canadian History. ARCTIC EXPLORATION JOHN RAE HUDSON BAY CANADIAN HISTORY. Catalogs: Canadian History. (Inventory #004687)

Ingstad, Helge, and Anne Stine Ingstad, *The Viking Discovery of America: The Excavation of a Norse Settlement in L'Anse aux Meadows*, Newfoundland, Breakwater Books, St. John's, 2000.

Kaye, Russell, text by W. Hodding Carter, *An Illustrated Viking Voyage: Retracing Leif Eriksson's Journey in an Authentic Viking Knarr*, Pocket Books, New York, 2000.

Kobalenko, Jerry, *The Horizontal Everest: Extreme Journeys on Ellesmere Island*, Penguin Group, Toronto, 2002.

Kreutz, K.J., P.A. Mayewski, L.D. Meeker, M.S. Twickler, S.E. Whitlow, and I.I. Pittawala, "Bipolar Changes in Atmospheric Circulation during the Little Ice Age," *Science* (1997).

Lampe, Davide, *Pyke: The Unknown Genius*, Evans Brothers, London, 1959.

Lapouge, Gilles, *Le bruit de la neige*, Albin Michel, Paris, 1996.

Leising, William A., O.M.I., *Arctic Wings*, Doubleday & Company, Garden City, NY, 1959.

London Illustrated News, March 2, 1946, 234–37.

Lopez, Barry, *Arctic Dreams*, Vintage Books, New York and Random House of Canada, Toronto, 1986.

Luckmann et al., *Géographie physique et Quaternaire* 53, no. 3 (1999).

McFarlane, Peter, and Haimila Wayne, *Ancient Land, Ancient Sky: Following Canada's Native Canoe Routes*. Alfred A. Knopf Canada, Toronto, 1999.

McGhee, Robert, *The Arctic Voyages of Martin Frobisher: An Elizabethan Adventure*, McGill-Queens University Press, Canadian Museum of Civilization, 2001, British Museum Press, 2002.

Morris, W.V., *Water*, Inland Waters Branch, Department of Energy, Mines and Resources, Ottawa, 1969.

Mowat, Farley, *The Top of the World Trilogy*, vol. 1: *Ordeal by Ice*; vol. 2: *The Polar Passion*, McClelland & Stewart, Toronto, 1960 [rev. 1973]; 1967.

Mowat, Farley, *The Alban Quest: The Search and Rescue for a Lost Tribe*, Key Porter Books, 1998.

National Research Council of Canada, Physics and Chemistry of Ice: 10TH International Conference on the Physics and Chemistry of Ice, *Canadian Journal of Physics* 81, nos. 1–2 (Jan./Feb. 2003).

Onfray, Michel, *Esthétique du pôle nord, Photographies d'Alain Szczuczynski*, Bernard Grasset, Paris, 2002.

Perutz, Martin, "Enemy Alien," *The New Yorker*, August 12, 1985, 35–54.

Petrella, Riccardo, *The Water Manifesto: Arguments for a World Water Contract*, trans. Patrick Camiller, foreword by Mario Soares, Fernwood Publishing Ltd., Halifax, 2001.

Pocock, Arthur, *Red Flannel and Green Ice*, Herbert Jenkins, London, 1950.

Siebert, Charles, "The Genesis Project," *New York Times Magazine*, September 26, 2004.

Spufford, Francis, *I May Be Some Time: Ice and the English Imagination*, Picador, New York, 1999; first published by Faber & Faber, London, 1997.

Stark, Peter, *Last Breath: Cautionary Tales from the Limits of Human Endurance*, Ballantine Books, New York, 2001.

Stark, Peter, ed., *Ring of Ice: True Tales of Adventure, Exploration and Arctic Life*, Lyons Press, New York, 2000.

Stefánsson, Vílhjalmur and Gisli Palsson, ed., *Writing on Ice: The Ethnographic Notebooks of Vilhjalmur Stefánsson*, University Press of New England, Lebanon, NH, 2001.

Steinbeck, John, *East of Eden*, Viking Press, New York, 1952.

Storey, Kenneth B., and Janet M. Storey, "Lifestyles of the Cold and Frozen," *The Sciences* (May 1999).

Troup, James A., ed., *The Ice-Bound Whalers: The Story of the Dee and the Grenville Bay, 1836–37*, maps by Anne Leith Brundle, Orkney Press in association with Stromness Museum, Orkney, 1987.

Wagner, Richard, *Designs on Space: Blueprints for 21ST Century Space Exploration*, with illustrations by Howard Cook, Simon & Schuster, New York, 2000.

"War on Ice?" *Newsweek*, March 11, 1946, 51.

Wharton, Thomas, *Icefields: Nunatak Fiction*, NeWest Press, Edmonton, 1995 [rprt. 2000].

Wightman, Gavin, *The Frozen Water Trade*, Hyperion, New York, 2003.

Willis, Clint, *Stories of Survival from Polar Exploration*, Thunder's Mouth Press, New York, and Balliet & Fitzgerald, New York, 1999.

Wylie, Betty Jane, *Letters to Icelanders Exploring the Northern Soul*, Macmillan Canada, Toronto, 1999.

INDEX

aboriginal people. *See* indigenous peoples
Adirondack Mountains, 16
Africa, 243
Agnello, Giovanni Battista, 110–11
Aid, 111
Akaitcho (Yellowknife chief), 143
Alaska, 52, 92, 221–22
   peoples of, 61, 84–85
   tourism in, 221, 234–35
Alaska, 153
albedo, 47, 307
Alberta, 210, 212, 277
Al-Biruni, 103
Alcock, Paul, 34
Aleut people, 84
Alexander Nevskii, 201
Alexander Nevsky (film), 201–2
Alexander the Great, 270
Alfred the Great, 107
algae, 33, 67, 319
Ali, Ameer, 102–3
Alutiiq-Aleut people, 84
Amazon River Basin, 44
American Association for the Advancement of
   Science, 44, 45–46
Amundsen, Roald, 135, 150, 165, 166
Anderson, R.M., 153
Anguikjuak, Ilkoo, 92
animals
   adaptation to ice, 61–62, 63–75
   with internal ice, 67–77
Anne (Queen of England), 216
Antarctica, 30–32, 80. *See also* South Pole
   exploration in, 150–52, 156, 159
   governance of, 167, 171–73, 247
   ice sheet over, 47, 80, 181–83
   research in, 167–69, 181–83
   tourism in, 244–47
Antarctic Treaty (1961), 171–73
antifreeze (natural), 72, 73, 75
Apollo 17, 191
Appalachian Mountains, 19
archaeology, 52–53, 119–20, 165, 166
Arctic. *See also* exploration; North Pole
   animals in, 63–75
   archaeology in, 52–53, 119–20
   definition of, 96, 307
   humans in, 79–83, 159–60
   ice pack in, 80–81, 115, 173–74

   ideas about, 95–97, 99, 124–25
   peoples of, 83–87
   plants in, 50–51, 61–62
   pollution in, 53, 177–78, 289
   research in, 5, 152–55, 163, 167–69,
     187–89
   time sense in, 119
   tourism in, 247
Arctic cod, 66–67
Arctic fox, 64
Arctic heath, 62
Arctic National Wildlife Refuge, 52
Arctic Ocean, 79
   on early maps, 95–96
   global warming and, 162–63
   research on, 164, 173–75
Arctic poppy, 62
Arduin, Dominick, 157–58
Aristotle, 26, 102
Arkhangelsk, 109
Arndt, Mike, 258
Asia, 44–45. *See also specific countries*
Athabasca Glacier, 30, 190–91, 223, 224–25
Athabascan people, 84–85
Atwood, Margaret, 197–98
aurora borealis/australis, 167–68, 169, 249–50,
   307
avalanches, 266

Baffin, William, 127
Baffin Island, 109–10, 117–19
Ball, Philip, 25
Balleny, John, 130
Bancroft, Ann, 139
barbarians, 199–201
Barents, Willem, 127
barnacles, 69
Barrette, Paul, 15, 25, 38–42, 193
Bartlett, Robert, 153, 155
bears, 93. *See also* polar bears
Beattie, Owen, 145
Beaufort Sea, 194
beer, 120–21, 276, 282
Belgium, 120–21
Bell, Alexander Graham, 18
Bentley, Wilson A., 27–28
bergy bits, 39, 308
Bering, Vitus, 127, 141
Beringia, 81

Bigjim, Fred, 79
biosphere, 16, 61–62
birds, 64, 67
Blechynden, Richard, 278
Bondar, Roberta, 196–98
Borchgrevink, Carson, 134
Borden, Robert, 153
Boston Bruins, 255
Bowman, Dale, 257–58
Bras d'Or Lakes, 18
Britain. See England
bumblebees, 18, 62
Burckle, Lloyd, 214
Burke, Edmund, 125
Bushoeven, Hermann von, 201
Bylot, Robert, 127
Byrd, Richard E., 136–38, 159

Cabot, John (Giovanni Caboto), 21, 106
Cabot, Sebastian, 107
Cagni, Lieutenant, 134
Cahill, Thomas, 200
Calvin, William H., 62–63, 177
Canada. See also specific locations,
  organizations and peoples
  and Arctic sovereignty, 153
  glaciers in, 222
  ice tourism in, 222–26, 229–34
  ice trade in, 269–70
  indigenous peoples in, 85–86, 92–93
  Inuit in, 85, 110, 114
  museums in, 224, 276–77
  research by, 170–71, 222
  seismic activity in, 17
  water resources in, 45
Canadian Ice Service, 170
Canadian Pacific Railway, 224
Canadian Shield, 16
caribou, 64
Carnaval de Québec, 235–36, 242–43
Cartier, Jacques, 106
cartography. See mapping; maps
Catherine de Medici, 270–71
C-CORE (Centre for Cold Ocean Resources
  Engineering), 22, 191, 193–95
Chancellor, Richard, 107–8, 163
Charcot, Jean-Baptiste, 134
Charles I (of England), 271
Chelyuskin, Vasily, 127
Chernobyl, 178, 183
Cherry-Garrard, Aspley, 117, 150–51
Chicks with Sticks, 264
China, 239–41
Chira, Mark, 243
Churchill, Winston, 207, 210, 212
Churchill (Manitoba), 247–50
Clarkson, Adrienne, 91
clathrates, 54–56, 309
Clean Air Act (U.S., 1972), 184

climate, 43, 47. See also climate change;
  environment; weather
  cryosphere and, 3–4, 47–48, 170–71
climate change, 4–5. See also climate; global
  warming
  and Africa, 243
  causes of, 180–81
  clathrates and, 55–56
  and humans, 5, 63
  predicting, 184–85
  research on, 163, 174–75, 179
  solutions for, 290
clouds, 53
colour
  of animals, 64
  of ice, 32–33, 36, 42
Columbia Icefield, 222–26
Columbus, Christopher, 106, 108, 126
comets, 55, 57
computers, 58
  in ice research, 171, 174–75
  models generated by, 184–85, 187
Confederation Bridge, 192–93, 194–95
Constantine (Roman emperor), 199
continental drift, 10, 11, 19–20, 187. See also
  tectonic plates
contrails, 53–54, 309
Cook, Frederick A., 49, 135
Cook, James, 121, 128, 141–42
Copper Eskimos, 91
Coupland, Douglas, 221
Couture, Clara, 269
Couture, Emile, 268
Craig, Dan, xv–xvi, 251, 253–56
Cree people, 85
Crowfoot Glacier, xi, 223
cryopreservation, 76–77
cryoprotectants, 72, 73, 75
cryosphere, 43, 44, 175
  and climate, 3–4, 47–48, 170–71
  importance of, 3–4, 47–48, 287–88

Daigle, Jeanine, 34, 35
Dall sheep, 64
Darwin, Charles, 155
Dash, Greg, 54
Davis, John, 117–19, 129
The Day After Tomorrow (film), 4–5
Dease, Peter, 130
DeLong, George Washington, 122, 133
dendochronology, 214
Dene people, 85, 309
Desbois, Jacques, 226–30
Descartes, René, 26–27
Desgroseilliers, 174
Dezhnev, Semyon, 141
Dickens, Charles, 146
Discovery, 196
disease, 88, 217

Disney, Walt, 76
Donev, Jason, 22, 25, 56–58
Dorset culture, 82, 83, 310
drumlins, 14–15, 310
Dumont d'Urville, Jules, 131
Dupras, Joseph W., Sr., 262

Earthwatch, 248, 250
Eastern Settlement, 100–101
ecotourism, 244–50
Edmonton Oilers, 253–54
Eisenstein, Sergei, 201–2
elephant seals, 64–65, 246
Eliasberg, Karl, 205–6
Elizabeth I (of England), 109, 110–11
Ellesmere Island, 197, 250
Ellsworth, Lincoln, 137
Emanuel of Bridgwater, 113
emigration, 81–82, 215–19
Endurance, 151, 152
Engel, Samuel, 115
England
    ice exploration by, 122–23, 142–43
    ice storage in, 271
    and Palatines, 216–17
    trade with Russia, 108, 109
    in World War II, 206–13
entropy, 26
environment, 50, 87. *See also* climate; pollution;
    weather
Environment Canada, 170
Eratosthenes, 102
Erebus, 144–45
Erik (the Red) Thorvaldsson, 100, 126
erratics, 20, 310
Eskimos, 5, 87, 90–91. *See also specific*
    Eskimo peoples; Inuit; Paleo-Eskimos
Europa, 58–59, 181
Europeans
    as explorers, 106–15, 122–23, 142–43
    and indigenous peoples, 87–91, 112–13,
        114–15
    and Inuit, 110, 114, 117–20, 150, 155
European Space Agency, 171
Ewing, George, 22
exploration, 105, 141–47
    in ancient world, 97–100
    in Arctic, 90, 122–23, 142–43
    beer and, 120–21
    by Europeans, 106–15, 122–23, 142–43
    ice and, 108–9, 115, 122–23
    for mineral resources, 110–13, 191
    polar, 123, 126–40, 150–52, 155–59
    stages of, 90–91
explorers
    health of, 121–23
    and Inuit, 110, 114, 117–20

Ferguson, Will, 37
Fiennes, Ranulph, 139
figure skating, 252–53, 254
firn, 29–30, 311
First Nations, 85. *See also* indigenous peoples
fish, 66–67, 74. *See also* ice fishing
    refrigeration for, 275
fishing shacks, 257–58
Fitzgerald, Betty, 40
Fitzgerald, Edwin R., 22
Fitzgerald, F. Scott, 237
Floki Vilgerdarson, 126
forests, 50, 51–52
Foxe, Luke, 124–25
Fram, xv, 163–64, 165–66
Franklin, Benjamin, 218
Franklin, Colleen, 124
Franklin, Jane, 144, 145
Franklin, John, 129, 131–32, 143–47, 149,
    155–56
frazil, 48, 170–71, 312
freezing
    and human body, 70–71
    nucleating agents in, 6, 71–72, 255
    process of, 2, 24, 26
Le Frigorifique, 275
Frobisher, Martin, 108–10, 111–14
    expeditions of, 117, 119–20
Frobisher Bay, 109–10
frogs, 67–75
Frontenac Axis, 16
frostbite, 74
Fuchs, Vivian, 138
Furbish, Kate, 18
Furbish lousewort, 17–18

Gabriel, 108–9, 111
Gaffer III, 34–35, 36–37
Gama, Vasco da, 127
gas pipelines, 55
Geiger, John, 145
Genz, Dave, 257, 258–59
Genz, Patsy, 259
geophysics, 186–87
German, Dave, 245
Gerritsz, Dirk, 127
Gjøa, 135, 165, 166
glacial flour, 223, 312
glacial rebound, 8, 9–10, 17, 20
glaciers, 312–13. *See also specific glaciers and*
    glacial formations; ice ages; ice sheets
    in Canada, 222
    colours in, 33–34
    deposits left by, 12–15, 20, 310
    effects of, 8–15, 20
    formation of, 29–30
    in Greenland, 37
    in Iceland, 99

glaciers *(continued)*
lakes under, 181–82
and landscape, 6–8
melting of, 46, 190, 225
movement of, 30, 36
and tourism, 221–26
water from, 39, 46
global warming
and Africa, 243
clathrates and, 55–56
cryosphere and, 47
and sea ice, 162–63
and sea levels, 9
solutions for, 290
glucose, 75
glycerol, 72, 75
Gokstad, 165
governance
of Antarctica, 167, 171–73, 247
for indigenous peoples, 85–86
Great Lakes, 9, 261
greenhouse gases, xiii, 55–56, 185. *See also*
global warming
Greenland, 100–101
glaciers in, 37
ice sheet over, 47, 80, 179–81
on maps, 95, 103, 104
peoples of, 82–83, 86, 88
research in, 179–81
Vikings in, 83, 184
Grissino-Mayer, Henri, 214
groundwater, 45–46
growlers, 39, 313
Gruben, Persis, 154
Grumpy Old Men (film), 257
Gulf current, 99
Gwich'in people, 84

Habbakuk, 206–13
Haida people, 84
Haimila, Wayne, 123
Hall, Charles Francis, 118–19, 132
Hall, Christopher, 110
Hansen, James, 290
Harbin, 239–41
Harper, Kenn, 88
Harris, Moira F., 238
Hayes, Derek, 161–62
health. *See also* medicine
of explorers, 121–23
Hearne, Samuel, 142
Hempleman-Adams, David, 140
Herbert, Wally, 139
Heyerdahl, Thor, 166
hibernation, 64
Hillary, Edmund, 138
Hitler, Adolf, 202, 203
hockey, 252–56
Holley, J. Gordon, 213

Honorius (Roman emperor), 199
Hortus Haren, 241
Hudson, Henry, 127
Hudson Bay, 9, 248
Hudson's Bay Company, 112, 142
humans
in Arctic, 79–83, 159–60
and freezing conditions, 70–71
ice and, 62–63, 282–84
prehistoric, 61, 63, 81–83
tool-making by, 82–83
water in, 2
hydrological cycle, 46–47

ice, 314. *See also specific forms of ice;*
freezing; ice cores; water
algae on, 33, 67, 319
amorphous, 56–58, 307
atmospheric, 53–54
beauty of, xiv, 192, 195–98
colour of, 32–33, 36, 42
convection in, 59
as cooling agent, 270, 276, 278–79
crystals of, 5, 26–29, 31
dangers of, 192–95, 257, 260–62, 266,
280
desserts made from, 270–71, 278–79, 282
extraterrestrial, xiv, 5–6, 55, 57, 58–59
flammable, 54–56
flotation of, 25–26
harvesting, 267–69, 271, 272, 277
high-pressure, 5
and historical events, 199–206
home delivery of, xiii, 274–75
and human body, 62–63, 282–84
imagery based on, 281–82
internal, 67–77
manufacturing, 275–76
melting of, 25
as mineral, 23–24
phases of, 5–6
pollutants in, 183–84, 279
research on, 4–5, 39, 40–42, 162–64, 281,
288–89
as semiconductor, 281
and space exploration, 182, 189–91
storing, 267–68, 271, 272
structure of, 5
theories about, 115
thin sections of, 40–42
vs. water, 24, 25–26
ice ages, 7–9. *See also* Little Ice Age
history of, 10–15
humans in, 63, 81
and pollutants, 93
Iceberg Alley, 34–37
iceberg cowboys, 39–40
icebergs, 3, 314
colour of, 36

icebergs (continued)
  explorers and, 108–9
  industrial use of, 39–40
  in Newfoundland and Labrador, 21, 34–37
  source of, 37, 308
  tongues on, 31–32, 322
  as tourist attraction, 34–37
  tracking, 170–71, 194
iceboxes, 275, 276–77
icebreakers, 193
ice climbing, 262–64
ice cores
  pollution in, 183, 287–88
  research on, 177, 178–83, 222
ice cream, 270–71, 278–79
iced tea, 278
ice fishing, 256–62
ice hotels, 226–35
icehouses, 267–68, 272
Iceland, 99
ice palaces, 236–39
ice plow, 72, 268
ice rinks, 253–56
ice roads, 260
ice sculpture, xv, 241–43
ice sheets (continental), 30–32, 47, 314.
  See also ice cores; Laurentide Ice Sheet;
  Wisconsin Ice Sheet
  in Antarctica, 47, 80, 181–83
  in Greenland, 47, 80, 179–81
  in ice ages, 7–15
  lakes under, 181–82
  in North America, 8–9, 20
  and plate tectonics, 187
  as time capsules, 178–83
ice shelves (coastal), 32, 314
ice storms, 280
ice tourism. See tourism
igloos, 226–28
Immen, Wallace, 221, 222
immigration, 215–19
India, 45–46, 273
Indiana, 256–57
indigenous peoples
  in Arctic, 83–87
  contributions of, 91–94
  disease among, 88
  Europeans and, 87–91, 112–13, 114–15
  exploration by, 100
  governance models for, 85–86
  origins of, 81–83
  racism towards, 114, 155
  terminology for, 84, 85
  time sense of, 93–94, 288
information processing, 58. See also computers
Innocent III, 201
insects, 62, 68, 74–75, 314
Institute for Ocean Technology, 21–22, 40–41
International Conference on the Physics and
  Chemistry of Ice, 15, 22, 23, 49, 53–54, 59

International Geophysical Year, 138, 168–69,
  171
International Meteorological Association, 167.
  See also World Meteorological Organization
Internet, 169–70
Inuit, 91–94, 315. See also Eskimos; Thule
  people
  in Canada, 85, 110, 114
  climate change and, 5
  culture of, 115
  Europeans and, 110, 114, 117–20, 150,
    155
  in Greenland, 83, 88
  kidnapping of, 88, 110, 114
  pollution and, 178
  and scientific research, 92
  technologies of, 115, 150, 155–56
Inupiat people, 84, 92
Inuvialuit people, 84, 85
irrigation, 45–46
Ivan the Terrible, 108
Ivry, Sara, 261
Izhor people, 86

James, Thomas, 124–25
Japan, 241–42
Jolly, Alison, 285
Jones, Stephen, 15
Jordaan, Ian, 15, 22, 192–93
July isotherm, 96
Jünger, Ernst, xi
Jupiter. See Europa

Kaiser, Ward L., 95
Kaloki, Michael, 243
Kamchadal people, 86
Karelien people, 86
Karluk, 153, 154–55
Kenya, 243
Kepler, Johannes, 26
Kerry, John, 252
King, Ernest, 212
kittiwakes, 67
Kobalenko, Jerry, 23, 156, 157–59, 265
Kodlunarn (Qadlunaat) Island, 118
Komi people, 86–87
Kon-Tiki, 165, 166

Lacelle, Guy, 262–63
Lake Erie, 9, 261
Lake Iroquois, 14
Lake Ladoga, xv, 203, 204
Lake Mille Lacs, 257
Lake of the Woods, 257, 259
Lake Ontario, 9
lakes. See also individual lakes; ice fishing
  subglacial, 181–82
Lake Superior, 9
Lake Vostok, 181–83
Lamont-Doherty Earth Observatory, 182, 214

L'Anse-aux-Meadows, 101, 315
Laptev, Dmitri, 127
latitude, 104, 105
Laurentide Ice Sheet, 9, 11, 20
Leif Eriksson, 101, 126
lemmings, 64
Leningrad, 203–6
Libbrecht, Kenneth, xiv, 28–29
Libya, 45
lightning, 54
Little Ice Age, 101, 155, 184, 213, 214–16
Lockwood, Lieutenant, 133
Lok, Michael, 108–9, 110–11, 113
longitude, 104
Lopez, Barry, 1, 3
lousewort, 17–18, 62

Macfarlane, John, 245–47
Mackinnon, Peter, 185–89
Macmillan, Margaret, xiii, 200–201
Madrid Protocol, 171–73
magnetic fields, 186–87
magnetic poles, 186, 316
magnetic storms, 167–68
Maine, 9
Malakhov, Misha, 157
mapping, 141–42, 144, 161–62. See also
   maps
maps, 95–96, 102–6. See also mapping
Marconi, Guglielmo, 21
Mary Sachs, 153–54
Maunder Minimum, 214–16
Mauro, Fra, 103
McFarlane, Peter, 123
McGhee, Robert, 114, 118–19
McGuigan, Leigh, 264
McKenna, Richard, 161, 192, 193, 195
M'Clintock, Leopold, 146
medicine, xiii, 282–84
   transplant, 70–71, 73, 75–76
Meier, Peg, 238
Memorial University, 15, 21–22, 192. See also
   C-CORE; International Conference on the
   Physics and Chemistry of Ice
Mercator, Gerhardus (Gerhard Kremer), 103–5
Mercer, Rick, 258
Messner, Reinhold, 264
methane, 55
Metis, 85
Michael, 108–9, 111
microprocessors, 58. See also computers
microscopy, 41–42, 56–57
mill holes, 190
Minik, 88
Minnesota, 236–39, 256
Mitford, Nancy, 150–51
molecules, 25–26
Montreal, 237, 252, 279–80
moon, 189–91. See also Europa

moraines, 15, 315, 316, 319, 321
moss campion, 51
Mountbatten, Louis, 207, 209, 211
Muscovy Company, 108, 109
museums
   in Canada, 224, 276–77
   in Norway, 164–65
   in Russia, 203
   in United States, 88, 118
music, 201–2, 205–6, 213–15
musk oxen, 62
mussels, 69

Nadolny, Sten, 149, 159–60
Nansen, Fridtjof, 133, 163–64, 166, 250
Napoleon I, 202
Nares, George, 132
NASA (US National Aeronautics and Space
   Administration), 169, 170, 189–90, 194
National Hockey League, 252, 253–56
National Research Council, 182, 212
   Institute for Ocean Technology, 21–22,
   40–41
National Science Foundation (US), 92
natives. See indigenous peoples
natural gas, 55, 194
Nautilus, 138
Nelson, Horatio, 142
Nero, 270
New Brunswick, 17
Newfoundland and Labrador, 19–21
   discovery of, 101, 106
   ice in, 20, 39–40, 191–92
   indigenous peoples of, 85
   tourism in, 34–37, 250
New York, 217–18
Niagara Escarpment, 9
nilas, 48, 317
Nine and a Half Weeks (film), 282
nitrates, 184
Nordenskjöld, Nils Adolf Erik, 132
Nordenskjöld, Otto, 134
Norsemen. See Vikings
North Dakota, 257
Northeast Passage, 107, 141
northern lights. See aurora borealis/australis
North Greenland Ice-core Project (North GRIP),
   179–81
North Pole, 103, 186
Northwest Passage, 106–7, 124–25, 141
   search for, 108–10, 142, 143–45
   travel through, 150, 166
Northwest Territories, 85
Norway, 163–66
Norwegian Polar Institute, 162–63
Nova Scotia, 18–19
nuclear waste, 93–94
nuclear weapons, 183
nucleating agents, 6, 71–72, 255

Nunavik, 85
Nunavut, 85–86, 92, 250
Ocean Ranger, 21
oceans. *See also* icebergs; sea ice; sea levels
   clathrates in, 55
   currents in, 99, 164
   glaciation and, 7–8
   icebergs in, 21
oil industry, 21, 52, 194
Olsen, Bob, 237
Ontario, 12–15. *See also* Toronto
Orion, 245, 247
Orkney Islands, 112
Ortel, Abraham (Ortelius), 103–4
Oseberg, 165
Ottar (Norse explorer), 107

pack ice, 317
   animal life on, 66–67
   explorers and, 109, 115
   tracking, 170–71
Palatinate, 215–16
Palatines, 216–19
Paleo-Eskimos, 82
pancake ice, 48, 98, 317
pan ice, 170–71
Pannigabluk, Fannie, 89–90
Pappalardo, Robert T., 22, 58–59
Parmenides, 102
Parry, William Edward, 90, 128–30, 143
Patagonia, 244
Patricia Lake, 210, 212
Patterson, W.S.B. (Stan), 187
Pauling, Linus, 26
Peary, Robert, 88, 135
Penn, William, 215, 216
Pennsylvania Dutch. *See* Palatines
Perito Moreno Glacier, 244
periwinkles, 69
permafrost, 50–53, 55, 318, 319
Perutz, Martin, 209–10, 213
Peters, Arno, 104
Peter the Great, 127
Petrenko, Victor, 22, 37–38, 281
Phipps, James, 117
photography, xiv–xv, 34, 41–42, 223–25, 248
photons, 32–33
Pilgrims, 121
Pindar, 96
pingos, 51, 318
Plaisted, Ralph, 139
planetary rings, 57
plants, 50–51, 61–62
plate tectonics. *See* continental drift; tectonic
   plates
Pleistocene era, 7, 313, 318
Pliny the Elder, 98
polar bears, 5, 142
   adaptation to ice, 64, 65–66
   in native spirituality, 82

pollution and, 177–78
tourists and, 247–50
Polar Years
   First International (1882–83), 133, 167
   Second International (1932–33), 137,
     167–68
pollution
   in Arctic, 53, 177–78, 289
   global effects of, 177–78, 183–84, 287–88,
     289–90
   in ice cores, 183, 287–88
   and ice trade, 279
   in Russia, 87, 289
   of water, 44, 53
polynyas, 82, 319
power generation, 281
Prokofiev, Sergei, 201–2
ptarmigans, 64
Ptolemy, 102–3
Pyke, Geoffrey Nathaniel, 207–12
pykrete, 207, 208–12, 213
Pythagoras, 102
Pytheas, 97–99, 126

Qadlunaat (Kodlunarn) Island, 118
qiviuk, 62
Quebec, 85. *See also* Montreal; Nunavik
   ice hotel in, 229–34
   winter carnivals in, 235–36, 237, 242–43

racism, 114, 155
radar, 189
radioactive fallout, 183
radio waves, 168, 189–91
Rae, John, 115, 146
Rasmussen, Knud, 81, 98, 115, 136
Rasmussen, Patricia, 29
The Red Violin (film), 213
refrigeration, 272, 275, 276, 279
Rensselaer Polytechnic Institute, 182
research. *See also* ice cores
   in Arctic, 5, 92, 152–55, 163, 167–69,
     187–89
   on Arctic Ocean, 164, 173–75
   computer modelling in, 184–85, 187
   in Greenland, 179–81
   indigenous people and, 92
   information sources for, 169–71
   international cooperation in, 167–69, 171,
     173–76, 180–81, 289
   and space exploration, 182
Rhine River, 199–200, 215
rime, 174
Ritter, Jerry, 236
Roman Empire, 199–200, 270
Ronne, Finn, 138
Roosevelt, Franklin D., 212
Ross, James Clark, 130, 131, 143
Rossiter, Jamie, 189–92, 206
Royal Navy, 142